Buying Bargains at Property Auctions

Howard R Gooddie MA (Cantab), DipTP, FRICS

Buying Bargains at Property Auction
by Howard R Gooddie

Published by
Law Pack Publishing Limited
10–16 Cole Street
London SE1 4YH

www.lawpack.co.uk

Printed in India

For convenience (and for no other reason) 'him', 'he' and 'his' has been used throughout and should be read to include 'her', 'she' and 'her'.

Contents

6 After the auction – what happens next? 77

7 The insider's guide to an auction house 85

List of figures

List of tables

List of illustrations

Tables of abbreviations

The following abbreviations are used commonly in advertisements and property literature:

adj.	adjoining
cr.	corner
d-h.	dwelling house
det.	detached
F.	freehold
f.g.r.	freehold ground rent
f.r.l.	full repairing lease
g.	gross, landlord paying rates
grd.	ground
L.	leasehold
l.g.r.	leasehold ground rent
lic.	licensed
Mod.	modern
n.	net, tenants pay rates
n.o.	not offered
nr.	near
OPP	outline planning permission
P	possession
PL	part let
PP	planning permission
pt.	part
p.a.	per annum
PAX	per annum exclusive
rev.	reversion
rr.	rack rental
rsv.	reserve price
RUP	residential upper part
R	repossessed
s.d.	semi-detached
sold priv.	sold privately
s.y.	square yards
sq. ft.	square feet
UT	unexpired term
w.	withdrawn
wk.	weekly rent
yrs.	years

Acknowledgements

When I have read acknowledgements in other books and noted that authors invariably thanked their typists, I never realised how indebted they were. It is only whilst composing this volume that I have come to appreciate exactly how much authors have to rely on the typing skills that back them up. My most sincere thanks in putting together this offering must firstly go to Diane Mercer-Brown in Longden & Cook Commercial who has had to suffer far more tribulation over the preparation of these pages than I have. She was thoroughly backed up by Pat Devlin, Olga Shaw and Liz Cummins who are or have been concerned with the promotion and co-ordination of auctions in Longden & Cook Commercial.

Debbie Patterson, Anne Fanning and David Crosby, all of Wyvern Crest Limited, were a constant support and encouragement as each of them took their part in the progressive development of the script. Anne Quirk and Gail Woodhall provided legal assistance when I needed it on the legal details, both of them partners in Vaudrey Osborne & Mellor. On a separate legal point, Grahame Lake from Wolstenholmes was particularly helpful and when I turned to accountancy skills, Peter Jeffery and Ray Lomax of Tunstall & Co in Warrington provided the expertise I needed from members of that profession.

Finally amongst the professionals, I must thank Rodney Schofield from Royles Surveyors in Manchester, for providing me 'at the drop of a hat' with an example of a typical structural survey.

The original concept of this work was put initially to the Property Auctioneering Skills Panel of the Royal Institution of Chartered Surveyors and my thanks must go to all members of that Panel for their support, co-operation, assistance and the contribution of some of the auctioneers' anecdotes. My thanks therefore to John Barnett of Sallmann Harman Healey, Richard H Auterac of Jones Lang Wootton, David J Hobbs of McDowalls, M W S Bax of Bax Standen, Gary C Murphy of Allsop & Co, A J Ridgeway of Symonds & Sampson, Benjamin Tobin of Strettons and Geoffrey van Cutsem of Savills International Property.

The world of property publishing is small and practitioners depend heavily upon the relatively few magazines for promotion and advertising and the relevant organizations have all been particularly helpful and willingly provided samples for mere acknowledgement of their copyright. My thanks therefore to the *Estates Gazette, Property Week* and *Under the Hammer* and in a slightly more modern form of information provider, Faxwise.

Thanks are also due to Barnard Marcus, Erdman & Lewis, Walter & Randall, HMSO, The Law Society of England Wales and The Solicitors Law Stationery Society Ltd for permission to reproduce extracts.

Without the assistance from all these people this work would not be in front of you now.

Howard R Gooddie

About the author

Howard Gooddie is head of auctions at Longden & Cook Commercial in Manchester. His father and grandfather were auctioneers before him and he grew up immersed in the world of auctions. During his boyhood he was a 'lotter' and clerk at many of his father's auctions. Howard's first property sale was in 1957 when he was 25. Legend has it that his audience only contained five people, of whom three were bank officials. In 1979 Howard returned to the auction world and started running quarterly auction sales, progressing to monthly sessions four years later. The firm's auction catalogue expanded rapidly when it started selling many lots on behalf of British Rail Property Board.

Novelty has always been part of Longden & Cook Commercial sales. The firm was the first to pioneer holding auctions simultaneously in London and Manchester, show pictures electronically of the properties being offered, introduce bidding paddles to property auctions and place the full catalogue on the Internet.

Howard Gooddie has conducted more than 210 composite auction sales and has offered nearly 13,000 lots, inspecting virtually all of them himself. He is a member of the auctioneering skills panel of the Royal Institution of Chartered Surveyors, and is a Master of Arts from Cambridge University with a Certificate of Proficiency in Estate Management. He also holds a Diploma in Town Planning and is a Fellow of the Royal Institution of Chartered Surveyors.

1 Auctions – the place to pick up a bargain

'The main advantage to me of buying at auction has got to be the price. Compared with the prices going through high street estate agents I paid 33% less.'
Don Lee, buyer of a residential property at auction.

The UK is awash with bargains

In two recent auction sales the following properties sold for prices that would not be found in any estate agent's window:

- A three-bed city flat in Birmingham sold for £8,500. Less than the price of a new car.

- A studio flat could be had in south London for only £9,000.

- £17,250 is all that was needed to obtain a two-bed flat in a Dower house within half a mile of the centre of Lincoln.

- A three-bed house in London with a private garden sold for less than £40,000.

These results demonstrate that there are plenty of bargain properties out there, if you only know where to look and how to go through the auction process.

What you will learn from this guide

In the following pages you will be shown:

- how auctions work;
- where to find auctions;
- how to spot a bargain;
- the price you should bid up to;
- the costs of buying at auction;
- how to handle the legal aspects of the purchase;
- how auctioneers operate;
- the best bidding tactics;
- how to sell at auction;
- what the pitfalls are;
- how to avoid losing a lot of money.

Auctions are full of mystique, but with the help of this guide, you will be taken inside how the auction process really works. It will enable you to have a clear idea of how to approach a property auction and it gives you the opportunity to pick up a bargain, saving you thousands of pounds compared with making a purchase through conventional channels.

Auctioneer's Anecdote: Repossessions at rock-bottom prices

Early in 1993 was a period when many building societies were using the auction room to dispose of their large portfolio of repossessed houses and flats. At the time, most auction houses were reporting successful sales of between 60 per cent and 75 per cent of the properties they were offering, but certain auctioneers publicised that they were having virtually a 100 per cent success rate in the sales of properties they were offering for one particular leading building society. To experienced auction dealers, this meant that many bargains were available and the reserve prices were set at attractive levels.

What types of auction are there?

Auctions fall into four categories according to their size:

- large composite
- medium composite
- smaller composite
- single lot.

Table 1.1 lists the relative sizes, the number of lots to expect, the size of the audience and where they may be held. A composite auction is one where a collection of different types of property are sold at the same auction.

Table 1.1 Size of auctions

	Number of lots	Likely audience	Likely venue
Large composite	100+	300+	Hotel/conference centre, theatre, meeting rooms
Medium composite	5–100	200–500	Hotel/conference centre
Smaller composite	2–5	10–100	Hotel, church hall, pub, restaurant, sale room
Single lot	1	10–75	Hotel, church hall, pub, restaurant

Large

Over the last 20 years there has been a move towards large and composite auctions, run not only in London, but also in the larger financial cities outside the capital. The auctions are generally run by one auction house although, on occasion, several firms may co-operate. These composite auctions run frequently on a regular published calendar and may contain up to 50 lots offered in just a morning or an afternoon right through to 300 or 400 lots offered over several days. The sales may be restricted to a special type of property, for example vacant possession houses, residential investments, retail investments, commercial investments, shops, factories, warehouses or land, or a blend of any or all of these types. Where there is a mixture, the different categories of property tend to be offered in consecutive lots sometimes with intervals between the various categories.

Advantages of composite auctions

Bringing together a number of lots in a composite auction produces economies of scale for the auction house. But from the seller's point of view a composite auction frequently generates more interest, a larger audience, more extensive marketing and generally a cheaper entry cost. If you are attending an auction for the first time, the scope of the catalogue

and the size of the audience may seem somewhat forbidding. But by following the steps in this book, you will be able to refine your interest down to only a few lots and will learn how to exercise your presence as a bidder at the vital moments in a crowded room.

Auctioneer's Anecdote: For any given lot, the higher the price the slower the bidding

Large composite auctions need to take place in rooms of sufficient size to cope with the expected audience which will probably exceed 300. For this reason, auction houses usually choose to use hotel or conference centres, theatres or meeting rooms which can be laid out in theatre style seating facing a single rostrum. A public address system with sufficient amplification is normal.

Medium

The medium composite auction is a smaller version of the larger composite auction, where either the lots will be restricted to a particular category, for example repossessed vacant houses and flats on behalf of finance houses or, alternatively, a mixture

'Subject to planning' – Where a property has development or redevelopment potential but there is no actual planning consent granted for that work then a buyer will need to obtain such a consent afterwards. It may or may not be forthcoming. An intending bidder may, by discussion with the development control officer at the local planning authority, be able to resolve any doubts he may have.

Thursday 11 February at 2-30 p.m. at The Sachas Hotel, Tib St., off Market St., Manchester.
LONGDEN & COOK COMMERCIAL (061-236 1114)
Bristol - Rent charges 375 collections. Total income £3,987.68 p.a.   w
Manchester - Vacant Land at Moston Rd., Middleton Junc'n Area 5.30a 1,468 sq yds with Ind'l Redev. Pot. suitable for B1, B2 or B8 users   F   P   w
Reddish - Land at Wayland Rd Sth., Gtr. Man. Site 16.4a apx. with Pot for apx. 7.7a Res. Dev (subj. to planning). Part occupied at a rent of £338.32 p.a.   F   P   w
Oldham - Land at Oaklands Rd., Greenfield. 2.74a. vacant Land (3,599 sq yds). PP for Res. Dev. refused F   P   **9,250**
Lower Darwen - Land at Fairfield Drive, Milking La., Lancs. Site with PP for 10 s-d d-h's.   F   P   w
do Land at Milking Lane, approx. 8.5 acres with PP for 80 Res. units and pot. to increase the density F   P   w
Manchester - Bracken House, Charles St. Mostly vacant modern City Centre Office Bdg. 31,060 sq ft on 8 fls. Pt. grd flr let 25 yrs from 1988 at £7,750 p.a. F   P   w
Stockport - Redhouse La., Disley, Gtr. Man. Commercial Invest. 4,160 sq yds comprising Goods Shed & Garage. Income from tenants £13,300 p.a.   F   pvt. *125,000*
Hyde - Land at Railway St., Gtr. Man. Site area 1a. 3,484 sq yds. Income £15,000 p.a. 7 yrs UT Planning prepared for Res. use with adj. 2.4a. site   F   w
Huddersfield - Vacant Land at Manchester Rd., Linthwaite, West Yorks. Area 0.9a. (4,356 sq yds)   F   P   n.o.
Bolton - Vacant Land at Greenwoods La., Hardy Mill Rd., Harwood, Gtr. Man. Agr. or amenity land with potential. Apx. 8.5a. and adjoins existing Res. Devel. F   P   **29,500**
do Land at Cox Green Rd., Dimple, Egerton. Apx. 45a. Agr. Land let on yr to yr agr. ten. £50.00 p.a. F   pvt. *22,000*

Illustration 1. Extract from Under the Hammer

of lots from a single geographical region covered by the auction house. This can be a suburb where the auctioneers specialise or a regional city such as Birmingham, Manchester, Liverpool or Edinburgh where there is a source of mixed lots available, but insufficient lots on offer at regular intervals to produce larger composite auctions.

This size of sale can still produce an audience of between 200 and 500 people depending upon the popularity of the lots being offered and the amount of marketing that has taken place. Therefore the auctioneers will need to choose a venue similar to that necessary for large composite auctions with similar facilities.

Small

There are occasions when a smaller number of related lots are appropriate for being auctioned consecutively at the the same place and at the same time. This may be a number of adjoining building plots or retail or domestic investment properties or land and agricultural property in a particular vicinity.

Look out for special themes

Thus the small composite auction will generally follow a theme. It may contain lots which result from the 'break-up' of an individual estate. Examples of this are:

- A large agricultural investment estate where the owners have decided that the best prices can be obtained by offering portions of the estate in small lots.
- The owners of a portfolio of residential investments in one particular suburb or of a row of shops in a particular centre may decide that they will obtain the best price by offering the properties individually.

In such cases it is logical for the auction house to bring together its marketing and advertising and produce a single brochure, one set of advertisements and run just one auction session. The number of people attending is likely to be less than those attending a larger auction and therefore there is no need for the auction house to organise a sale in a large venue. The auction room may well be a smaller hotel, church, village hall or similar sized building.

The single lot

If a vendor (also called the seller) chooses to offer a single lot, it is often because the auctioneer believes there will be a tremendous demand for the property.

The costs of promoting a single lot sale will be considerably higher than for a composite auction. This extra cost must be justified by the belief that the property is one for which there is a spectacular demand. The audience may only be between 10 and 75 people and the auction room will need to be of a corresponding size.

What properties are offered for sale by auction?

Thatched cottages

Some rural and suburban firms of auctioneers specialise in offering for sale by auction country cottages of which the 'thatched cottage' is the prime example. These are usually sold in single lots and occasionally in small, themed sales. Even when other types of auction during the 1950s were unpopular, the 'thatched cottage' sales were still held quite frequently, as both vendors and auction houses believed that considerable competition could be engendered between would-be-buyers, by offering this type of property for sale by auction. That belief was furthered by the belief amongst valuers that it was almost impossible to judge precisely what price such a property would realise. From the owner's point of view, therefore, the possibility of a crowded auction in a hotel or public room one evening with bidders fighting to buy was irresistible. Although the romantic cottage exemplifies the type of property which vendors feel are best offered for sale by auction, it should not be forgotten that other types of property which are particularly attractive, for whatever reason, may also benefit from the 'thatched cottage' syndrome, and realise a high price in the auction room as a result of exceptional competition.

Why not pick up an exceptional property?

Other properties that might benefit from exposing themselves to exceptional competition include:

- houses that are unique because of their historical associations or their exceptional position;

- building or development prospects which are in pockets of exceptional interest or demand;
- investment properties of a type which are particularly in vogue at the time;
- plots or buildings which hold the key to development or profit-making prospects;
- sites or buildings appropriate for uses which follow fashions of the time. (Over the years these have included post offices, launderettes, petrol stations, food take-aways, nursing homes, bowling alleys, multi-screen cinemas and docklands, to name a few.) Dealers and entrepreneurs who have spotted the next trend or vogue will already be combing the auction rooms for their future stock.

Properties that are almost unsaleable

The auction route has often proved more successful than the private treaty sale method in the disposal of properties that are nearly unsaleable. Presumably this is because at auctions there is an element in the audience who are able and willing to 'chance their arm', particularly if they feel that a lot is apparently a bargain.

The sale rooms have seen the successful disposal of various properties that have been:

- derelict;
- subject to compulsory purchase orders;
- subject to major disrepair or fabric failure;
- subject to local authority repair notices;
- subject to closing orders;
- offered with unsatisfactory legal titles;
- sold without access;
- sold with major fencing, paving, drainage or other similar responsibilities;
- sold subject to easements, covenants or restrictions which prevent their satisfactory use;
- in derelict or unpopular areas.

Auctioneer's Anecdote: Read the particulars carefully

There is a long-standing joke in the auctioneers' profession that those auctioneers who sell land on behalf of Railtrack need long thin catalogues because of the long thin pieces of land which they have to offer. One particular piece, first offered by their Property Board, was near one of the conurbations and was three-quarters of a mile long

but only several yards wide. It was disclosed in the catalogue and in the title for sale that the land had no access other than through other people's land, was being sold with no access from the railway line and the purchaser had to erect a new fence along the entire three-quarter mile length adjoining the line. These factors did not inhibit some enthusiastic bidding when the property was offered. No doubt the bidders felt that around the £1,500 mark they could 'not go wrong'. Three months later the auctioneer was approached by the successful buyer to re-offer the land because it had no access and because the fencing convenant was about to be enforced. The land sold a second time at a slightly lower price at auction. Over the next two years, the auctioneer was instructed to offer and succeeded in selling the land no less than five times in total and not always at steadily reducing prices. Presumably, the only parties to whom any of the transactions gave a satisfactory result were Railtrack and the auctioneers.

LOT 52

First Floor Flat, 5 Victoria Road, Folkestone, Kent

HALIFAX

BY ORDER OF MORTGAGEES IN POSSESSION

A Leasehold First Floor Flat

TENURE
Leasehold. The property is held on a lease for a term of 99 years from 1st October 1987 (thus having approximately 93 years unexpired) at a current ground rent of £50 per annum.

LOCATION
The property is located on the west side of Victoria Road close to its junction with Broadmead Road in an established residential area close to Folkestone British Rail Station and within reach of the town centre.

DESCRIPTION
The property comprises a first floor flat situated within a mid terrace building.

ACCOMMODATION
Reception Room
Two Bedrooms
Kitchen
Bathroom with WC and wash basin

How much would you pay for a two-bed flat on the south coast? £50,000, £75,000 or £100,000? This one sold at auction for only £14,000.

Repossessed houses

Unfortunately for their previous owner-occupiers, this category of property continues to feature considerably in many auctioneers' catalogues in the waves of repossessions that occur from time to time. Whilst feeling for those that have been dispossessed, there is no doubt that auction houses, speculators, builders and new owner-occupiers all benefit from such situations. The losses registered by the finance houses and the insurers may only be the result of a drastic domestic property revaluation or may also have been occasioned by the surfeit of vacant houses offered in the sale rooms because of a high level of repossesions at any one time.

But there is no doubt, there are some very good value-for-money properties to be purchased at auction. 'Repossession' is not to be considered synonymous with 'bargain'. You should still thoroughly research your target property.

Investment properties

Properties that are owned for the benefit of the income they produce are frequently included in auction catalogues. Investors cover a range of buyers from large pension funds and commercial investors at one end, through to medium-sized investment companies and smaller private pension funds, right down to individual investors, looking for a satisfactory return on their money.

The range of properties includes:

- office investments;
- shop investments;
- domestic investments (single houses, blocks of flats and portfolios of houses);
- ground and chief rents;
- investments in land;
- investments in easements;
- reversionary investments (where the investor is concerned with long term income or growth in it).

What affects the price of investment properties?

Prices paid for investments depend on many factors which include:

- security of the covenant of the payer of the rent;
- the quality and position of the property;
- the potential growth or variation of the income collectable;
- the frequency of rent reviews;
- the investor's view of the future of the money market and future interest levels;
- the investor's view of the yield which is appropriate for the type of property;
- the nature and responsibilities of the landlord;
- the nature and responsibilities of the tenant;
- other factors which could affect the future income of the property favourably or adversely.

A portfolio of lots being sold by property dealers

You should be aware that occasionally the same properties feature in different auctions at different times. A tenanted shop in Liverpool may first of all sell at an auction in that city and then some time later reappear at an auction in London. A vacant repossessed house may be sold at an auction just outside the capital and subsequently reappear in the hands of a local auctioneer in the town in which the property is situated. A portfolio of domestic investments may be offered 'en bloc' in the capital, appear in another auction in that city six months later broken up into smaller units and then perhaps 50 per cent of that portfolio will be represented in individual lots in, for example Manchester, Birmingham or Liverpool 12 months later.

Do not be totally discouraged from being interested in these dealing lots, but do watch out for them by combing auction advertisements frequently. If you see a property which interests you, approach it with care and only after thorough research.

The auction houses

The principal firms of property auctioneers are listed in Appendix 7, with a great many firms offering their services throughout the country. There is no way you can monitor all their auctions, their results and their withdrawn lots.

Select firms that cover your area

You will have to select the firms you examine acknowledging there are:

i) varieties of specialist firms who only deal with

particular types of property and who are generally London-based;

ii) other auction houses in the capital who cover a wider range of properties, generally in composite auctions but occasionally in specialised ones as well;

iii) London-based firms who deal with property throughout the UK, sometimes only offering it in the capital but occasionally running sales in the regions;

iv) auction houses based upon the larger cities and towns throughout the country who run regular composite auctions, generally specializing in properties in their area rather than specializing in particular types of property; and

v) local firms who run smaller auctions on demand.

Within these broad divisions, as you become acquainted with the auction field, you will discover that there are certain specializations and subspecializations which various firms have developed through design or their past history and it is only by research that you will establish which auction houses to patronise, as a buyer or as a seller.

How to choose which firms to follow

1 Visit a few local auctions of any kind.
2 Decide upon the type of property in which you are interested.
3 Decide upon the geographical area you propose to cover.

4 Research auction advertisements in the property and local press.
5 Respond to those advertisements with specific requests for specific properties in which you are interested.
6 Subscribe to the mailing lists of firms who specialise in your type of property in your area.
7 Start visiting the auctions of your chosen firms on a regular basis.

By and large you will find that the sales of the majority of the firms are conducted in a similar manner. British auction houses are relatively traditional in their manner of offering with only minor variations in style, speed of selling, presentation and marketing.

> **KEY POINT:** *Whether you are a dreamer or a speculator, an entrepreneur or an investor, a would-be owner-occupier or a developer, an intending purchaser of many lots or only one, good luck in your hunt for bargains. Remember they will only come with thorough research and plentiful experience. Follow the advice that follows and you should not go wrong.*

'From a purchaser's point of view, I would have said you were going to get quite a good deal at auction, particularly in this climate.'

Michael Kirby, Chartered Surveyor.

2 How to find your bargain property

'I was living in Manchester and noticed there were a number of run-down properties in the inner city part of Manchester. They had been built as private houses and there had been problems with them simply because the people who had bought them could not pay their mortgage. They were quickly vandalised and went down in value like the rest of the property market. I negotiated a price of £12,000 for it after the auction and it only needed another £1,000 to put it into liveable condition. I was surprised they did not go for more.'

Don Lee, buyer of a residential property at auction.

First, find your bargain

Finding your bargain property can be immensely enjoyable. First, you need to know what steps to take to find your bargain and once found, how to decide what price to pay for it. The following checklist gives the key steps (from your initial search right up to going to auction) to help ensure you are successful in obtaining a bargain property.

PRE-AUCTION CHECKLIST:
For the bargain hunter

1. Find the newspapers that advertise auctions in the area that interests you.
2. Go on auctioneers' mailing lists. ☐
3. Subscribe to *Property Auction News*. ☐
4. Subscribe to the *Estates Gazette* and *Under the Hammer*. ☐
5. Look out for For Sale boards. ☐
6. Comb the auction catalogues. ☐
7. Inspect the properties that interest you. ☐
8. Find out the guidelines and reserve price (if possible). ☐
9. Appoint your solicitor. ☐
10. Instruct your surveyor. ☐
11. Consult your builder. ☐
12. Read the conditions of sale. ☐
13. Decide on your maximum bid. ☐
14. Consider a 'dummy run'. ☐
15. Take your accountant's advice. ☐
16. Arrange the finance. ☐
17. Don't forget your other buying costs. ☐
18. Look out for pitfalls. ☐
19. Consider putting in a bid before the sale. ☐

Finding your property – the first steps

Where can I find out about auctions?

The auctioneer has a responsibility to his owner to give as much publicity about his auctions as possible. You would think, therefore, that all auctions are extensively advertised. In practice, since advertising is expensive and auctioneers' budgets are limited, auction adverts may not receive tremendous exposure. As a bargain lot hunter, you would be wise to take other steps to ensure you hear about all the properties that are being offered in the area that interests you. Appendix 7 lists the majority of auctioneers' firms in the United Kingdom who advertise their auctions regularly. But no reader should treat this list as comprehensive, particularly since some firms may stop auctioning and others are likely to enter the market.

How to get on a mailing list

Most auctioneers maintain a mailing list of potential buyers to whom they send details of forthcoming auctions. Certain firms require a nominal payment to receive details, which in most cases is worth paying. However, many firms provide this service free of charge. Since servicing a mailing list is an expensive operation, auctioneers revise their lists at frequent intervals. It is worth checking how long each auctioneer will keep you on their list. Alternatively, check at least every six months whether your name is still on their list and how long they will continue to send you details.

Narrow down your choice of firms

You will often find that auctioneers specialise in certain types of property or certain regions. By telephoning a number of auctioneers and asking if they offer properties of the type you are seeking, you will be able to narrow down the number of mailing lists you go onto. This way, it is possible to reduce the number of wasted catalogues that come through the letter box.

Where auctioneers do not maintain a mailing list, the only reliable way of finding out the date, location and type of property being offered is to ring them up at frequent intervals.

Questions to put to an auctioneer:

* Do you have a mailing list?
* Do you charge for names to go on your mailing list?
* How long will you keep me on your list?
* Will you tell me if my name is about to be removed?
* What types of property do you auction?

Where are auctions advertised?

Two major property magazines are published weekly. The *Estates Gazette* and *Property Week*. *Property Auction News* is published monthly. Table 2.1 lists their addresses, telephone numbers and subscription charges. A fourth magazine *Under the Hammer* is the specialist trade magazine for auctioneers and is published fortnightly.

Each of the four property magazines has a slightly different approach to the auction world. None of the magazines focuses solely on residential or commercial properties or any specific part of the market.

The major property magazines

Property Auction News has become the best-selling publication dedicated to property auctions in the UK. Thousands of readers have bought cut-price property after learning about the potential of auctions through its pages; invaluable and highly recommended. Every major property auction listed every month, together with excellent advice, tips and background information.

The *Estates Gazette* provides a page every week of commentaries on sales that have taken place coupled with a calendar of auctions proposed for the forthcoming week and a schedule of the results of all auctions throughout the country. Its only disadvantage is that it does not publish details of lots that have been withdrawn.

Table 2.1 The major property magazines

Publication	Address	Published	Price	Subscription
Property Auction News	Streetwise, Riverside House, Claire Court Rawmarsh Road, Rotherham S60 1RU Tel: 01709 820033	Monthly		£45 for first year subscription
Estates Gazette	Oakfield House, Perrymount Road Haywards Heath West Sussex RH16 3DH Tel: 01444 445335	Weekly		£130 for a year's subscription
Property Week	Exchange Tower, 2 Harbour Exchange Square London E14 9GE Tel: 020 8309 3629	Weekly	£2.40 per week	£125 pa
Under the Hammer	70 Rowheath Road, Kings Norton Birmingham B30 2EX Tel: 0121 680 6832	Fortnightly		£150 for a year's subscription

Property Week publishes a weekly page with past news from the auction scene followed by a calendar of auctions for the following week. It does not publish a list of auction results.

Under the Hammer only deals with auctions and provides no news commentary whatsoever. It provides a fortnightly list for separate regions throughout the UK of all the properties which are to be offered by auction in the near future. A brief description of each lot is given. A second list gives results from auctions which have taken place during the previous fortnight indicating the price at which particular lots have sold. Details of all the lots that have been withdrawn are included and occasionally the price at which they are available. *Under the Hammer* also produces an annual digest of results analysed by property type and region.

Figures 2.1, 2.2 and 2.3 illustrate extracts from some of these magazines.

Apart from the specialist property press, certain newspapers are known for their auction advertisements. They often specialise in their regions or in the types of property that they cover. There is no alternative in your search for auctions to combing local and national newspapers and the Internet until you have discovered which ones carry advertisements for auctions of the type of property that interests you.

Other publications also advertise and list auctions but almost invariably they relate to the sale of chattels rather than properties. They are thus, to the property buyer, of no use.

What else will help in the search?

For Sale boards

Many estate agents, if pressed, will admit that more than half of their initial enquiries from successful purchasers come from a sale board erected on site. This high level of response is not as usual for auction properties but, nevertheless, most auctioneers will erect a sale board (or at worst put up a poster), at the property being offered. If you are looking for a property in a particular area, For Sale boards can be very useful. It may be worth trawling frequently through that area to look for boards.

Cottons
CHARTERED SURVEYORS
Auction Department

AUCTION SALE

To be held at the Grand Hotel, Colmore Row, Birmingham

on

Wednesday 6th December

43 Lots

To include a range of Residential and Commercial Vacant and Investment Property, along with Freehold Building Land and development opportunities comprising:

- 8 Residential Investment properties.
- 20 Freehold Vacant Houses.
- 2 Leasehold Vacant Houses.
- 2 Residential Building Plots.
- 2 Residential Development opportunities.
- 2 Freehold Shop Premises with Vacant Possession.
- 3 Freehold Shop Investments.
- 1 Freehold Office Premises with Vacant Possession.
- 2 Freehold Ground Rent Investments.
- 1 Styled Title and Legend 'Lord & Lady Weoley' In the County of Worcestershire.

To register for a catalogue please contact the Auctions Department 0121 247 2233 361 Hagley Road, Edgbaston, Birmingham B17 8DL E-mail: auctions@cottons.co.uk

47/473499

Figure 2.1 Estates Gazette advertisement

Cheshire

Roy Pugh & Co at Manchester, 18 Oct

Dunham-Warrington Rd. F agricultural land, 3.68 acres. Vacant	13,000
Northwich-Cuddington Station House, Warrington Rd, Cuddington. F house, 2 floors, 6 rooms and ancil, rooms, garage/s and land, part vacant, RR - CRR £2,158 pax.	50,000
Greenbank Station House, Chester Rd, Hartford. F house, 2 floors, 7 rooms, garden, yards, UM. Vacant	46,500

Bigwood at Birmingham, 19 Oct

Warrington-1, 3, 7, 9, 11 & 13 Alfred Rd, Lowton. F GR/s on 6 house - CRR £35 pax.	550

East Sussex

Austin Gray at Hove, 13 Oct

Brighton-8 College Rd. L 1st/2nd floor mais, 4 rooms, garage/s, UM. Vacant	104,500
45 Ladysmith Rd. F residential land, OPP, house. Vacant	45,750
73 Shaftesbury Rd. L G/F converted flat, 2 rooms, AST - CRR £4,940 pax.	52,500
Heathfield-Tilsmore Lodge, Cross in Hand. F detached house, 2 floors, 10 rooms, garden, 3 garage/s, 6 acres, OPP, 2 detached houses. Vacant	720,000

Fox & Sons at Hove, 17 Oct

Bexhill-on-Sea-The Old Church, King Offa Wy. F detached former church/chapel, 2 floors, dev pot. Vacant	102,000

Figure 2.2 Excerpt from Estates Gazette auction results

Allsop's market domination hammered home in 1999

Allsop extended its command of the market as commercial property auctions reached a record high in 1999

Auction results analysis - 1999

1999	Value of lots sold (£m)	1998	Value of lots sold (£m)
Allsop	519.8	Allsop	335.5
Royal & SunAlliance	151.0	Jones Lang LaSalle	122.1
Jones Lang LaSalle	145.7	Royal & SunAlliance	116.3
Nelson Bakewell	122.7	Healey & Baker	74.2
Healey & Baker	106.0	Harman Healy	59.0
Harman Healy	98.3	Nelson Bakewell	56.4
Andrews & Robertson	88.3	Andrews & Robertson	52.0
Conrad Ritblat*	73.2	Strettons	43.1
Countrywide	67.7	GA Property Services	43.0
Strettons	51.1	Countrywide	42.7

Source: Focus Information Services 020 7839 7684

By Liz Hamson

ALLSOP UNDERLINED ITS ABSOLUTE dominance of the auctions market last year by posting £520m sales – more than three times the amount raised by the second-placed auctioneer.

The auction powerhouse raised 55% more than in 1998 and a phenomenal 244% more than the 'combination of effective marketing, presentation and strong auctions'.

He also commented on his rivals: 'I'm surprised JLL didn't do better. It looks like carelessness against the 50% increase in total value raised by auctions last year.'

The comparison was downplayed by JLL auctioneer Peter Cunliffe, who highlighted the achievable – I would want to develop on the success we had last year.'

The top six auctioneers predicted further growth in 2000. Moir commented: 'There is a strong investment market generally. As investors find it more difficult to buy larger lot sizes, and if they're chasing higher yields – which they have to if they're small property companies – they may

Figure 2.3 Extract from Property Week

While travelling through the district you may find that the auctioneers have also used poster sites for the erection of For Sale bills, which gives details of their auctions and a brief summary of the properties that are available. The use of such bill-posters is an old habit that seems to be dying out, so you should not rely on this source of information.

It will only be the most inefficient auctioneer – or one suffering a very limited advertising budget – who will rely only on a For Sale board. Combing the columns of local newspapers and the Internet will generally be quite as effective as combing the district. You may well consider this 'armchair' approach much easier!

How to unearth a bank or building society repossession

'Years ago it wasn't the done thing to buy property at auction but now it is more the norm, especially on repossessions and investments. It's a quick way to buy a property. It gets the deal done.' Michael Kirby, Chartered Surveyor.

Look for the clues to repossessions

Some banks and building societies are very coy about the public knowing that they have repossessed properties and take considerable steps to avoid it being known that properties included in auctions are the result of repossessions. Other societies and banks are quite open. You can look for the clues.

In the initial advertisements, the auctioneers may disclose that certain properties are being sold as a result of repossession. The advert may contain a general list of the clients for whom they are selling which will then include the names of the societies and the banks. This information may be repeated in the auction catalogue itself, either in a general statement or on the relevant lots. The catalogue may give less specific references with phrases such as 'On behalf of mortgagees in possession', 'By order of .... Building Society', 'On the instructions of an LPA Receiver' or 'On the instructions of a liquidator' or similar.

Without these clues there can be more subtle indications. The solicitor acting may have as his address that of the head office of a building society or bank. Even without that direct indication it is possible that the name of the building from which the solicitor operates is an indication of the society for which he works. It may even be possible to link up the solicitor's telephone number quoted or that quoted for access to the property.

If all else fails, an outright enquiry at the auctioneer's office or at the co-agent's office may tell you if the lot you are considering is as a result of a repossession.

What information will an auctioneer give me?

The property details (or particulars)

You will probably be accustomed to the standard estate agents' particulars. Similar particulars are always produced by auctioneers and will invariably contain, apart from the normal property details, information about the date, time and venue of the auction. The Property Misdescriptions Act 1991 has made it a criminal offence for an estate agent to give misleading details about a property. Even before the existence of this Act, auctioneers were expected to provide more reliable details of the lots being offered than estate agents' particulars usually gave. For this reason, and following the 1991 Act, details provided in auction catalogues are usually brief, but they can be relied upon for accuracy despite the 'saving' clauses that vendors and auctioneers often incorporate in their Conditions of Sale. Figure 2.4 shows an example of an auctioneer's particulars.

AUCTION BUYERS GUIDE

All intending purchasers should note that the information relating to the properties in this auction brochure has been provided by the vendors or lessors to the auctioneer and has not been checked by the auction house or by the auctioneer personally.

Before you come to our auction you will need to be in a position to buy, be in a position to purchase outright independent of any other transaction and be able to finance your purchase.

Contracts and special conditions of sale (and probably local searches) are already available for a quick check by your solicitors.

If you cannot attend the auction we can arrange for the auctioneer to bid up to your specified maximum amount. A deposit cheque will need to be left with us beforehand.

When the gavel falls and you are the successful bidder the property is yours - you should insure it straight away - and you will have avoided the problems of chains, vendors changing their minds & gazumping.

At the sale you pay a 10% deposit or £500 whichever is the greater, by cash or cheque, and exchange contracts immediately. Completion is usually one month later.

Allied Dunbar financial advisers attend every auction to help you if you wish. In the event of a successful introduction Longden & Cook Commercial will share in their commission.

In the lot descriptions, there is only a brief precis of such items as planning consents and leases. Copies of these and similar items can only be appreciated properly when they are read in detail and all intending purchasers are encouraged to inspect the copies available at the auctioneer's or solicitors' offices.

Reproduction of maps should not be assumed to be to any specific scale and all calculations of areas should be assumed to be approximate.

Longden & Cook Commercial for themselves and for vendors or lessors of these properties, whose agents they are, give notice that:

(i) the particulars are set out as a general outline only for the guidance of intended purchasers or lessees, and do not constitute, nor constitute part of, an offer or contract;

(ii) all descriptions, dimensions, references to condition, necessary permissions for use and occupation and other details are given without responsibility and any intending purchasers should not rely on them as statements or representations of fact but must satisfy themselves by inspection or otherwise as to the correctness of each of them;

(iii) no person in the employment of Longden & Cook Commercial has any authority to make or give any representation or warranty whatever in relation to these properties.

(iv) All sales are subject to the General, Additional General & Special Conditions applicable to each particular lot.

SOLD AND WITHDRAWN LOTS - AUCTION HOT LINE - ANSWERPHONE 061-236 1117

All would be buyers are invited to check with us at any time during the 24 hours prior to the auction that the lots in which they are interested will be offered.

The attention of all intending purchasers is drawn to all the General and Additional General and Special Conditions of Sale detailed in this brochure. All purchasers interested in lots are invited to obtain copies of the Special Conditions of Sale from the solicitors specified in the catalogue in relation to each lot.

Figure 2.4 Auctioneer's instructions to buyers on how to proceed at auction

The catalogue

Do not be excited by the change in name! The catalogue contains the same information as the individual auctioneer's particulars but produced in a bound form, in lot order. In most cases these will be provided by auctioneers where there are more than three or four lots to be offered on one occasion. The lots' details are still likely to be brief but accurate. They are usually accompanied by relatively comprehensive instructions to buyers on how to proceed at the auction. Figure 2.5 gives an example of these instructions.

The catalogue almost always contains the particulars and the conditions of sale which are referred to in greater detail on page 29. It is this kind of comprehensive catalogue that you are likely to receive from auctioneers who maintain a mailing list and who despatch such magazines or booklets one month to three weeks before their sales.

Understanding the jargon

The effect of the Property Misdescriptions Act has been to reduce considerably the 'estate agentese' in which all property particulars and auction particulars were previously clothed. Nevertheless, if you are accustomed to picking the detail out of sheets prepared by agents for private treaty sales you will find no difficulty in understanding the contents of auctioneers' catalogues.

With the changes that the Property Misdescriptions Act 1991 have brought, you can be pretty sure that estate agents' descriptions do not mislead and you should find that their particulars give a clear description of the property. You are unlikely to find exceptional exaggeration or hyperbole. But do note that every single description in the particulars will have been carefully judged and 'weighed' by the auctioneers, before being included in their description.

Scrutinise the wording carefully

You should therefore scrutinise very carefully the wording in the particulars, noting especially:

- the situation of the property;
- any descriptions of its condition, for example 'refurbishment' should be contrasted with 'modernisation' while 'restoration' should indicate

For a basic house, you might find commentary such as:

VACANT TERRACED HOUSE FOR REFURBISHMENT	
Situation:	A–Z Map Reference 4F 51. Off Old Road.
Construction:	Brick and slate
Tenure:	Freehold or long leasehold subject to a nominal annual rent charge.
Accommodation:	
Ground floor:	2 rooms
First floor:	2 bedrooms, bath/wc
Exterior:	Rear yard
Note:	The property needs complete restoration.
Viewing:	By arrangement with the auctioneers.
Vacant possession:	On completion
Solicitors:	Available from the auctioneers.

For a better quality house, you might easily find details such as:

LUXURY 4-BED DETACHED HOUSE IN APPROX HALF ACRE	
Situation:	A–Z Map Reference 1E 13. Travel north east along A623 for 2 miles from town centre.
Tenure:	Freehold
Accommodation:	
Ground floor:	Porch; entrance hall with seating area; study; fully tiled cloaks with wc and vanity unit; dining room; 3 reception rooms one with fixed bar unit; kitchen/breakfast room including hob, extractor, double oven, microwave, fitted refrigerator and freezer; 4 berth sauna/solarium with shower cubicle, sun bed.
First floor:	Landing with access to balcony overlooking rear garden; 4 fitted bedrooms; fully tiled and pine ceiling bathroom with jacuzzi, shower cubicle, basin, wc, bidet; child's tiled bathroom with miniature bath and twin wash basins set in vanity units.
Exterior:	Double length garage with parking for 2 cars, fitted cupboards, sink, utility area and plumbing for washing machine; front and rear gardens with automatic flood lighting, electric fountain at rear.
Outbuilding:	Snooker room with snooker table.
Note:	This fine traditionally built family home is fitted and decorated to the highest of standards and includes all carpets, curtains and snooker table.
Viewing:	By arrangement with the auctioneers.
Vacant possession:	On completion
Solicitors:	Available from the auctioneers.

Figure 2.5 Auctioneer's particulars and catalogue details

LOT 69
13 Eversleigh Road, East Ham, London E6

BY ORDER OF MORTGAGEES IN POSSESSION

A Freehold Mid Terrace House

TENURE
Freehold

LOCATION
The property is located on the south side of Eversleigh Road in an established residential area within reach of the facilities of East Ham.

DESCRIPTION
The property comprises a mid terrace house arranged over ground and first floors beneath a pitched roof with a private rear garden.

ACCOMMODATION

Ground Floor	First Floor
Double Reception Room	Three Bedrooms
Kitchen Area	
Bathroom Area	

A three-bed house in London with a private garden for under £40,000? Not possible? This one sold at auction for £38,250.

the need for an even more extensive schedule of major repairs;
- in a property with tenants, the exact terms of tenure and any special references to irregularity or lack of payments of rent;
- the extent and nature of the accommodation and the use of adjectives rather than size to describe it;
- any other special elements that are particularly relevant to the type of property offered in the lot.

What price should my top bid be?

This is the fundamental question everyone asks themselves when bidding at auction. It is also one of the most difficult to answer. The situation partially depends upon why you are buying the property.

What type of buyer are you?

Entrepreneur: A true 'wheeler-dealer' looking to buy a bargain and make a profit.

Builder: Someone experienced in the building trade who can take advantage of their connections and knowledge to refurbish a property and sell it on at a profit, giving them an investment with a high yield.

Investor: An individual or company looking to 'tuck away' cash in a property which will give a strong flow of income with a commensurate yield.

Home owner: An individual seeking a property for their own occupation, which they can buy hopefully with more certainty, speed and at a cheaper price than can be bought in the normal private treaty market.

Short-term investor: A combination of an investor and entrepreneur aiming to buy cheaply, improve their income flow and resell the investment to take a profit.

Are you an entrepreneur, experienced or hoping to become experienced in property who will rely on your own opinion of value? Are you a person experienced in building or construction, who is happy to assess any likely costs of bringing the property up to a satisfactory condition? Are you an investor already deeply involved in the investment market who already has a yield in mind or are you an individual purchaser seeking to buy just one lot at one auction?

Judging the market

As an entrepreneur you will probably already have taken steps to obtain the 'feel' of the market. You may have narrowed down the type of property which interests you and perhaps researched the subject. Everyone, whether amateur or professional, can only endeavour to judge the 'right' price by comparing the lot at auction with the prices that have been paid for comparable properties in the past. This is fundamental to seeking out your bargain property. If you are an entrepreneur you may even be prepared to make your own judgement on the condition of the building or the nature of the investment or the likely problems that could arise on development or redevelopment. It may well be that you already have an informal chain of contacts in the various trades or professions to give you assistance.

Get a good feel for the market

If, of course, you have experience in the building trade, the assessment of structures and the ability to estimate costs, you may still need a smaller chain of contacts to make your decision, but you must still rely on that essential 'feel of the market' which can only come from research into recent, past transactions. Even then, in the phrase popular with the financial services industry: 'past performance is not necessarily a guide to future performance!'

As an investor, the eventual net yield of your investment in relation to its quality is what is going to matter to you, although other bidders may take different views from you on the quality of that investment, the yield sought and the quality of the agreement with the tenant.

All these categories of prospective bidders may feel they are experienced or entrepreneurial enough to make their own decision on price.

> **KEY POINT:** *If you are a one-off buyer looking for your single purchase at auction, you are well advised to obtain a professional valuation.*

How to decide on your top bid

The easiest way to do this is to obtain a professional valuation of your target property. The auction market is a particular test of a valuer's skill, since the competition to buy exists in the present and the purchase is immediate. You are asking the valuer to use his experience of a general market and to come to a conclusion following the results of his research

of past transactions. Even when applied with maximum skill, this will not necessarily give the accurate answer you are seeking, since he is only endeavouring to put himself into the minds of two or more hypothetical bidders, with all the uncertainties that that creates. Nevertheless, his experience and assessment from past sales must be of invaluable assistance to you in making a final decision as to your maximum bid.

You should choose a Chartered Surveyor or a member of the Society of Valuers & Auctioneers. If you can find one in the district of the property who also has experience of auctions, do obtain their assistance. You must expect to pay a non-returnable fee which will vary according to the type of report that you require. Details of the fees are given in Table 2.2.

> **KEY POINT:** *If you are satisfied that you can make your own judgement as to the condition of the property, then you only need to ask your surveyor and valuer for a non-structural report on open market value.*

A non-structural valuation report may be sufficient

You will need to provide him with as much information as you can obtain. Advise him about the exact nature of your interest and the extent of your enthusiasm for the particular lot you nominate. Be ready to put him in touch with the auctioneers. An extract of a non-structural valuation report is shown in Figure 2.6 and the general terms and conditions regarding the report are shown in Appendix 3.

Table 2.2 Fees for survey and valuation reports

Valuation range	Sample fee ranges		
	Non-structural valuation	House Buyers Report	Structural survey
Up to £50,000	£200–300	£150–250	£300–450
£50,001–£150,000	£300–450	£250–350	£400–550
£150,001–£250,000	£400–600	£350–450	£550–700
£250,001–£500,000	£600–800	£450–550	£700–1,000
£500,001–£750,000	£800–1,100	£550–750	£1,000–1,500
Over £750,000	£1.50 per £1,000	£1 per £1,000	£2 per £1,000

This scale is given for guidance only. Specific quotes should always be obtained prior to instructing surveyors.

REPORT UPON VALUE OF PROPERTY AT
81 Blossom Road, Buckford

INTRODUCTION

We thank you for your recent instructions in accordance with which we have carried out an inspection of the above mentioned property for valuation purposes.

We have not carried out any form of structural survey of the building and our inspection was intended to be for valuation purposes only. It is therefore assumed that the property is not affected by any serious defects other than those noted in this report.

In particular we have not carried out any investigations to ascertain the presence of high alumina cement or calcium chloride additive and are unable to report whether the property is free from risk in this respect.

GENERAL DESCRIPTION

The property consists of a mid-terrace, two-storey house built in the early 1990s, part of a terrace of similar properties including both original and modernised houses.

LOCATION

Blossom Road is off Bloomfield Road, close to its junction with Charles Road (A756), a continuation of Blakemore Road which joins the A6, Blair Street at Buckford precinct.

This is a reasonably popular residential area, generally convenient for most amenities and with good communications offering access to both Manchester and Buckford City Centres.

ACCOMMODATION

Briefly, the accommodation includes:
Ground floor:
Through lounge/dining room Fitted kitchen (single storey extension)
First floor:
2 double bedrooms, one with fitted wardrobes Bath/wc/basin
Exterior:
Paved rear yard

SERVICES

Mains gas, water, electricity and drainage are laid onto the property. A burglar alarm has been installed and there is an Economy 7 heating system.

TENURE

Assumed to be either freehold or long leasehold subject to a nominal annual charge.

CONSTRUCTION

Of traditional construction with external walls of brick and a pitched slate roof. The roof to the kitchen extension is partially flat and partially pitched under a mineral felt covering and was re-covered during 1992 to rectify rainwater ingress.

CONDITION

As mentioned above, our inspection was of a limited nature intended to be for valuation purposes only. We have not carried out any form of structural survey nor inspected any area not normally visible without the use of ladders or opening up of any part of the structure.

The cosmetic condition of the property is generally good but we would draw your attention to the following:

i) We have referred to the re-roofing of the kitchen extension and note that the underside of the ceiling shows evidence of the original leak; the bottom right hand corner of the kitchen requires decoration to complete the work.

ii) The area to the right of the first flow window to the front elevation was wet at the time of our inspection and subject to constant dampness from a leak resulting from broken guttering (photograph 1, appended).

iii) A number of the slate roof tiles have slipped and require relaying.

iv) The porch area above the front door is damp, as a result of the broken gutter referred to above.

GENERAL OPINION

There are a number of houses for sale in the area, both modernised and original and prices tend to fall in the range £20–30,000, subject to condition. Our enquiries confirm that values have fallen in the last 2/3 years although there appears to be reasonable demand for modernised properties in mortgageable condition from first time buyers. A number of the properties are let, either to regulated tenants who may have been in occupation for some considerable time, or an assured shorthold tenancies to students at the nearby Buckford College.

VALUATION

Taking all the above facts into account, we consider the present open market value of the above described property, with the benefit of vacant possession, to be in the region of:
£25,000 (Twenty Five Thousands Pounds)

MICHAEL F LEWIS BA (Hons) ARICS

Figure 2.6 Extract of a non-structural valuation report

KEY POINT: *If you have any doubts at all on the quality of the structure of the property, then you have no alternative other than to ask for a full structural survey.*

Getting a full structural survey

You should ask the surveyor to give a full structural survey and an opinion of the price at which the property might sell. Your surveyor will carry out a far more detailed inspection of the building and provide you with a relatively comprehensive report on the nature of the structure and any problems that he considers might develop. An extract of a full structural survey report is shown in Figure 2.7. The surveyor may suggest you obtain approximate costs for bringing the property up to a reasonable condition in the light of the report before making conclusions about the price. You will appreciate that this procedure will take some time and both your surveyor and repair estimator must be made to realise the urgency of your request and be warned of the auction date deadline.

The House/Flat Buyers' Report and Valuation

If you are considering a one-off purchase of a house or flat, there is an intermediate level of report which you may consider obtaining which will cost less than the full structural survey. This House/Flat Buyers' Report and Valuation is provided by certain Chartered Surveyors and Society of Valuers & Auctioneers' members, but not by all of them. The cost of such a report can sometimes be a little less than the normal valuation report and will certainly be less than the fees charged for a full structural survey.

How is property valued?

Judging the value of a property is not an exact science. However, there is a number of key techniques that professional valuers use to reach an assessment of a property's value and which you can use to decide what price you should bid up to. The valuer's checklist illustrates (in a slightly simplified version) the key points you need to consider.

VALUER'S CHECKLIST:

1 Obtain as much preliminary information about the property as possible, in particular:
- tenure of site; ☐
- any tenancies; ☐
- size and extent of accommodation and site; ☐
- any peculiarities of the district or situation; ☐
- recent sales, purchases or lettings of the building. ☐

2 Thoroughly inspect the property inside and out. ☐

3 Ascertain outstanding defects and deficiencies that need remedying to bring the property up to normal standards. ☐

4 Make a provisional estimate of the costs of curing those defects and deficiencies. ☐

5 Judge the effect of those costs on the mind of a hypothetical buyer. ☐

6 Obtain as many recent transactions concerning comparable properties as possible. ☐

7 Adjust those transactions for any rise or fall in the market over the period in which they have taken place. ☐

8 Compare and adjust the information from the 'comparables' so that it relates as closely as possible to the property being valued. ☐

9 For vacant properties use as far as possible transactions of vacant 'comparables'. ☐

10 For investment properties, consider rental levels as well as yields of 'comparables'. ☐

11 Allow for differing states of repair with particular reference to step 3 above. ☐

12 Come to a conclusion in the light of your analysis which you hope will equal that of a would-be-buyer. ☐

STRUCTURAL SURVEY,
VALUATION, OPINION,
REPORT, SCHEDULE,
DILAPIDATION, SURVEY,
INVENTORY

RODNEY SCHOFIELD, F.R.I.C.S. F.S.V.A. M.C.B.A
FELLOW OF THE ROYAL INSTITUTION OF CHARTERED SURVEYORS.
FELLOW OF THE INCORPORATED SOCIETY OF VALUERS AND AUCTIONEERS.
MEMBER OF THE CERTIFICATED BAILIFFS' ASSOCIATION.

ROYLES, CHARTERED SURVEYORS

REEDHAM HOUSE, 31/33 KING STREET WEST, MANCHESTER M3 2PW.
TEL No. 061-834 2663
FAX No. 061-832 5706

Structural Survey of a plot of Land and Two Storey Grade II Listed End Terraced Cottage situate and known as 3 Windy Hill, Framsham, FR7 6AU.

TERMS OF REFERENCE

In accordance with your recent instructions and confirmation and Standard Terms of Reference forwarded to you recently, in which we detailed the scope and extent of the Survey we duly attended the property on the 16th January 1994.

At the time of the inspection the weather was dry, cold and bright following a prolonged period of wet and inclement weather during the early autumn and winter months.

We have not inspected woodwork or other parts of the Property which are covered unexposed or inaccessible and we are unable to report that such parts are free from defective; we report only on such parts which are clearly visible.

Observations are made if Structural movement is suspected and comments are made on the structure, accessible roof timbers and other parts of the interior and exterior where visible. It must be noted however that the external survey was limited to one from ground level or via short ladders where possible.

Reference may be made as to the condition of the services but specific testing was not carried out except where stated. At the time of inspection the property was occupied and all the furniture and floor covering were in situ, and in this context it should be mentioned that in most of the rooms the carpets were nailed down or the carpets were stretched over carpet grippers and due to the placement of furnishings no inspection was possible in these areas.

The Inspection of floor and floor areas was therefore restricted to only a very limited series of spot and random checks where possible; therefore we cannot give assurances that the timbers are free from rot but from what we were able to inspect it seems reasonable to assume that the floor timbers are reasonably sound, we would suggest that once the floor coverings are removed a more detailed inspection is carried out.

INTRODUCTION

The property comprises of a two storey listed end terrace cottage constructed in 1724; one of a terrace of three cottages within a small hamlet within a Conservation Area. The property retains many of its original features; no major additions or structural alterations have been made since construction, with the exception of the rear porch entrance which appears to be of a later construction.

Internally there have been no structural removal of walls or chimney breasts but some of the chimneys have been reconstructed or repaired in brick and the flue to the dining room appears to have been sealed at first floor level and smoke test revealed that this is not at present useable for an open fire and if it is intended to use an form of gas convector fire within this property a copex lining should be fitted.

The property is set within an irregular shaped plot with garden frontage and access via a small gate over which there are common rights of way; the boundaries are not strictly defined other than by the low stone walling to the gable elevation; at the rear there is a small raised garden area on which are set a number of mature trees; and an open court yard which is common to this and the other properties with Public Rights of Way and a semi-detached Garage which is constructed in salvaged stone and blockwork and set with a stone tiled roof.

The property lies in a residential area and has views of open countryside and old mill properties and lies approximately half a mile from the village centre local shopping and amenities.

CONSTRUCTION

The property is constructed by traditional methods typical of the period with eighteen inch solid stone walls set on stone footings; the main elevations are faced in local random stone and have been repointed fairly recently in sand and cement mortar using a flush pointing method. These walls due to their age have a bowed appearance particularly on the gable and rear elevation and this is to some effect highlighted by the recent pointing; but no significant structural movement was noted and any deflections are to be expected in a property of this nature and age.

The floors to the ground floor are of solid construction and where exposed and visible are surfaced in asphalt; due to the presence of fitted floor coverings only a limited surface inspection was possible this revealed there were no abnormal signs of rising dampness or cold bridging but it is not possible to tell if the floor has a damp membrane without excavation; the original floor is likely to have been constructed with stone flags. The first floors are of hollow construction and are of suspended timber type with one inch edge to edge pine boarding overlaid on timber joist which span the width of the property and are set into the gable elevation walls, floor levels run out in the majority of the first floor area, in some places the floors have dropped some quarter to half and inch from the skirting level, this is most likely due to the general settlement which has taken place since the property was built and due to its age and the drying out of some of the timbers, and one can normally expect this in a property of this age in this locality.

Figure 2.7 Extract of a full structural survey report

How to estimate what price to pay for a house

The following example illustrates how a house in a suburban street of identical properties is valued.

Four houses in the same street have been bought with vacant possession within the last 12 months. The values of each property are affected by three items:

- the market is judged to be rising at 0.25 per cent per month;
- the even numbers in the street are more popular because they back onto a park;
- the lower numbers in the street are always thought to be the better end of the street.

The prices paid and repair costs for each house were:

House No.	Date bought	Price paid	Repair costs
No. 20	January	£200,000	£30,000
No. 66	March	£190,000	£12,000
No. 85	June	£140,000	£35,000
No. 46	September	£174,500	£40,000

What price should be paid for No. 54 in December where repair costs are £60,000? Table 2.3 illustrates how to calculate what price to pay given the variable information.

Four steps are followed:

Step 1 Find the value of each property by adding the cost of repairs to the price paid.

Step 2 Add or deduct the adjustments for date purchased, side of street and the end of street the property is situated in to give you a comparable value.

Step 3 Add the comparable values of each property together and divide by the number of properties to give you an average comparable value.

Step 4 Deduct the repair costs needed to bring No. 54 up to scratch from the average comparable value and you have a valuation of the property and a good idea of what price you should bid up to.

How to calculate the rent and value of a shop

An investor is looking to purchase a shop in a prime high street location and wants to calculate what the rental income should be and how much the shop is worth. The following information has been gleaned about similar shop investments.

Table 2.3 Calculating the value of a surburban house

House No		20		46		66		85
Price paid		£200,000		£174,500		£190,000		£140,000
Repairs		+£30,000		+£40,000		+£12,000		+£35,000
		£230,000		£214,000		£202,000		£175,000
Bought in	Jan		Sept		March		June	
Adjustments:								
Date	+3%	+£7,000	+1%	+£2,145	+2.5%	+£5,050	+1.5%	+£2,625
Side of street	nil	–	nil	–	nil	–	+10%	+£17,500
End of street	−10%	−£23,000	−3%	−£6,435	+4%	+£8,080	+10%	+£17,500
Comparable value		£214,000		£210,000		£215,130		£212,625

Adjusted comparable values	No. 20	£214,000
	No. 46	£210,210
	No. 66	£215,130
	No. 85	£212,625
	£851,965	(divided by four)
Average comparable value	£213,000	
Applied to No. 54 deduct repair costs	£60,000	
Value in December	£153,000	

1. Three shops have sold in the street in the last month.

2. These three and the one to be valued:
   • are in identical positions;
   • are held on identical leases;
   • have been maintained in good order.

3. No adjustment is needed to compare:
   • position;
   • date of the transaction;
   • differences in tenure;
   • condition.

The shops are different in size and the quality of the covenants of the tenants varies.

Shop A
Has a floor area of 800 sq ft.
The rent is £16,000 per annum.
The tenant is a well-known multiple.
It sold subject to the tenancy for £232,000.

Shop B
Has a floor area of 1,100 sq ft.
The rent is £23,000 per annum.
The tenant is a popular local baker.
It sold for £255,000.

Shop C
Has a floor area of 1,500 sq ft.
The rent is £32,000 per annum.
The tenant is unknown and of doubtful quality.
It sold for £228,500.

Shop D
Is to be sold in auction shortly.
It has 1,253 sq ft.
It is in good repair.

Question 1 What rent can be expected for Shop D?
To work out the rent for shop D, calculate the average rent per square foot of each of the other shops (£20.74) and multiply it by the number of square feet of shop D (1,253 sq ft). Table 2.4 gives the figures needed to make the calculation.

Table 2.4 Calculating the average rent

Shop	A	B	C
Rent	£16,000.00	£23,000.00	£32,000.00
Floor area sq ft	800	1,100	1,500
Rent per sq ft	£20.00	£20.90	£21.33
Average rent	£20.74 per sq ft		

Table 2.5 Investment yields

Shop	A	B	C
Sale price	£232,000	£255,000	£228,500
Rent	£16,000	£23,000	£32,000
Yield on investment	6.9%	9%	14%
Quality of covenant	Excellent	Fair	Poor

Answer 1
Shop D 1,253 sq ft. Likely rent at £20.74 per sq. ft is £26,000 per annum.

Question 2 How much is it worth?
Assuming it can be let within 6 months to a local retailer who has a chain of 12 shops, you need to work out what the annual percentage yield is on the investment by dividing the rent by the sale price and multiplying it by 100. The yields for shops A, B and C are given in Table 2.5.

The yield from a local retailer with a chain of 12 shops will be around 8 per cent – just between the yield for shops A and B. (It is worth noting that the better the quality of covenant, the lower a yield an investor will accept. Conversely, if the tenant seems a higher risk, or poorer quality of covenant, then the investor will expect a higher yield.)

If the yield is 8 per cent and the rent £26,000, then the value is the sum that £26,000 is 8 per cent of. This can be calculated by taking 100 divided by the percentage yield of 8 per cent (12.5) multiplied by the rent of £26,000.

Answer 2
The value is therefore £325,000.

But a buyer needs to discount this amount to allow for:

• the 6 months he has to wait for his rent	£15,000
• his costs	£5,000
• his risk	£25,000
	£45,000

Net Value (£325,000 minus £45,000)　£280,000

UNDER THE HAMMER
REPORT NUMBER 0022 **MONDAY 6 NOVEMBER 2000**

AUCTIONS
AREA 3

ABBREVIATIONS

a-acre accomm-accommodation adj-adjoining agr-agricultural as-arranged as
AST-assured shorthold tenancy av-available at bed-bedroom bldg-building
bment-basement CH-central heating comm-commercial conv-conversion
cott-cottage cnr-corner ctb-council tax band C-freehold with a rent charge
det-detached dev-development DG-double glazing d-h-dwelling house
F-freehold fm-farm fmr-former frct-forecourt frl-full repairing lease
gdn-garden gge-garage gnd-ground gp-guide price GR-ground rent
ho-house imp-improvement ind-industrial inv-investment L-leasehold
lge-large lic-licensed LL-long leasehold LU-lock up m-metre mod-modernised
n/o-not offered nr-near off-office OPP-outline planning permission
P-vacant possession pa-per annum pax-per annum exclusive PH-public house
pkg-parking space PL-part let pot-potential PP-planning permission
PPA-planning permission applied for prems-premises pt-part pvt-sold privately
r-river R-repossessed ren-renovation req-requiring res-residential ret-retail
reg ten-registered tenancy rr-rent roll rsv-reserve price
RUP-residential upper part ⁄-rising/upward only sc-self contained
SC-service charge s-d-semi-detached SPP-subject to planning permission
terr-terraced UT-unexpired term V-vacant possession v-virtual w-withdrawn
xLA-ex Local Authority yd-yard yr-year
#-number ☎-head office ~-range of non-sequential numbers

All sizes and distances are **approximate**

GREATER MANCHESTER

Monday 6 November at 6.30pm
at the Village Hotel & Leisure Club, Cheadle Rd, Cheadle
MAIN & MAIN   01 614 916 666
Gatley   The Old Coachouse, 145 Styal Rd.
   2-bed coach ho in need of mod   summerho
   0.25a ctyd & gdns (gp£115,000)   F   P   ....
Fallowfield   240 Moseley Rd.
   3-bed mid-terr d-h in need of tot refurb
   (gp£40,000)   F   P   ....
Levenshulme   12 Westminster St.
   3-bed s-d d-h (gp£16,000)   F   P   ....
Bury   38 Haymarket St.
   shop with res accomm over (gp£65,000) F P   ....
Stockport   337 Wellington Rd Nth, Heaton Chapel.
   prop as shop with res accomm over
   shop with A3 use granted (gp£45,000) F P   ....
Cheadle Hulme   76 Grove Lane.
   2-bed d-h in need of tot mod (gp£75,000) F P ....
Longsight   13 Giles St.
   2-bed mid-terr d-h in need of further imp
   (gp£8,500)   F   P   ....
Whalley Range   20 Wellington Rd.
   5-bed s-d d-h in need of complete refurb
   suit conv to flats poss grant avail
   (gp£25,000)   F   P   ....
Swinton   31 Cromwell Rd.
   3-bed s-d d-h in need of tot mod
   (gp£28,000)   F   P   ....
Longsight   20 Meller Rd.
   3-storey 3-bed mid-terr d-h (gp£19,500) F P ....
Levenshulme   32 Belvoir Avenue.
   3-bed s-d d-h (gp£14,000)   F   P   ....
Levenshulme   30 Agnes St.
   2-bed mid-terr d-h in need of imp
   (gp£8,500)   F   P   ....
Levenshulme   65 Barlow Rd.
   3-bed end-terr d-h poss flat conv
   (gp£14,000)   F   P   ....
Sale Moor   14 Baguley Rd.
   2-bed mid-terr d-h in need of mod
   Fgdn (gp£57,500)   F   P   ....
Levenshulme   22 Dorset Rd.
   3-bed s-d d-h in need of mod (gp£8,500) F P ....

Tuesday 7 November at 10.00am
at the Café Royal, Regent St W1
ALLSOP & CO   02 074 943 686
Burnley   35 Herbert St.
   2-bed mid-terr d-h
   L895yrUT GR£16.4s.6d (gp£3-8,000)   LL   P ....
Burnley   35 & 43 Fielden St & 5 Duke St.
   3 x 2-bed mid-terr d-h's
   L999yr 1869/1889 GR£peppercn
   (rsv£10,000)   LL   P ....
Moston   20 Summerville Av.
   2-bed mid-terr d-h
   let AST prod £3,120pa (gp£5-10,000)   F   ....
North Burnley   12 Athol St.
   2-bed mid-terr d-h
   let AST prod £3,120pa (gp£5-5,000)   F   ....
Oldham   16 Chaffinch Cl.
   2-bed modern s-d d-h Fgdn pkg
   (gp£20-25,000)   F   P ....
Rochdale   6 Union Rd.
   2-bed mid-terr d-h (gp£17-22,000)   R F   P ....
Stockport   *Wellington Apartments,*
   Wellington Mill, Wellington Rd South.
   8-storey grade II listed fmr mill bdg
   as 3-storey hat museum with possesion of
   45 sc flats on 5-storeys over   2 p-lifts
   44 let/1 void prod £216,300pa
   (gp£1.9-2m)   F   ptP ....
Wigan   9 Scott Av.
   3-bed mid-terr d-h frct
   (gp£25-30,000)   R F   P ....
Wigan   11 Georgian Sq, Platt Bridge.
   3-bed mid-terr d-h Fgdn
   let AST £5,200pa (gp£25-30,000)   F   ....
Worsley   80 Manchester Rd, Walkden.
   3-storey prop as off accomm Fgdn
   conservatory pot for conv to res accomm
   L999yr 1874 GR£peppercn   LL   P ....
Worsley   15 Bridgwater Rd, Walkden.
   2-storey end-terr prop as off accomm
   pot for res conv SPP
   rent chge £2.63pa   C   P ....

Wednesday 22 November at 11.00am
at the Radisson SAS Portman Hotel, London W1
COLLIERS CONRAD RITBLAT ERDMAN   02 079 354 499
Longsight   *Kingfisher Garage,* 441 Stockport Rd.
   0.176a site shop petrol frct
   let 10yr 1997 rv3yr £17,500pax   F   ....
City Centre   *Mellor House,* Mellor St.
   5-storey fmr cotton mill
   PP for conv & addition of 2 further flrs
   to provide 94 flats with pkg   F   P ....

acknowledgments to all who helped in the compilation of this issue

1
auctions continued

Figure 2.8 Extract from Under the Hammer

Understanding the auctioneers' guidelines on price

Many auctioneers will give their opinion of the price range in which a property falls. These guidelines are occasionally published as part of the auction advertisements or part of the auction catalogue. Other firms only respond to a direct enquiry. Virtually all auctioneers will give limited guidance on the price expected.

> **KEY POINT:** *The bottom guideline is usually relatively close to what the auctioneer has fixed or expects to fix as his reserve. The top guideline is normally a slightly optimistic forecast.*

How to track what properties fetch at auction

There can be nothing more valuable to you than forming your own conclusions about the price from doing your own research. To do this, you will need to analyse the prices that have been paid for similar properties at previous auctions. Analysing past figures in the light of the present state of the market and the nature and true comparability of the properties can only come with practice. Obtaining the results of past auctions is sometimes not easy. Occasionally, auctioneers publish past results in their next catalogue and if you are on their mailing list you will be able to collate these figures.

Magazines that publish auction results

There is also a fortnightly publication known as *Under the Hammer* which publishes all auction results in sections for different parts of the country. The publication is provided mainly to professionals on subscription, but anyone can subscribe to it. *Under the Hammer* can be obtained direct from the publishers at 70 Rowheath Road, Kings Norton, Birmingham, B30 2EX, Tel: 0121 680 6832, Fax: 0121 680 6888. *Under the Hammer* also publishes an annual digest of auction results in book form divided into regions which is also usefully divided into categories of property. An extract from *Under the Hammer* is shown in Figure 2.8.

If you decide to subscribe to the *Estates Gazette* you will find that their auction pages analyse all auction results weekly, again on a geographical basis. They also publish a weekly schedule of all the property auctions taking place throughout the country. An example is reproduced in Figure 2.9 on page 22.

Faxwise Plc, of 7 Old Town, London SW4 0JT, Tel: 020 7720 5000, reports on every London property auction by fax to their subscribers. The results are available on the evening of the auction. To complement this service, the results are also available on request from a premium rate telephone number.

The service is in the process of being extended to principal regional auctioneers. Details of this service are shown in Table 2.6. An example of their information is shown in Figure 2.10 on page 23.

Auctioneer's telephone information

Some auctioneers also provide answerphone services. In many cases, auction catalogues can be ordered by leaving your name and address on their answerphone. In other cases, auctioneers give details of their auction programme on a recorded message and, shortly before the auction, provide recorded information of lots that have been amended, sold or withdrawn.

Figure 2.9 Faxwise auction results service

AUCTION ANNOUNCEMENTS AND RESULTS FAXLINE

call

09067 110241

To receive the guide prices of the lots prior to auction, and the results after the auction, dial the above number from the handset of a fax machine. If you do not have a handset, set the machine to 'poll receive mode'.

(calls are charged at 50p per minute at all times.)
Service provided by Faxwise Plc, 020 7720 5000

AUCTION RESULTS

SUFFOLK

O A CHAPMAN & SON at Cambridge, Feb 23
Lowestoft — Commercial Rd. Commercial/
indust site 2.90 a, various offices, w/shops,
stores, let £19,550 PA, 1 shop, store & 3 indust
units with P. F — 250,000
Newmarket — Green Rd. Bdg site 1.10 a with
brick bdg, OPP res development. F, P — 165,000

SURREY

WINKWORTH & CO at London W8, Feb 23
Redhill — 164 Station Rd, Flat 4. 1st floor
studio flat. L, P — 13,500
South Croydon — Sanderstead Rd,
3 Claremont Villas. Flat, 3/4 rms. L, P — 26,500
Sutton — 45A Lower Rd. RUP flat, 2 rms. L, P — 24,500

SUSSEX

WILLMOTTS at London NW1, Feb 24
Brighton — 34 St Michaels Place. Terr hse as
5 flats, 4 LGR & 1st floor, 2 rms, let at
£2,020 PA. F — 16,000

WEST MIDLANDS

WINKWORTH & CO at London W8, Feb 23
Coventry — 14 & 18 Winston Close, Henley
Green. Terr hse, 3 bed, adj linked flat, 2 rms, in
poor order. F, P — 10,500
Kingswinford — 82 Sandhurst Rd, High Acres.
S/D hse, 2 bed, garage. F, P — 28,500

**EDGE EDWARDS & TROMANS at Walsall,
Feb 24**
Walsall — 55 William St. Terr hse, 2 bed. F, P — 18,000

WILTSHIRE

WINKWORTH & CO at London W8, Feb 23
Chippenham — 56 Hillcorner Rd. Flat, 2 rms.
L, P — 14,250

YORKSHIRE

DUNLOP HEYWOOD at Leeds, Feb 23
Cudworth — Newland Ave. Bdg land 1.00 a,
OPP 6 dwellings. F, P — 20,000
Doncaster — East Lane, Stainforth. Bdg land
5.83 a, PP office/industrial development, part site
let £750 PA. Mainly P — 50,000
Thorne Rd, St Georges Bdgs. 2 office bdgs,
4 floors, 13,180 & 17,045 sq ft, parking, site
1.04 a. F, P — 350,000
Kilnhurst — Wharf Rd. Ex rail sidings, 1.23 a.
F, P — 18,800
Methley — Barnsdale Rd. Ex rail track 2.47 a,
possible PP res development. P — 25,000
Mexborough — Wath Rd. Ex rail cutting,
10.87 a, part let at peppercorn — 280,000
Normanton — Altofts Rd. Grassland, 15.00 a,
footpath access only. F, P — 30,000
South Hiendley — Brierley Rd. Ex rail cutting,
19.02 a. F, P — 60,000
Sowerby Bridge — Sowerby St. Ex goods yard
as storage land, 5.08 a with bdgs, let £20,574
PAX — 200,000
Thorne — South End, Thorne South Stn. Bdg
land, 3.80 a, possible PP res development, part
let at £47 PA. Mainly P. F — 40,000

WINKWORTH & CO at London W8, Feb 23
Dewsbury — 41 Moorside Ave, Dewsbury
Moor. S/D hse, 4 bed, vandalised. F, P — 17,000

Halifax — 11 Francis St. End hse, 1 bed, attic
rm. F, P — 8,500

WALES

**THE WILLIAM RICKETTS PARTNERSHIP at
Porth, Feb 22**
Blaenllechau — 29 Commercial St. Terr hse,
3 bed. F, P — 4,000
Ferndale — 32 Duffryn St. Terr hse, 3 bed. F, P — 6,000
Penygraig — 71 Amos Hill. Terr hse, 3 bed.
F, P — 9,500
Tonypandy — 21 Kenry St. Terr hse, 3 bed. F, P — 9,250
Tylorstown — 26 Brynbedw Rd. Terr hse,
2 bed. F, P — 5,000
5 East Rd. Terr hse, 3 bed. F, P — 7,500
102 East Rd. Terr hse, 3 bed. F, P — 5,500
196 East Rd. Terr hse, 2 bed. F, P — 8,000
Tynewydd — 94 Gwendoline St. Terr hse,
2 bed. F, P — 5,500

ABBREVIATIONS – adj. adjacent. CHR chief rent.
F freehold. FRL full repairing lease. FGR freehold
ground rent. GR ground rent. hse house. k 1,000.
L Leasehold. LGR leasehold ground rent. Lit litres.
mais maisonette.
MQ milk quota. OPP outline planning permission.
PA per annum. PAX per annum exclusive.
P possession. PP planning permission.
REV reversion. RR rack rent. R/O rear of.
RUP residential upper part
S/C self-contained. UP upper part.

Results of sales held in London compiled with the
assistance of FAXWISE.

FORTHCOMING AUCTIONS

Date		Auctioneer	Phone No	Venue	Time
Mar	29	CONNELL PROPERTY AUCTIONS	0525 372838	Sachas Hotel, Manchester	2.30 pm
	29	GODFREY-PAYTON	0926 492511	The Plough, Warmington, Warwicks	6.30 pm
	29	WRIGHT-MANLEY	0829 732151	Crown Hotel, Nantwich	7 pm
	30	ANDREWS & ROBERTSON with EDWIN EVANS	071-703 2662 071-228 5864	Four Seasons Hotel, W1	11.30 am
	30	CROWN & CO	0222 594238	The Park Hotel, Cardiff	6.30 pm
	30	DEDMAN PROPERTY SERVICES	0702 467000	Cumberland Suite, Westcliff on Sea	3 pm
	30	GA PROPERTY SERVICES	0705 872312	Royal Scot Hotel, Edinburgh	12 noon
	30	STAGS	0392 55202	The Devon Motel, Exeter	3.30 pm
	30	WALTER & RANDALL	0634 841233	Inn On The Lake, Shorne, Kent	3 pm
	30	WRIGHT-MANLEY	0829 732151	The Swan Hotel, Tarporley	7 pm
Apr	6	HAMBRO COUNTRYWIDE	0245 344133	Stifford Moat Hse, Grays, Essex	2 pm
	7	AUSTIN GRAY	0273 207575	Dudley Hotel, Hove	3 pm
	7	BARTONS	0222 777756	Aztec West Hotel, Bristol	7 pm
	7	HAMBRO COUNTRYWIDE	0245 344133	Moor Lodge Hotel, Branston, Lincs	2 pm
	8	HAMBRO COUNTRYWIDE	0245 344133	Airport Ambassador Hotel, Norwich	2 pm

Figure 2.10 Estates Gazette auction results and forthcoming auctions

AUCTION	**CONNELL**		**RESULTS of SALE**			
Phone No.	0793 480028		Lots Offered	145		
Auction Venue	PARK LANE HOTEL PICCADILLY		Lots Sold Prior	52		
			Lots Sold in Room	71		
			Total Lots Sold	123		
Copyright FAXWISE Plc. 1993			Percent Sold	85%		
	Tel: 020 720 5000 Fax: 020 720 5030		Total Raised	£4,040,745		

faxwise
Your information advantage

Publication Date :
19.4.94

Numbers in Brackets [ ] indicate LOTS that did NOT Sell :

Lot Nº	PROPERTY ADDRESS	Gross Income £ 000's	Property Description Code	1st. Bid £ 000's	Sold [Last Bid] £ 000's	Remarks / Available £ 000's
1	45 St Aidans Rd,E Dulwich,SE22		Lh.1stFl.Flt.2Rm.V	10	19	
2	4 Emperors Gate,S Kensington,SW7		Lh.3rd/4thFl.Mas.3Rm.V	Sold Prior	157.5	
3	Flt 3,2 Beaumont Cres,W Kensington		Lh.Gnd.Fl.Flt.1Rm.V	Sold Prior	52	
4	54 Crouch Hill,Crouch End,N4		Fh.Gnd.Fl.Flt.3Rm.Gar.CG.V	Withdrawn Prior		
5	74 Sylvan Ave,Wood Green,N22		Lh.Gnd.Fl.Flt.3Rm.V	Sold Prior	32	
6	85 Tudor Cl,Brixton Hill,SW2		Lh.2ndFl.Flt.1Rm.V	10	18	
7	24 Greenland Quay,Plough Wy,Rotherhithe,SE16		Fh.Ter.Hse.2Fl.3Rm.Gdn.PS.V	35	[47]	55
8	102 Gloucester Ter,W2		Lh.Bas.Flt.3Rm.V	Sold Prior	60	
9	57 Gleneldon Rd,Streatham,SW16		Lh.2ndFl.Flt.3Rm.V	Sold Prior	25	
10	16 Compass Ct,Horselydown Sq,Shad Thames,SE1		Lh.PB.2nd/3rd/4thFl.Apt.3Rm.V	Sold Prior	104	
11	197A Edgware Rd,Colindale,The Hyde,NW9		Lh.PB.1stFl.Flt.3Rm.V	8	18	
12	59B Palmerstone Cres,Palmers Green,N13		Lh.Gnd./1stFl.Mas.3Rm.V	Sold Prior	38	
13	11 Station Approach,Coulsden,Surrey		Fh.Ter.Hse.	40	47.5	
14	Flt 4,30 Mount Ephraim Rd,Streatham,SW16		Lh.Flt.4Rm.V	25	30.5	
15	38 St Marys Rd,Harlesden,NW10		Lh.SC.1stFl.Flt.4Rm.V	20	[28.5]	30
16	10 North Rd,Surbiton,Surrey		Lh.Bas.Flt.3Rm.Gdn.V	Sold Prior	50	
17	Familo Rd,Walthamstow,E17		Lh.1stFl.Flt.3Rm.V	20	22	
18	29 Wrottesley Rd,Willesden,NW10		Fh.Det.Hse.2Fl.8Bs.Gdn.Gar.V	Withdrawn Prior		
19	71 Northwood Rd,Thornton Heath,Surrey		Fh.Gnd.Fl.Flt.2Rm.Gdn.V	10	17	
20	20A The Broadway,Tolworth,Surrey		Lh.PB.2ndFl.Flt.3Rm.V	20	33	
21	70 St Hildas Way,Gravesend,Kent		Fh.Ter.Hse.2Fl.4Rm.Gdn.V	Sold Prior	40	
22	30 Green La,Chessington,Surrey		Lh.1stFl.Flt.3Rm.CG.V	Sold Prior	40	
23	Flt 3,Whales Yard,West Ham La,Stratford,E15		Lh.PB.1stFl.Flt.3Rm.PS.V	20	25	
24	Flt 5,Whales Yard,West Ham La,Stratford,E15		Lh.PB.2ndFl.Flt.3Rm.PS.V	20	25	
25	16B Green La,Hersham,Surrey		Lh.1stFl.Flt.2Rm.V	20	[22.5]	23
26	50 Oval Rd,Croydon,Surrey		Fh.EoT.Um.Hse.4Rm.Gdn.V	Sold Prior	36	
27	2 Boyne Rd,Hastings,E Susx		Fh.SD.Hse.2Fl.4Rm.Gdn.V	Sold Prior	25	
28	16 Adelaide Rd,High Wycombe,Bucks		Fh.SD.Hse.2Fl.4Rm.Gdn.Gar.V	Sold Prior	42	
29	Flt 5,1 Clarendon Ter,Kemp Town,Brighton,Susx		Lh.2ndFl.Flt.1Rm.V	Sold Prior	5	
30	403 Goffs La,Goffs Oak,Herts		Fh.Hse.2Fl.6Rm.Gdn.Gar.V	100	[120]	130
31	52A Cheapside,Luton,Beds		Lh.1st/2ndFl.Apt.3Rm.V	Sold Prior	19	
32	8 Church Cl,Brandon,Suff		Fh.SD.Bw.3Rm.Gdn.V	15	20	
33	Cottesmore Ct,Leigh on Sea,Essex		Lh.PB.1stFl.Flt.3Rm.V	20	20	
34	19 St Johns Rd,Chelmsford,Essex		Fh.Ter.Hse.2Fl.4Rm.Gdn.Gar.V	Sold Prior	49.995	
35	492 London Rd,Brands Hill,Slough,Berks		Lh.PB.Gnd.Fl.Mas.3Rm.Gdn.Gar.V	Sold Post	30	
36	Doveport Lodge,Nr Haddon,Peterborough,Hants		Fh.Bw.4Rm.Gdn.Dbl.Car Port.V	50	[65]	75
37	Roxton Hill Hse,Great Barford,Beds		Fh.Det.Hse.2Fl.5Bed.&Ext.Pool.14.5Ac.V	100	[115]	280
38	6 Empire Ct:Pole Barn La,Frinton on Sea,Essex		Lh.1stFl.Flt.3Rm.3PS.V	16	18	
39	2,2A&2B Woodlands Pde,Maidstone,Kent	7.1	Fh.Sh.GRs.onMas.&Flt.	45	52	
40	Beecholme,54 Codicote Rd,Welwyn,Herts	17.91	Fh.Hse.AA.7Flt.1V.RR.'94	150	180	

Figure 2.11 Auction results from Faxwise

'I have bought properties that are in some state of disrepair. They always wanted modernising and bringing up to date. In deciding what price to bid I tend to take an overall view. I check local sale prices and work out how much it will cost me to bring it up to date. I am usually prepared to pay so much at auction and if it goes for that price, I will buy it.'

Michael Roe, buyer of residential properties.

3 Clearing the contracts and arranging the finance before the auction

'You must ask why the property is going for sale at auction and what (if anything) is wrong with it and satisfy yourself that you are not buying a pig in a poke. You have got to be prepared to do your own research. For example, I had to check that I was not buying a property over a coal mine. I knew the reason for sale – that the property was foreclosed and put up for auction by a building society.'   Don Lee.

As soon as you have found your chosen property, you must take a careful look at the legal and financial issues to make sure you can finance the transaction and commit to exchanging contracts as soon as you succeed in your purchase. This chapter examines these issues and other pitfalls to watch out for in the run-up to attending the auction.

When to use a solicitor

Choosing your solicitor

Your solicitor should be someone in whom you have confidence and whom you are sure will make reasonable charges for the service provided. Your solicitor should undoubtedly be someone who has experience in property conveyancing. If you can find one that has extensive experience of auction procedures this will be a bonus. Finally, you must be sure that they can move quickly since the time scale from when an auction is announced to when it occurs is often only three or four weeks.

Solicitor's fees

Competition between solicitors for conveyancing work has recently driven down the charges for it. Nevertheless, fees charged by solicitors vary considerably and are dependent upon the amount of work which will be necessary and the size of transaction. It is more important to have a solicitor in whom you can trust, who knows auction procedures and who will act with speed, rather than

save yourself £100 in conveyancing fees. Most solicitors will give a general quotation of the price band in which their fees will fall for any specific transaction. Do ask for one before instructing them to begin work. Table 3.1 gives an example of solicitor's conveyancing fees.

Table 3.1 Solicitor's conveyancing fees

Purchase at auction (excluding disbursements)	Fee range
Up to £50,000	£200–£300
£50,001–£150,000	£250–£450
£150,001–£250,000	£300–£500
£250,001–£500,000	£450–£1,200
£500,001–£750,000	£1,000–£1,500
Over £750,000	0.25%–0.35%

> **KEY POINT:** *You must be positive that the solicitor you choose understands the meaning of the word urgency.*

What advice should I seek?

Hopefully, by the time you have absorbed the contents of this book, you will know as much or more about auction procedures than your solicitor and you will probably not need to visit or ring him to discuss what you need to do at an auction. However, as soon as you have decided to make a bid, you should immediately approach your solicitor for advice. Ideally, you should give him a copy of the catalogue and, at this first stage, discuss the condition being applied to the sale. The conditions of sale are examined on page 29. Your solicitor will check that the conditions do not contain any unusual or surprise clauses that could penalise you. As soon as you have his reassurance that he is happy for your to go and bid, you need him to start researching the lot or lots in which you are interested.

LOT 80

Flat 1, 44 Elm Park Gardens, Chelsea, London SW10

BY ORDER OF MORTGAGEES IN POSSESSION

A Leasehold Raised Ground Floor Flat

TENURE
Leasehold. The property is held on a lease for a term of 125 years from 29th September 1982 (thus having 113 years unexpired) at a current ground rent of £10 per annum.

LOCATION
Elm Park Gardens is situated off Fulham Road, midway between St Stephens Hospital and Brompton Hospital. Fulham Road provides access to Knightsbridge and a full range of shopping facilities.

DESCRIPTION
The property comprises a raised ground floor flat situated within a terraced house which overlooks the communal gardens of Elm Park. Access is from a communal entrance hall.

ACCOMMODATION
Reception Room with Integral Kitchen
Bedroom
Bathroom with WC

Would you like a flat in Chelsea without breaking the bank? You could have picked this one up for only £68,000.

What information does my solicitor need from me?

Your solicitor will need detailed information about your prospective property including:

1 A copy of the auction catalogue.

2 A copy of all the conditions of sale.

3 Any further details of the lots you are interested in. For example:
   - a copy of the valuation/survey/builder's report;
   - a copy of the lease (if relevant);
   - a copy of any further letters/details from the auctioneers;
   - notes of answers to queries already put to the auctioneers;
   - the name and address of the solicitors acting for the seller.

4 Who is making the purchase. For example,
   - the full name and address of you and your partner;

Priors and posts bolster Erdman result

Erdman Lewis raised a total of £4.17m from its 21-lot auction at the Meridien Hotel in Piccadilly, W1, but only seven of the 16 successful lots were sold under the hammer.

Six were knocked down prior, raising £1.375m, and a further three went immediately after the auction, contributing £841,000.

Five out of six High Street shops, which are currently let to Foster Brothers Clothing, were snapped up, mainly by private investors, at net initial yields ranging from 8.14% to 10.53%. The one remaining lot was close to selling this week.

The properties are all let on leases of more than 20 years from August last year, when Foster Brothers completed a management buyout from Sears. Lot sizes ranged from £171,000 for 79 High Street, Bideford, Devon, to £300,000 for 17 Sheep Street, Bicester, Oxfordshire.

Auctioneer John Townsend commented that the good response to the shops meant that the company would be offering a further tranche in its June auction. The June catalogue will also contain 13 Barclays Bank sale and leasebacks, which have proved to be popular in previous sales.

The largest lot to go under the hammer at last week's sale was an Italian restaurant with flats above in Market Street, Brighton, East Sussex,

which fetched a price of £433,500. The annual income from the building is £43,600, reflecting a net initial yield of 9.79%.

A shop in Hampstead High Street, NW3, trading as Hobbs fashionwear, was knocked down prior, fetching approximately £600,000 — the same price that the vendor paid when he bought it at an Edward Erdman auction three years ago.

A freehold redevelopment opportunity in Princes Street, W1, went in the room for £385,000. The Grade II listed building on basement, ground and three upper floors provides 3,790 sq ft of office accommodation.

Planning consents for the site, which is only 200 yards from Oxford Circus, exist for office, restaurant and residential uses.

Townsend said that there were signs of confidence among bidders which has been lacking for some time.

"Investors are obviously eager to pick up valuable properties and expect competition for them in the room," he said.

'Sale and leasebacks' – Owners of (generally commercial) properties occasionally wish to realise capital from that ownership whilst remaining in occupation. They do this by creating a lease back to themselves and then selling the freehold with the entitlements to collect the newly created rent on the new lease.

'Knocked down prior' – 'Knocked down' is a colloquial way of expressing the fall of the gavel and/or the exchange of contracts. 'Prior' is before the auction.

Illustration 2.
Estates Gazette report on an Erdman Lewis auction

- Partnership details, if a partnership is buying the property.
- Details of the business, if a business of limited company is buying the property.

5   Financial arrangements:
  - how the property is being paid for;
  - name and address of the mortgage provider;
  - your accountant and/or financial broker (if relevant);
  - status of any sales or other assets which will be linked to the purchase.

What questions will my solicitor put to the vendor's solicitors?

Almost invariably the solicitors acting on behalf of the sellers are noted in the catalogue but, if not, the auctioneer's firm can advise you who is acting. Your solicitor should then approach them with the appropriate questions covering in particular:

1. The quality of the title

The ownership of land in England is well catalogued and formulated. Many titles and their details are recorded at the Land Registry, who provide a log book style document with a plan giving concise details of what a landowner holds. The log book shows:

- whether the title is freehold or leasehold (and its length);
- the current ownership;
- a brief history of the previous ownerships;
- covenants, restrictions or easements that affect the property and normally any major charge registered against the land.

Not all titles, however, are as thoroughly catalogued and ownership of land is not always as secure. It is not unusual for auctions to be used as places for the disposal of properties where the title may be questionable and where the vendor hopes, that by submitting the property for sale in this manner, the purchaser will be less than thorough in ensuring that his solicitor makes the necessary investigations. The possibility of such a problem should not stop you from considering buying properties at auction, but should encourage you to ensure that before buying, you have the title checked.

How to own property without buying it!

As a rather extreme example of the sort of problem that can arise under English law, it is possible for someone who does not initially own a plot of land or property to become its owner by occupying it for at least 12 years without anyone – and particularly the true owner – raising any objection whatsoever during that period. After 12 years, the occupier usually becomes the landowner with an appropriate title to sell.

To obtain such a 'statutory title' (also sometimes known as a 'squatter's title'), the proper procedures must be followed meticulously for the title to be perfect. If, as a buyer of such a title, you have not had the process of development of ownership thoroughly checked, it could be possible that the possessory title is not supported by suitable affidavits or has not been created because of some inadequacies in the occupation. In such extreme circumstances, a buyer at auction may find that he has purchased a property and is subsequently unable to register his title or to defend it against an original and previous owner.

2. The nature of any covenants, restrictions or easements

Land is frequently subject to drains, culverts or water courses underneath it; electricity, gas or similar services running on, over or under it; rights of way, bridle paths, footpaths and roads running across it and many similar 'easements'. Occasionally, one hears of people discovering that rights of way exist that run right through their garden or even right through their property. It is an unlucky bidder who discovers only after a contract has been exchanged, that his lot suffers such an impediment.

Can you use your property for the intended purpose?

Covenants and restrictions on use of land can be even more complicated. If you are buying a piece of building land to develop and do not research it adequately, it might result in your buying a piece which has covenants preventing the land from being developed for the intended purpose. For example, a buyer intending to erect a multi-storey block might find covenants preventing the erection of such a building. Alternatively, the buyer of a piece of land beside a railway line or road might discover they have acquired a responsibility to erect an expensive wall or fence.

3. Any adverse details revealed in the local search

The local search is a set of questions submitted to the local authority in which the property is situated. All sorts of planning (for example, highway and transport plans) may affect a lot. Building or planning regulations may not have been observed when the building on a lot was erected. The local authority environmental departments may be critical of items in the buildings or on the site which could have expensive repercussions after you have bought the property. All property is subject to detailed building and planning regulations under the auspices of the local authority. The local search should reveal if any problems are present.

With luck, the solicitor acting for the seller will have obtained a local search or be in the process of obtaining one prior to the auction. But it could be that the local search may not be available. If the local search has not been obtained, it would be wise for either you or your solicitor to enquire with the relevant local authority, if there are any adverse proposals or notices affecting the property. Appendix 2 reproduces the Enquiry to Local Authority form listing all the questions you will need to ask them about your target property. If any planning consents affecting the lot are of interest to you, the local authority will generally provide a copy at a nominal cost or, alternatively, make available for inspection at their offices the relevant planning register.

4. Any other appropriate legal points.

KEY POINT: *When you attend the auction, if you find the solicitor for the seller is present, check with him to see if there have been any subsequent alterations or changes and also to read through whatever literature he can provide.*

If you are unsure in your bidding or if your solicitor has been unable to obtain any details before the auction itself, you may feel it is worthwhile employing him to accompany you to the auction, to make whatever research is possible at the time and to assist you in your bidding when the lot comes up for sale. You must realise that he will charge an additional fee for such a service, probably on an hourly basis. Do obtain from him a quotation of the cost for attending the auction. You can expect such a charge to be between £80 and £200 per hour depending upon the nature and level of expertise of the person you are employing and the size, calibre and address of the firm you are using.

The following checklist illustrates the stages your solicitor will go through from initial instruction through to completion.

SOLICITOR'S CHECKLIST:
Acting for a Buyer

1 Request the contract, searches and replies to pre-contract enquiries plus auction catalogue. ☐

2 Ask the client how he is financing the transaction and explain the pitfalls of buying at auction. ☐

3 Investigate title and raise any appropriate enquiries on that and any other matters and also raise such pre-contract and personal searches as may be necessary, for example, personal local search, British Coal search etc. ☐

4 Report to the client and establish his maximum offer and advise of the deposit amount he must take to the auction. ☐

5 A few days before the auction, see if there are any amendments with the seller's solicitors or auctioneers and, if so, relay those to your client. ☐

6 If the client so wishes, attend the auction with him or as his agent. ☐

7 Re-check the details received from the seller's solicitors and see if there are any amendments. If so, notify the client. ☐

8   Bid as instructed, or monitor the client's bidding.   ☐

9   Ensure the contract is signed correctly and exchange of contracts is recorded properly.   ☐

10 Obtain signed contract received by client and liaise with seller's solicitors, as normal, up to completion.   ☐

Conditions of sale

What are the conditions of sale?

These are the terms on which the successful bidder will buy the property. They regulate not only the bidding, but also any obligations the bidder must fulfil. They give a full and definitive description of the property and prescribe what happens after your bid is successful.

Check for onerous liabilities

If you are interested in bidding for a lot, you should ask to see these before doing so – otherwise you may end up buying something that is different from what you thought. You may be left with some heavy liabilities or the property may be subject to various covenants, for example a requirement to fence the borders of the property.

It is usual for an auctioneer to draw your attention to serious matters affecting the property, either in the auction catalogue itself and/or on the day in his introductory remarks. However, his remarks are very often only a summary. It is up to you to inform yourself and look at the conditions carefully. They will always be available from the auctioneer or from the owner's solicitors.

What types of conditions are there?

The bidder at auction will usually find up to four conditions to watch out for:

- the general conditions
- the additional general conditions
- the special conditions
- any other conditions under whatever name

These conditions may appear in several guises and in several places. You may find all the relevant conditions applicable to a lot are dealt with in the auction catalogue. Alternatively, you may find only some conditions in the catalogue, normally called 'General Conditions'. An example is shown in Figure 3.1.

Where an owner has a number of lots in an auction and he or his solicitor thinks it advisable to have certain conditions relating to all those lots or most of them over and above the general conditions, he can arrange for these to be printed in the catalogue and they will be headed 'Additional General Conditions' or something similar. An example is shown in Figure 3.2.

Watch out for hidden conditions

An owner's solicitor may need to draw up extra conditions to cover points that are not covered in the general conditions or additional general conditions, or he may find that the general conditions do not achieve what his client needs – in that case he will draw up special conditions.

Frequently, these will not be printed in the catalogue, as the catalogue will have been sent for printing before the owner's solicitor has even seen the title deeds. They will only be available from the auctioneer and the owner's solicitors. Figure 3.3 on page 32 shows an example of special conditions.

> **KEY POINT:** *You should always check to make sure that before you bid, you have seen and understand any conditions that apply to the purchase. All these conditions form the contract on which any lot is knocked down to you.*

What do the general conditions mean?

The general conditions (as shown in Figure 3.1) will usually cover the following:

1   **Most of the current Law Society Standard Form of Contract for sale of property but often with variations in the owner's favour!**

The main points in the Law Society's Standard Form to note are:

(a)   the seller sells the property subject to any matters affecting it whether they are

General Conditions of Sale applicable to all Lots insofar as they are not inconsistent with the Special Conditions of each Lot

1 (a) The property is sold subject to the following conditions ('The General Conditions') and to the Standard Conditions of Sale (3rd Edition) ('The Standard Conditions') so far as they are not inconsistent with the General Conditions and in the event of any conflict between the General Conditions and the Standard Conditions then the General Conditions shall prevail.

   (b) Each Purchaser shall be deemed to purchase with full knowledge of all the conditions subject to which the property is sold.

   (c) The Standard Conditions are amended as follows:-

   (i)   Reference in the Standard Conditions to 'the Seller' shall mean the Vendor' and to 'the Buyer' shall mean 'the Purchaser'.
   (ii) The Contract rate referred to in Standard Condition 1.1.1(g) is 4% above Lloyds Bank Plc base lending rate from time to time.
   (iii) The Standard Conditions 3.1.3, 3.3.2(c) and 4.3.2 shall not apply.
   (iv) The Standard Condition 5.1 shall not apply and on and from the date of the Contract the property shall be at the sole risk of the Purchaser who shall insure it from such date in its full reinstatement value against all usual risks and perils with an insurance company of repute.
   (v)   The words 'without delay' shall be deleted from Standard Condition 3.2.2.(b).
   (vi) In Standard Condition 7.3.4 the words 'if he does so he cannot claim compensation under Condition 7.3.1 as well' shall be deleted.
   (vii) The words 'with an Absolute Title' shall be deleted from Standard Condition 8.2.4.
   (viii) Standard Condition 8.3 shall not apply.

   (d) Where the property transferred is leasehold the Transfer shall contain a declaration in the following terms "the covenant implied by the Transferor transferring in this deed with limited title guarantee" is varied as follows:- Section 4 of The Law of Property (Miscellaneous Provisions) Act 1994 shall not apply.

2 If a person attending the sale intends to bid on behalf of some other person or company, he shall before the sale commences hand the Auctioneer a note of the name and address of that other person or company failing which the Auctioneer shall be entitled, at any time prior to completion, to treat the bidder as the contractual purchaser whether or not the Auction Contract was signed for or on behalf of some other person or company.

3 On each Lot being knocked down the successful bidder must, upon being asked by the Auctioneer or the Auctioneer's Clerk, give his name and address or the name and address of the person or company on whose behalf he has been bidding and in default the Auctioneer shall be entitled to re-offer that property for sale as if it had not previously been knocked down.

4 (a) Bidding. All bids are to be made clearly. The Auctioneer reserves the right to regulate bidding and to refuse undesirable bids. The Vendor reserves the right to bid up to the reserve price or to authorise the Auctioneer to do so. In the event of any dispute in respect of the conduct of the auction the Auctioneer's decision is final.

   (b) Each lot is offered subject to a reserve price unless otherwise stated.

   (c) All bids are deemed to be exclusive of Value Added Tax.

5 The amount of the deposit shall be 10 per cent of the purchase price or £1000 whichever sum shall be the greater and shall be paid to the Auctioneers, Longden & Cook Commercial, as agents for the Vendor and Standard Condition 2.2 shall be varied accordingly.

6 If a cheque given for the payment of a deposit is dishonoured on presentation or if the successful bidder fails to pay such deposit, the Vendor shall be entitled (but shall not be bound) to treat such dishonour or failure as a repudiation of the Contract and to sell the property to some other person but without prejudice to the Vendor's right to claim against the successful bidder damages for repudiation of the Contract.

7 The date for completion of the purchase shall be on (or before) four weeks from the date of the contract at the offices of the Vendor's Solicitors or as they shall direct.

8 The tenure of each Lot and the estate or interest sold is as stated in the Particulars and Special Conditions of Sale for the Lot. In the case of land registered at HM Land Registry the title shall be deduced in accordance with section 110 of the Land Registration Act 1925. In the case of land not so registered the title shall be deduced as provided for in the Special Conditions of Sale. The Vendor sells as Beneficial Owner with full title guarantee unless otherwise provided.

9 Each Lot is believed to be and shall be taken as correctly described and any incorrect statement, error or omission found in the Auction Particulars or Special Conditions of Sale shall not annul the sale or entitle the Purchaser to rescind the Contract nor shall the Purchaser claim or be allowed any compensation in respect thereof.

10 The Purchaser shall be deemed to have made all searches and enquiries normally made by a prudent Purchaser and to have knowledge of all matters which would have been disclosed thereby and shall purchase subject to such matters. In particular the Purchaser shall buy subject to any existing or future notices claims acquisitions requisitions proceedings orders acts or requirements (whether registered or not) or any tribunal or local or other authority in relation to the property or any part thereof.

11 From the date of the Contract the property shall be at the sole risk of the Purchaser.

12 The Auctioneer reserves the right to hold the Memorandum of Contract or the Contract signed by them on behalf of the Vendor until the Purchaser's cheque for the deposit has been cleared.

13 No objection or requisition shall be raised as the permitted user of the property for the purposes of the Town and Country Planning Act or any Act or Acts for the time being amended or replacing the same.

14 The Purchaser acknowledge that (a) no statement or representation which may previously have been made to him or any person concerned on his behalf by or on behalf of the Vendor whether orally or in writing induced him to enter into this agreement (b) any such statement or representation does not form part of this agreement and (c) any liability of the Vendor in respect of any statement made to the Purchaser at law or in equity is hereby excluded to the extent authorised by the Misrepresentation Act 1967.

15 The Purchaser shall be deemed to purchase with full knowledge of the state of repair and condition of the Lot and notwithstanding anything in these General Conditions or in the Particulars and Special Conditions no representation,warranty or condition is made or shall be implied either as to the said state or condition of the Lot or any part thereof or as to whether the same is subject to any sanitary or Public Health Notice or notices, or intimation notice or notices or proposals under the Housing Acts or any of them. The Purchaser shall be deemed to purchase in all respects subject thereto whether or not he makes any enquiry and neither the Vendor nor the Auctioneers shall be required or bound to inform the Purchaser of any such matters whether known to them or not and the Purchaser shall raise no enquiry requisition or objection thereon or thereto.

16 Each Lot is sold (as mentioned in the Particulars and Special Conditions) either with vacant possession of the whole or part or subject to and with the benefit of the tenancies leases or other occupancies referred to in the Particulars and Special Conditions. The Purchaser shall take the Lot as he finds it and shall accept that Vacant Possession is given of the whole or any part offered with Vacant Possession notwithstanding that there may be furniture fittings or effects remaining therein and shall not be entitledto require the removal of any such furniture fittings or effects or object to taking the same on the ground that the existence thereof does not constitute Vacant Possession as such.

17 The fact (if such be the case) that the Lot is a house or part of a house which may not legally be used for immediate residential occupation shall not annul the sale or entitle the Purchaser to rescind the sale or claim damages or diminution in the price.

18 No representation is made that the rent payable in respect of any Lot or any part thereof is the rent properly chargeable under any Acts of Parliament or Statutory Instruments or Regulations regulating or controlling the same. The only representation made or intended to be implied by or from the Particulars and Special Conditions is that the rents referred to therein are the rents actually being paid by the Tenants to the Landlord and no objection or requisition shall be taken or made as to any matter arising under any such Acts Instruments or Regulations. The Purchaser shall not be entitled to raise any requisition or objection as to any rent limits or net rents or fair rents or the present or former regulated rents payable in respect of the property nor to the liability of the Vendor to produce copies of statutory notices of increase and notices to quit (if any) which may have been served. In the case of a regulated tenancy under the Rent Acts no objection shall be made on the grounds that the rent referred to is not the fair rent or that it may exceed the rent registered under the Rent Acts or that the rent has not been registered. No objection shall be taken by a Purchaser as to whether or not a notice of increase of rent has or has not been validly served or as to whether or not a Certificate of Disrepair has been obtained by the Tenant authorizing a reduction of rent nor shall the Purchaser object to the existence or terms of any counter-notice served upon or by a Tenant.

19 In the case of a Lot let, no representation is made as to whether or not there is any sub-tenant except where expressly stated in the Particulars and Special Conditions.

20 The Vendors shall not be required to assure the whole or any part of the property to any person other than the Purchaser and by one assurance.

21 The Vendor makes no representation as to the ownership of electric wiring and fittings and gas fittings and installations or central heating installations which may be on hire or hire purchase from the supply companies. In such case the Vendor accepts no liability for any payments that may be outstanding in respect thereof and the lot is sold subject thereto.

22 Each Lot is sold subject to Special Conditions of Sale of which each purchaser shall be deemed to have knowledge regardless of whether or not he has taken the opportunity that is available to inspect them or consult with the solicitors acting for the Vendor in each individual case. Wherever possible the Special Conditions of Sale will be available for inspection at the place of auction for at least three quarters of an hour before the sale.

23 Upon each Lot being knocked down, the successful purchaser shall as soon as practicable after the successful bid and in any event before leaving the auction room sign a form of contract or memorandum of the terms of the Contract at the table of the solicitors or that of the Auction Administrator. In default thereof, the Auctioneer shall be and is hereby authorised (but is not obliged) to sign on his behalf.

Figure 3.1 Auctioneer's general conditions

Note: The Royal Institution of Chartered Surveyors is close to completing a modernised version of these General Conditions which they hope will be used generally by solicitors shortly.

Additional General Conditions of Sale

Additional General Condition of sale applicable to Lots specified insofar as it is not inconsistent with the Particulars and Conditions of Sales of each lot.

24   The Solicitors for the Vendors are:

25   General Condition 8 shall be read if:

(a) The words 'and the Purchaser shall not investigate or make any requisition or objection in respect of any earlier Title' had been added after the words or provided by the Special Conditions of Sale.

(b) Where the Lot is in a compulsory registration area under the Land Registration Acts or the Title is already registered at H.M. Land Registry the Vendor will nevertheless after completion of the purchase without expense to the Purchaser produce to the Chief Land Registrar all documents and do all acts and things required by the Registrar to enable him to accept the application of the Purchaser for registration of his Title to the Lot.

26   The purchaser shall execute and deliver to the Vendor within 14 days after completion of the purchase a duplicate of the Assurance of the Lot to the Purchaser such duplicate to be engrossed perused executed stamped and denoted by and at the expense of the Purchaser.

27   The Vendor shall not be required to execute more than one Assurance of the Lot.

28 (a) There are not included in the sale of any Lot (unless otherwise provided in the Particulars and Special Conditions of Sale):

(i)   any mines or minerals under the property or any right of support from any mines or minerals whatsoever.

(ii)   any easements of light air or support or other easements or right which would restrict or interfere with the free use by the Vendor or any person deriving Title under it for building or any other purpose of an adjoining or neighbouring land of the Vendor (whether intended to be retained or to be sold by it).

(b) There shall be reserved to the Vendor:

(i)   the right at any time to erect of suffer to be erected any building or other erections and to alter any building or other erection now standing or hereafter to be erected on any part of its adjoining or neighbouring land in such a manner as to obstruct or interfere with the passage of light or air to any building which is or may be erected upon the Lot and any access of light and air over the adjoining land of the Vendor shall be deemed to be enjoyed by the licence or consent of the Vendor and not as of right;

(ii)   the right of support from the Lot for the adjoining property of the Vendor;

(iii)   the right to have maintain repair cleanse use reconstruct alter and remove any drains pipes wires cables and work on over or under the Lot now used for the benefit of the adjoining property of the Vendor;

(iv)   full right and liberty for the Vendor and its Successors in Title with or without workmen and equipment at all reasonable times to enter upon the Lot for the purpose of exercising the right reserved by paragraph (iii) of this sub clause;

(v)   full right and liberty for the Vendor and its Successors in Title with or without workmen and equipment at all reasonable times to enter upon the Lot for the purpose of maintaining repairing renewing reinstating altering or amending any fences walls or retaining walls and other works of the Vendor on its adjoining or neighbouring land, the Vendor making good any damage occasioned to the Lot by the exercise of the rights of entry reserved by paragraph (iv) and (v) of this sub-clause.

(c) Where under the Condition of Sale for any Lot of the Purchaser is required forthwith after completion or within a specified period thereafter to carry out any works to the Lot or its services or boundaries the Assurance of the Lot shall additionally reserve to the Vendor and its Successors in Title to its neighbouring land the right in the event of the Purchaser failing to carry out any such works by the due date to enter upon the property at any time within 10 years thereafter (after giving not less than six weeks notice in writing of its intention to exercise such right) for the purpose of carrying out any such works and the costs thereof shall be payable by the Purchaser on demand with interest thereon at the Contract rate.

(d) Exceptions reservations or declarations giving effect to the provisions of sub-clause (a) (b) and (c) of this Condition shall be incorporated in the Assurance to the purchaser.

29   Where under the Particulars and Special Conditions of Sale for any Lot a right of way is to be granted to the Purchasers over an adjoining roadway owned by the Vendor and reference is made to this condition in the Special Conditions the grant shall be in the following terms: 'The Vendor hereby grants in fee simple to the Purchaser and his Successors in Title to the property and his and their agents servants and licensees a right of way (in common with the Vendor and all others entitled) on foot or by vehicle at all times and for all purposes over and along the adjoining roadway of the Vendor coloured brown on the plan so as to enable access to be gained to the property and vice versa subject to the Purchaser or his Successors in Title observing and performing the covenants relating to the said roadway hereinafter contained'.

30   The Purchaser shall in the Assurance to him release the Vendor from all its obligations (if any) as to fencing and drainage in relation to the Lot and in addition covenant with the Vendor to indemnify it against its liability (if any) in respect of any such fencing and drainage.

31   The Assurance to the Purchaser shall contain the following declaration: 'it is hereby agreed by the Purchaser that the carrying on by the Vendor of its undertaking on its adjoining or neighbouring land in exercise of its powers and subject to its statutory and common law obligation shall not be deemed to be a breach of the covenant for quiet enjoyment implied herein by reason of the Vendor being expressed to convey as Beneficial Owner nor to be in derogation of its grant'.

32   The Assurance of the property shall contain a covenant by the Purchaser with the Vendor (by way of indemnity only) thenceforth to observe and perform the covenants (if any) subject to which the property is sold by virtue of the Particulars and Special Conditions (and including but without prejudice to the generality of the foregoing any covenants by the Vendor in its capacity as Landlord in relating to any of the tenancies leases or other occupancies referred to in the Particulars and Special Conditions of Sale) and to indemnify the Vendor against any actions costs claims expenses demands and liabilities brought against or occurred by the Vendor as a result of failure by the Purchaser of his Successors in Title to observe and perform the same.

33   Where the original of any agreement or counterpart of any lease or tenancy agreement subject to which the property is sold cannot be located by the Vendor the Purchaser shall accept in lieu a copy certified on the Vendors behalf as a true copy to the best of the Vendors knowledge.

34   Where in the Special Conditions of Sale for any Lot (or these General Condition as they apply to the Lot) reference is made to a plan this shall mean the plan forming part of the particulars in the copy of the special conditions held by the Auctioneer of the Lot in question.

35   IT IS HEREBY AGREED that except where the context forbids (a) words importing the singular number shall include the pluml and vice versa and (b) where there are two or more persons included in the expression "the Purchaser" covenants expressed to be made by the Purchaser shall be deemed to be made by such persons jointly and severally.

Figure 3.2 Auctioneer's additional general conditions

SPECIAL CONDITIONS OF SALE

AS TO LOT 1

4a-18b Kenerne Drive, Barnet, Herts.

Solicitors: Taylor Walton, Hart House, 6 London Road, St. Albans, Herts. AL1 1NG Telephone: 01727 845245 (Ref. KNM).

1 The Property consists of:
- (1) FIRSTLY All that Freehold Property known as 4A and 4B and 6A and 6B Kenerne Drive Chipping Barnet in Greater London and
- (2) SECONDLY All that Freehold Property known as 8A 8B 10A and 10B Kenerne Drive Chipping Barnet Greater London and
- (3) THIRDLY All that Freehold Property known as 12A and 12B and 14A and 14B Kenerne Drive Chipping Barnet Greater London and FOURTHLY All that Freehold Property known as 16A and 16B 18A and 18B Kenerne Drive Chipping Barnet Greater London

2 Title to the Property FIRSTLY described is registered with Title Absolute under Title No. P162341 and Title to the Property SECONDLY described is registered at H.M. Land Registry with Title Absolute under Title No. NGL312988 and as to the Property THIRDLY described is registered at H.M. Land Registry with Title Absolute under Title No. NGL312776 and as to the Property FOURTHLY described at H.M. Land Registry with Title Absolute under Title No. NGL312777.

3 The Property FIRSTLY described is sold subject to and with the benefit of Entries Numbers 1 to 3 inclusive of the Charges Register of the said Title

and as to the Property SECONDLY described subject to Entries Numbers 1 to 3 of the Charges Register of the said Title

and as to the Property THIRDLY described subject to Entry No 1 of the Charges Register and as to the Property FOURTHLY described subject to Entry No 1 of the Charges Register of the said Title.

4.1 The Property FIRSTLY described is sold subject to and with the benefit of the following Leases:
- (i) 4A – a Lease dated 23 May 1967 made between Wodehouse Estates Limited (1) John Edward Green (2) for a term of 99 years from 25 March 1967 at a yearly rent of twelve pounds twelve shillings.
- (ii) 4B – a Lease dated 14 October 1966 made between Wodehouse Estates Limited (1) Sonia Elizabeth Pounds (2) for a term of 99 years from 25 March 1966 at a yearly rent of twelve pounds twelve shillings.
- (iii) 6A – a Lease dated 6 September 1989 made between Ronald John Cawley Roffe Richard Jeremy Golland (1) Grainne Cecilia Spain (2) for a term of 120 years from 25 March 1989 at an initial yearly rent of fifty pounds rising to four hundred pounds.
- (iv) 6B – a Lease dated 30 September 1971 made between Ronald John Cawley Roffe Jack Alexander Allerton (1) William George Edwards Marion Patricia Edwards (2) for a term of 99 years from 25 March 1970 at a yearly rent of fifteen pounds seventy five pence.

4.2.1 The Property SECONDLY described is sold subject to and with the benefit of the following Leases:
- (i) 8A – a Lease dated 24 May 1957 made between Frederick John Randall George Frederick Randall (1) John Porter Stretton (2) for a term of 99 years from 25 March 1957 at a yearly rent of five pounds five shillings.
- (ii) 10B – a Lease dated 22 June 1983 made between Ronald John Cawley Roffe Richard Jeremy Golland (1) Susan Elspeth Laithwaite (2) for a term of 99 years from 25 March 1983 at a yearly rent of twenty five pounds rising to seventy five pounds.

4.2.2 The Property SECONDLY described is sold subject to and with the benefit of the following Regulated Tenancies:
- (i) to L M Piper with a Registered Rent of £38.00 per week effective from 13 August 1990.
- (ii) to F L Harding with a Registered Rent of £33.00 per week effective from 13 August 1990.

4.3 The Property THIRDLY described as sold subject to and with the benefit of the following Leases:
- (i) 12A – a Lease dated 25 May 1984 made between Ronald John Cawley Roffe Richard Jeremy Golland (1) Paul Alexander Conway (2) for a term of 99 years from 25 March 1984 at a yearly rent of twenty five pounds rising to seventy five pounds.
- (ii) 12B – a Lease dated 21 May 1971 made between Ronald John Cawley Roffe Jack Alexander Allerton (1) Alan Bell (2) for a term of 99 years from 25 March 1970 at a yearly rent of fifteen pounds and seventy five pounds.
- (iii) 14A – a Lease dated 18 October 1965 made between Wodehouse Estates Limited (1) Martin Charles Curran and Patricia Curran (2) for a term of 99 years from 24 June 1965 at a yearly rent of twelve pounds twelve shillings.

- (iv) 14B – a Lease dated 26 April 1985 made between Ronald John Cawley Roffe Richard Jeremy Golland (1) Susan Carol St James (2) for a term of 99 years from 25 March 1984 at a yearly rent of fifty pounds rising to one hundred pounds.

4.4 The Property FOURTHLY described is sold subject to and with the benefit of the following Leases:
- (i) 16A – a Lease dated 14 August 1970 made between Ronald John Cawley Roffe Jack Alexander Allerton (1) Geoffrey Henry Howard and Jean Howard (2) for a term of 99 years from 25 March 1970 at a yearly rent of fifteen shillings.
- (ii) 16B – a Lease dated 24 October 1977 made between Ronald John Cawley Roffe Richard Jeremy Golland (1) Trevor William Skinner and Angela Joy Booth (2) for a term of 99 years from 25 March 1970 at a yearly rent of fifteen pounds seventy five pence.
- (iii) 18B – a Lease dated 24 June 1991 made between Ronald John Cawley Roffe Richard Jeremy Golland (1) Nicola Le Moine and Raymond Vella (2) for a term of 125 years from 25 March 1989 at a yearly rent of seventy five pounds rising to four hundred pounds.
  AND
  18B – a Regulated Tenancy to J H Simpson with a Registered Rent of £33.00 per week effective from 13 August 2000.

5 The Vendor's Solicitors are Messrs Taylor Walton of Hart House 6 London Road St Albans Herts. AL1 1NG Telephone No 01727 845245 reference KNM). Copies of the Title Deeds, recent Local Authority Search Certificate and replies to Standard Form Enquiries before Contract are available for inspection at the offices of the Vendor's Solicitors in accordance with General Condition X.

6 Vacant Possession of the Property will not be given on completion.

7 The Vendor is not aware of any written Tenancy Agreements in respect of the Regulated Tenancies and the Purchaser shall not raise any objection or requisition thereto but shall accept as conclusive evidence a copy of the Rent Register which is available for inspection at the offices of the Vendor's Solicitors.

8 The Vendor has served no notice of disposal on the Tenants in accordance with Section 5 of the Landlord & Tenant Act 1987 and the Purchaser takes subject to the Tenant's rights under such Act. The Purchaser shall not raise any objection or requisition thereto but shall complete the Purchase of the Property notwithstanding that the Vendor has not served such Notices. Forthwith after Completion of the Purchase the Purchaser shall give Notice to all Tenants in accordance with Section 3 of the Landlord & Tenant Act 1985 (as amended by Section 50 of the Landlord & Tenant Act 1987) and shall indemnify the Vendor against any damages costs claims or other liabilities falling upon the Vendor by virtue of any delay or failure to do so.

9 The Purchaser shall in the Transfer (which shall be executed in duplicate) covenant with the Vendor to observe and perform the covenants and conditions contained in the Leases on the part of the Landlord and to keep the Vendor's estate and effects fully and effectually indemnified from all future costs claims demands and expenses in respect of any breach or non-observance thereof and if the Purchaser shall be a limited company it shall procure that at least one director of good financial standing personally covenants with the Vendor in the manner aforesaid.

AS TO LOT 2

75 Ashurst Road, North Finchley, London N12

Solicitors: Taylor Walton, Hart House, 6 London Road, St. Albans, Herts. AL1 1NG Telephone: 01727 845245 (Ref. KNM).

1 The Property consists of FIRSTLY All that Freehold Property known as 75 Ashurst Road Friern Barnet in the London Borough of Barnet and SECONDLY the Freehold passageway at the rear of 75/91 (odd numbers) Ashurst Road Friern Barnet in the London Borough of Barnet.

2 Title to the Property FIRSTLY described is registered at H.M. Land Registry with Freehold Title Absolute under Title No. MX193617 and as to the Property SECONDLY described Title to the Property is registered at H.M. Land Registry with Title Absolute under Title No. MX318831.

3 The Property FIRSTLY described is sold subject to and with the benefit of Entries Numbers 1 and 2 of the Charges Register of the said Title and as to the Property SECONDLY described subject to the Entries Numbers 1 to 10 inclusive of the Charges Register of the said Title.

4 As to the Property SECONDLY described the Purchaser shall raise no requisition or objection regarding the absence of the Conveyance dated 13 January 1970 referred to in Entry No 1 of the Charges Register.

5 The Property FIRSTLY described is sold subject to and with the benefit of a Regulated Tenancy to P E Watson with a Registered Rent of £210.00 per month effective from 13 August 1999.

Figure 3.3 Auctioneer's special conditions

discoverable or not, either on inspection or through local search against the property.

For example, if the property has dry rot and you buy it, you are presumed to know about that rot. If the property has a compulsory purchase order against it, which is something that shows up on a local search, **and the vendor does not know about it**, then you are presumed to know about it.

(b) A deposit of 10 per cent is payable on exchange of contracts. The general conditions will usually specify a minimum figure. For example: 10 per cent or a fixed sum – often £500 – whichever is the greater.

(c) Risk of deterioration/disrepair should be the seller's responsibility, but the general conditions will usually alter this so the purchaser has to insure the property from the date when contracts are exchanged.

Hidden terms are no excuse to cancel a contract

(d) The purchaser is presumed to have investigated title prior to exchange of contracts. If the title has an oddity in it, which you discover after contracts have been exchanged, then you cannot use this to cancel the contract. You are presumed to have examined the title documents and know about the peculiarity. Examples of peculiarities that can arise are: someone other than the owner is claiming title to a part of the property or there is a covenant preventing you developing the site without consent from a third party.

(e) There is a timetable laid down for completion. For example: no later than 2.30pm on a working day four weeks after the contract has been exchanged.

(f) The purchase price must be paid by cleared funds, so a personal or building society cheque is not acceptable, whereas a banker's draft is.

2 **Conditions about the bidding and formal paperwork.**

(a) The owner can bid for his own lot up to (or beyond) the reserve or the auctioneer can do this on his behalf.

(b) The bidder has formalities to complete before and after bidding. For example:

- completing a form giving your name and address,

- signing the memorandum of contract, which is a record of the terms on which the purchaser has bought at the fall of the gavel. (The memorandum of contract is discussed in greater detail on page 48 and an example is shown in Figure 4.2 on the same page.)

(c) Bids are exclusive of Value Added Tax.

(d) If the bidder fails to sign the memorandum of contract then the auctioneer may do this on his behalf.

What do the special conditions mean?

The special conditions deal with the following:

1 The owner's identity and whether the property is being **sold** with or without vacant possession as owner, trustee or mortgagee.

2 The identity of the property. Strictly speaking, this will be found under the heading 'Particulars' but 'Particulars' tend to be presented with 'Special Conditions'.

3 Any new covenants the purchaser is to enter into with the owner (or any other party) on completion. You are most likely to come across this where a lot forms part of a larger piece of land owned by the vendor.

Special conditions imposed by a vendor

For example: A private landowner owns fields to the rear of his house. He puts these in an auction hoping that a builder will buy them. However, he wishes to protect his own comfort and so the

LOT 186

119 Corporation Road, Gillingham, Kent

BY ORDER OF MORTGAGEES IN POSSESSION

A Freehold Mid Terrace House

TENURE
Freehold.

LOCATION
The property is situated on the east side of Corporation Road, in an established residential area to the north east of the town centre which is within walking distance.

DESCRIPTION
The property comprises a mid terrace house arranged over ground and first floors beneath a pitched roof with a rear garden.

ACCOMMODATION

Ground Floor	First Floor
Reception Room	Three Bedrooms
Kitchen Area	
Bathroom with WC and wash basin	

A house in the heart of Kent for only £17,000.

special conditions provide that whoever buys the site must:

- erect a large fence and fast tall-growing conifers to screen off the development;

- only build private houses of a type to be approved by him;

- not use the new buildings other than as private residences.

4 Any tenancies affecting the lot.

5 Any rights the owner reserves.

Taking the same example as in 3 above of a sale of land for development, the owner would probably want to reserve all rights of light and air so his house enjoys the level of sunshine it currently has.

Where an owner has a number of similar lots with

similar concerns, many of these points may be covered in the catalogue as 'Additional Conditions'.

Are these special conditions not unlawful?

The Unfair Contract Terms Act 1977 prevents a person drawing up an agreement from inserting terms which are unfair. However, this Act does not apply to contracts for the sale of land so, **no matter how onerous the contract is, the purchaser and the owner are obliged to abide by its terms.** There are two exceptions to this principle:

1 If an interest rate or penal arrangement for payment of the price is too onerous, it may be struck out by a court as being contrary to rules in equity on penalty clauses. These are separate from the 1977 Act and are unlikely to apply to most auction contracts you will come across.

Circumstances that may allow you to cancel a contract

2 If a seller makes a misrepresentation about the property prior to the contract and then in the contract itself disclaims any liability for that misrepresentation, the disclaimer may be unlawful. You may be able to withdraw from the contract if you have placed reliance on the misrepresentation the seller has made, or sue for damages. It depends on how the disclaimer is phrased.

For example, an owner advises a purchaser that the property has planning permission for six semi-detached buildings. In fact, the planning permission is for two detached houses. In the information pack available in the auction room, there is a copy of the planning permission. There is also a set of replies to standard enquiries which a purchaser would normally make before exchanging contracts and these reiterate that the property enjoys planning permission for six semi-detached houses. The successful bidder does not bother to read any of the information pack, nor does he speak with the auctioneer or the owner's solicitors before bidding.

Can he withdraw from the contract?

The bidder may be able to withdraw in the following circumstances:

(a) If the special conditions do not refer to the planning permission or indicate the purchaser is presumed to buy with knowledge of the property or its use.

(b) If the special conditions do not refer to the planning permission but state:

> *The purchaser acknowledges that it has not entered into this agreement in reliance upon representations made by or on behalf of the vendor other than such written representations as the vendor's solicitor may have made and then save only as to such (if any) as were not susceptible of independent verification by inspection and survey of the property, by enquiry of the local authority, the local planning authority and any other competent authority of by inspection of documents made available to the purchaser before this agreement (whether or not the purchaser has made such inspection survey search or enquiry).*

In this case the owner has misrepresented information but this clause tries to prevent the purchaser claiming he has relied on that.

Does this clause work and is it lawful? The property world believes it does work and is legitimate. Usage of this clause (and similar) is widespread – **bidders beware!**

Damages will not be payable

In this example, the estate agent or auctioneer may be criminally liable under the Property Misdescriptions Act 1991 for making a misleading statement. But do remember, this does not give you any right to damages.

If you can't stand the heat, get out of the kitchen!

At this stage, before the auction, the owner is making all the rules. The buyer has no opportunity to change them and no alternative but to purchase under the conditions that are laid down.

KEY POINT: *If the conditions make the property 'too hot', whatever sort of bargain it appears, don't bid at the auction.*

Before bidding, every potential purchaser should make very sure that all the conditions (in whatever guise) have been read, checked and are acceptable. Since conditions are frequently clothed in 'legalese' you should take your own solicitor's advice about the significance of any conditions - particularly those that appear at all unusual.

Hidden pitfalls to watch out for

Major arrears

Frequently the sellers of tenanted properties find that their tenants do not pay as regularly as they should. Once they have sold a property, it is relatively difficult for them to press the tenant (with whom they no longer have regular contact) for outstanding arrears. It is therefore common for a vendor to provide in the contract of sale a clause stating that the purchaser pays a sum over at completion equal to any arrears outstanding. Although this 'balances the books' for the seller, it leaves the buyer in the invidious position of having paid out money in full against the right to collect it back in arrears from the tenants. Those arrears may prove to be uncollectable or it may be necessary to spend a lot of time and money to retrieve from the tenant, the cash already paid over to the seller.

KEY POINT: *Your responsibility to pay over outstanding arrears to the seller at completion may be revealed in the part of the catalogue that refers to the relevant lot or may only be mentioned in the conditions of sale.*

Before bidding on any property where this condition applies, you should make detailed enquiries to establish your chances (and costs) of collecting the outstanding money from tenants. Irregularity in payments may be reflected in the outstanding arrears and it should warn you to check on the past payment record. After such enquiries, you may decide that you should trim the size of your top bid accordingly. Alternatively, you may decide not to buy because the arrears are such that you can have no confidence in the future ability of the tenants you are about to acquire to pay their rent.

> **KEY POINT:** *In every case where you are buying a tenanted property, you should be positive before you buy that the actual tenant is in occupation of the property and has not 'done a moonlight flit'. An inspection just before the auction is always wise, whether the property is tenanted or not.*

Local authority charges, public health and other notices

Where the local search reveals a local authority charge against a property, you should expect the vendor to pay off that charge at completion. You should ensure that the conditions of sale provide for this. If they do not, reduce your highest bid by the amount of the charges that you will have to pay on owning the property.

Are you required to carry out repairs?

The local search may reveal other public health and similar notices which can range from requirements to carry out certain repairs, right through to closure or demolition notices. Auctioneers encourage their clients to reveal the existence of such notices. They are usually mentioned in the sale catalogue or amendment sheets or by the auctioneer (if he is aware of them) at the time of sale. Nevertheless, you should not rely on this. Instead, you or your solicitor should ensure that by suitable enquiry to the local authority in which the property is situated that no notices or charges are outstanding.

They should reveal if any compulsory purchase orders are in existence or pending and indicate how the property is affected by any planning proposals, warning you of any similar drawbacks to the lot.

Do not take plan sizes for granted

As plans pass between owners, solicitors and auctioneers, they are often subjected to copying and re-copying. Sometimes, plans are deliberately shrunk to fit on pages for faxing, printing or other use.

Plans reproduced in the auctioneer's catalogue should never be relied upon to be accurate, even if a written scale is shown on the plan. Sometimes the auctioneer's catalogue includes a saving clause, acknowledging that plans may not be accurate. Omission of this clause from the catalogue does not mean the plan sizes can be relied upon. If you have an opportunity to check the actual size of any land or property that you are buying, you should do so or, at worst, take suitable measurements and make your own calculations from an original of the Ordnance Survey.

View, view and view again

Viewing any lot you are thinking of buying should not be difficult. Almost invariably the auctioneer's catalogue will indicate the viewing arrangements. Occasionally, specific days and times for viewing are shown where the lot particulars are printed. Alternatively, viewing may be by direct arrangement with the auctioneer's office or by collecting the keys where it is appropriate. Occasionally, the auctioneers can only arrange viewing subject to the consent of the tenants. Whatever means of inspecting the property is provided, you should take advantage of it.

> **KEY POINT:** *If a full inspection of your lot is reasonably feasible but is refused, you should be highly suspicious and make your decision whether or not to bid accordingly.*

Financing the purchase

Will I need an accountant's advice?

An accountant may be needed at the very early stages for more general than specific advice. It is not the purpose of this book to give detailed help on accountancy and taxation matters.

Nevertheless, you will need to make an early decision once you have become interested in a property, whether you are going to buy and sell personally or through a private company or whether, by appropriate planning, you can take advantage of schemes such as self-administered pension funds, overseas companies and other measures to reduce your tax liability.

The advice and assistance that an accountant can provide you with in terms of accountancy and taxation matters depends very much on the use to which the property is to be put.

Tax allowances for investment properties

If the property is to be rented then such income is taxable under Schedule A, unless the property is let as furnished accommodation in which case tax is charged under Schedule D, Case VI. A person is charged the tax under Schedule A by reference to the rents or receipts to which he becomes entitled in the tax year concerned. Payments that are actually made during the chargeable period may be deducted if they fall within the definition of 'permitted deductions'. These include maintenance repairs, insurance and other services which the owner was obliged to provide and for which he received no separate payment. As far as maintenance or repairs are concerned there is a whole host of types of expenditure which are normally allowable, including interior and exterior repairs and decorations, cleaning, upkeep of gardens and the costs of rent collection.

Capital allowances may also be claimed in respect of plant and machinery belonging to the landlord. These will include items of office equipment such as computers and machinery that have become part of the building, such as a lift.

Interest on a loan to purchase a property or carry out improvements may be set against Schedule A income. Where the qualifying interest exceeds the amount of Schedule A income, the excess may be carried forward and set against subsequent years' Schedule A income. Tax relief is available on interest paid on a loan to purchase an investment property provided that certain conditions are satisfied including:

- The property must be let at a commercial rent.
- In any 52-week period, the property must be let for more than 26 weeks and when not being let, the property must be available either for letting or prevented from being available because of construction work or repairs.
- The property must be situated in the United Kingdom or the Republic of Ireland.

Tax relief for holiday property

If the property being let represents furnished holiday accommodation, then it may be treated as a trade, provided certain conditions are satisfied, including the following:

- It must be let on a commercial basis.
- It must be let as furnished accommodation.
- It must be available for commercial letting to the public as holiday accommodation for at least 140 days in a 12-month period.
- It must be let for at least 70 such days.
- It must not normally be occupied by the same person for more than 31 consecutive days at any time during a period of 7 months within the 12-month period.

If a property is treated as being let as furnished holiday accommodation, then interest on loans used to purchase the property and finance the lettings will qualify as an expense. If this gives rise to a loss for tax purposes, it may be offset against other taxable income. In addition, equipment and furniture and fittings may attract capital allowances. Profits from furnished holiday lettings may qualify as 'relevant earnings' for the purposes of personal pension contributions and retirement annuity premiums. For capital gains tax purposes, roll over and retirement relief may also be available.

Double your exemption from capital gains tax

On disposal of the investment property, capital gains tax may be payable on the chargeable gains arising. However, an annual exemption can be deducted from the chargeable gains, which for the income tax year 2000/2001 was £7,200. If husband and wife jointly own the property, then each is entitled to this annual exemption against their proportion of the chargeable gain. It may, therefore, be advantageous to consider acquiring the property jointly between the husband and wife to benefit from this exemption. One further advantage of this is that any rental income assessable is divided between the husband and wife for income tax purposes. As each spouse is assessed separately for tax purposes, then subject to any other taxable income, each is entitled to set their personal allowances against the rental income. Any remaining liability is subject to the 10 per cent or 22 per cent tax rate band with the remainder chargeable to higher rate tax at 40 per cent. In this way, personal allowances and lower rate tax bands can be utilised by both spouses.

LOT 191

Flat 1(c), 1 Ridsdale Road,
Anerley, London SE20
BY ORDER OF MORTGAGEES IN POSSESSION

A Leasehold Ground Floor Flat

TENURE
Leasehold. The property is held on a lease for a term of 99 years from 25th December 1987 (thus having approximately 93 years unexpired) at a current ground rent of £100 per annum.

LOCATION
The property is situated on the west side of Ridsdale Road to the east of its junction with Anerley Road (A214). Local amenities are available in Anerley itself and the further facilities of Beckenham are within reach. British Rail services run from Anerley Station.

DESCRIPTION
The property comprises a self contained flat situated on the ground floor of a mid terrace house arranged over ground and two upper floors under a tile clad roof.

ACCOMMODATION
Reception Room
Two Bedrooms
Kitchen
Bathroom with WC and wash basin

This base in London could have been yours for only £16,000.

The consequences of a company acquiring the property as an investment need to be examined carefully by your accountant, as there are significant differences in the taxation treatment of companies and individuals. For example, the annual exemptions for capital gains tax previously mentioned are not available to companies.

It is also possible for the property to be acquired by a small self-administered pension scheme which is linked to the company, provided certain criteria are met. The Inland Revenue requirements regarding such pension schemes will need to be discussed in detail with your accountant; however, they do offer the opportunities to mitigate the incidence of tax both on a corporate and personal level.

The VAT minefield

VAT on property is a minefield. At present, most properties are sold exclusive of VAT. However, the ramifications of this tax are extensive and they should be discussed in detail with your accountant.

KEY POINT: *The acquisition of property as an investment involves both tax planning opportunities and pitfalls. It is essential that you discuss the matter in detail with your accountant before undertaking the purchase.*

The deposit and balance

It is important to remember that on the day of the auction you will be required to make a deposit of 10 per cent of the purchase price. You must ensure that you are able to pay both this deposit and the balance of the purchase price 28 days later. Table 3.2 shows the different deposit amounts to be paid for sample purchase prices.

If you are using a finance broker, bank or building society to provide the funds you should have the financing agreed, lot by lot, prior to the auction. The finance house will want to be satisfied that the valuation of the property is acceptable to them.

Table 3.2 The purchase price, deposit and balance payable

Price	Deposit	Balance
£350	£350	Nil
£500	£500	Nil
£1,000	£500	£500
£3,000	£500	£2,500
£5,000	£500	£4,500
£8,500	£850	£7,650
£12,000	£1,200	£10,800
£20,000	£2,000	£18,000
£30,000	£3,000	£27,000
£50,000	£5,000	£45,000
£100,000	£10,000	£90,000
£150,000	£15,000	£135,000
£250,000	£25,000	£225,000
£500,000	£50,000	£450,000
£1,000,000	£100,000	£900,000

Table 3.3 Total purchase costs

The purchase price £	Deposit £	Balance £	VAT if payable on purchase price £	Surveyor's fees full structural £	Plus VAT auction incl VAT £	Solicitors attending £	Solicitors' fees £	Plus VAT £	Stamp duty £	Your expenses £	First insurance initial repairs £	Making secure £	Tenant's arrears fees £	Finance House £	Total £
£350	350	nil	61	–	–	–	200	35	nil	150	200	200	?	–	£1,196
£500	500	nil	88	–	–	–	200	35	nil	150	200	200	?	–	£1,373
£1,000	500	500	175	–	–	–	200	35	nil	150	200	200	?	–	£1,960
£3,000	500	2500	525	200	35	176	200	35	nil	150	200	200	?	–	£4,721
£5,000	500	4500	875	200	35	176	200	35	nil	150	200	200	?	–	£7,071
£8,500	850	7650	1,488	250	44	176	200	35	nil	150	250	300	?	–	£11,393
£12,000	1,200	10,800	2,100	250	44	176	250	44	nil	250	250	300	?	150	£15,814
£20,000	2,000	18,000	3,500	300	53	176	250	44	nil	250	300	300	?	200	£25,373
£30,000	3,000	27,000	5,250	300	53	176	300	53	nil	250	350	400	?	300	£37,431
£50,000	5,000	45,000	8,750	400	70	176	300	53	nil	250	450	600	?	500	£61,549
£100,000	10,000	90,000	17,500	500	88	176	350	61	1,000	350	800	800	?	1,000	£122,625
£150,000	15,000	135,000	26,250	600	105	176	400	70	1,500	350	1,200	1,000	?	1,500	£183,151
£250,000	25,000	225,000	43,750	800	140	176	500	88	2,500	450	2,500	1,500	?	2,000	£304,404
£500,000	50,000	450,000	87,500	1,200	210	176	1,000	175	15,000	550	4,000	3,500	?	4,000	£617,311
£1,000,000	100,000	900,000	175,000	2,000	350	176	2,500	438	40,000	650	8,000	7,000	?	3,500	£1,239,614

What other costs should I allow for?

You have already planned to meet professional fees for your valuer, your solicitor and your accountant. If your bid is successful you will have the full conveyancing fees to pay to your solicitor and if your purchase is above the relevant level, Government stamp duty at one per cent of the purchase price for properties over £60,000.

Your cash flow is now fully prepared for the 10 per cent deposit payable at the auction, for the balance of the purchase price, plus VAT if it applies, 28 days later and for all your other costs. Table 3.3 lists the possible total costs incurred for buying a property priced between £350 and £1,000,000. Depending on the individual property, there may be other costs to pay that are not mentioned here, but it gives a useful guide.

Table 3.4 is a purchase costs checklist giving all the items for which you might have to budget.

Table 3.4 Purchase costs checklist

- [ ] Deposit
- [ ] Balance
- [ ] VAT on purchase price
- [ ] Credit to vendor for tenants arrears
- [ ] Surveyors' fees and VAT
- [ ] Professional fees and VAT for attending at auction (if appropriate)
- [ ] Finance House commitment fee and VAT
- [ ] Solicitors' fees and VAT
- [ ] Local search fees
- [ ] Stamp duty (see left)
- [ ] Vendor's fees and costs (if charged)
- [ ] Repayment of grants
- [ ] Planning application fees
- [ ] Building regulation application fees
- [ ] Covenant buyout
- [ ] First insurance premium
- [ ] Contractor's bill for making secure/initial repairs
- [ ] Champagne

Financial catches to watch out for

- Remember that finance houses frequently require a commitment fee, not to mention their interest charges and their capital repayments.

- As you interpret the conditions of sale, make sure you know what amount you could have to pay for items such as tenants' arrears.

- Ensure that you and your solicitor are aware of any outstanding local authority charges or grants. These can often be made the responsibility of the purchaser to repay.

- If you are hoping to explore the planning potential of your purchase, remember that planning and building regulation applications may require the payment of a fee to the local authority.

- Be sure that you have made allowance to buy out any covenants if such a procedure is appropriate. For example, if you are buying a site for development there could be covenants preventing you from carrying out your proposals until the person holding the benefit of these covenants has agreed to your proposals and been paid a sum for their amendment.

- Finally, always leave sufficient margin for the champagne celebration after you have successfully purchased a lot at your price.

4 Going for your bargain

'I went to auction a couple of times before to get the feel for it and to see what the prices were like. I thought just before Christmas would be a good time to buy because people haven't got a lot of spare money and have other things on their mind and as it turns out I was proved right.'

Don Lee, buyer of a residential property at auction.

Doing a dummy run

Get the feel for how an auction works

Although you can be armed with the information in this guide and be made aware of what happens in an auction, nothing can be better than experiencing several auctions before you go to the first one at which you intend to bid. Doing a 'dummy run' is highly recommended. Ideally, this should extend way beyond merely calling at one or two auctions to see how matters proceed. Earlier on in the previous chapter, you read the recommendation that you approach your solicitor and accountant at an early stage for the relevant pieces of advice that they can give. You could focus your enquiries to them by indicating a general interest in a lot in an auction during your dummy run. By doing so, you will be able to develop and research the enquiries and questions you will put to them when your 'run' is for real.

Key points for the dummy run

1. Choose a specific lot to focus your interest.

2. List and rehearse the questions you would wish to ask your professional advisers.

3. Visit your dummy property and make a thorough inspection as if you were intending to buy. (You may find that you can discuss it with a surveyor without charge, if you warn him that this is a dummy run but that you are looking to develop mutual business in the future.)

4. Ask the seller's solicitor the questions that your solicitor would put to him.

5. Look at a copy of the local search or ring the relevant local authority if the search is not available.

6. Read carefully the conditions of sale, general and additional conditions and auctioneer's conditions. This will prepare you for similar research when it really matters.

7. Contact the auctioneer's office. Consider having a trial negotiation with them to practise your negotiating skills. Your experience with them in such negotiations may cast a revealing light on their approach and the reality of their guideline figures.

8. To avoid fees, you will probably not wish to ask your solicitors to research the title of the dummy lot.

No play takes place without rehearsal.

Cut out the competition and buy your bargain before auction

'I always try to do a deal beforehand because you never know what opposition you are going to come up against at auction. But you should never show your hand in case it does go to auction. The vendor is generally only going to accept a higher price before the auction.'

Michael Kirby, Chartered Surveyor.

Move in before the auction happens!

Negotiating the purchase of a lot before auction is not at all unusual. Do remember that all the steps previously recommended should be undertaken. Before the day of the sale, you may feel confident enough to risk negotiating for the property. Lucky buyers can acquire bargains in this way but they do run the risk of 'disclosing their hand' to the auctioneers and they can be passing the initiative to them. Whether you take up such an initiative is undoubtedly a gamble. Only you can decide whether it is worthwhile in the light of your desire to buy the lot and to beat the competition that might take place on auction day. On the other hand, by revealing your interest so soon, you can lose what would otherwise be a strong position in your bidding at the auction.

Before you start such negotiations you will no doubt have decided how much you wish to pay for the property. If you are endeavouring to buy before auction, this must be either because you wish to buy the property noticeably cheaper than the amount you are ready to pay on auction day, or because you want the lot so badly that you do not want anybody else to have the opportunity to purchase and 'bid you up' on that day. The decision is entirely yours.

'chief rents' – These rents are also known as perpetual annual rent charges which are payable by the owners of freehold land annually. In the main, the rents only exist in the Greater Manchester, Bristol and Channel Isles' districts. The period over which they can now be collected is restricted by statute.

'OP.' – This is an acronym for 'outline planning permission'.

FRANK R MARSHALL & CO at Nantwich, Apr 7
Shavington — Green Bank Farm, B5071 Rd. Arable/pasture farm. Hse, 10 rms, 3 attic rms, tradn bdgs, loose boxes, stores, barns. 106.10 a. F, P 400,000

BIGWOOD at Birmingham, Apr 8
Goostrey — Buckbean Way etc. Chief rents on 57 units at £1,140 pa. 6,000
Holmes Chapel — Danefield Rd etc. Chief rents on 80 units at £1,299 pa. 6,500

DENTON CLARK & CO at Rowton, Apr 14
Ashton — Gable Cottage, Kelsall Rd. Terr cottage, 2 bed. F, P 66,500
Cuddington — Cuddington Barn, B5069 Rd. Barn with PP conversion to hse, 4 bed, adj cottage, 1 bed. Stables/store. 2.62 a. F, P 65,000
Marbury — School Hse, School Lane. Cottage, 3 bed. Adj bdg plot with OPP 1 dwelling. F, P 60,000
Tilston — Constabulary Cottage, Church Rd. Det cottage, 3 bed. F, P 66,500
Adj garden land, 110 ft x 50 ft. F, P 8,500
Apr 15
Helsby — Off A56 Chester Rd. Accom pasture, 13.07 a. F, P 52,000
Accom pasture, 10.73 a. F, P 26,000
Accom pasture, 28.54 a. F, P 28,500
Paddocks, 2.99 a. F, P 5,000
Manley — Manley Rd, Riley Bank. Pasture/conservation land, 27.95 a. F, P 35,000
Morley Lane, Dunham Heath. Pasture, 10.02 a. F, P 20,000

Illustration 3. Estates Gazette auction results

> **KEY POINT:** *You must realise that disclosing your interest and your figure at this time gives the auctioneer and the seller an opportunity to adjust the reserve and take into account the amount which they believe you are prepared to bid.*

> **KEY POINT:** *By bidding before the auction you are likely to remove any opportunity of buying the property any cheaper than your pre-auction bid. But this has to be balanced against the advantages of cutting out the competition.*

Contracts must be exchanged quickly for pre-auction sales

If you decide to bid before the auction, you must be prepared to negotiate quickly and if your bid is successful, to sign a contract and pay your deposit even faster. The auctioneer will require you to exchange contracts before the auction (and probably by several days in advance). *You have an even greater need for speed.* If you have decided to buy before the auction, you must be aware that there could be other people who have a similar desire to buy early. If, therefore, you have agreed a pre-auction purchase, you should not then leave your solicitor to exchange contracts or memoranda in the normal course of 'legal' time. You should press him to complete his enquiries at top speed and to exchange contracts or memoranda as a matter of urgency. You will have to provide your 10 per cent deposit at the time the exchange takes place.

Many auctioneers are willing to allow you to leave your deposit with them and to complete and exchange memoranda or contracts in their office. This will speed the passage of the sale but it is not recommended unless your solicitor is satisfied with his enquiries about the title and background to the property. Only those who want a lot so badly that they are prepared to risk irrevocably committing themselves to a purchase before their solicitor is satisfied should proceed before then. Having exchanged, if you then decide to 'go back' on the purchase, legal sanctions (including loss of your deposit and other responsibilities to meet damages) will follow. The same sanctions apply if you succeed with a bid on the auction day itself and subsequently withdraw. The extent of your likely loss and damages is explained on pages 78–79.

> **KEY POINT:** *You must realise that a purchase prior to the auction does not change any of the procedures, responsibilities or actions detailed in this book other than those that relate to attending and bidding at the auction itself.*

Buyer's timetable

For most auctions, you will have about a month from the initial advertisement to the auction itself to carry out all your preparations. The following timetable provides a useful guide for buyers on when you need to make the necessary arrangements prior to the auction.

Days prior to and after the auction	Action
30	See advertisement and apply for auctioneer's catalogue.
28	Receive catalogue
26	First inspection of property Check auctioneer's particulars
25	Instruct valuation surveyor
23	Read and understand the conditions of sale
20	Receive surveyor's report
19	Instruct solicitor Visit accountant Arrange finance
17	Second inspection of property Assess quality of tenants
6	Consider a pre-auction purchase
5	Check solicitor's report on title Check availability of finance
3	Decide on your maximum bid
1	Final visit to property prior to the sale
Auction day	Attend auction Bid successfully, Exchange contracts or memoranda Pay 10 per cent deposit
1	Insure property Revisit property Check security Meet tenants
1/3	If your lot was withdrawn on the day, negotiate to buy
28	Complete purchase Pay balance of purchase monies Pay stamp duty Pay solicitor's fees

Attending the auction

'You always feel a little apprehensive before you go in. You go in with nothing and come home with something else.'

Michael Roe, buyer of residential properties.

You have picked out your lots, you have done your research, you have spoken to your solicitor, accountant and other advisers and your finance is arranged. You have settled in your own mind the maximum figure you are prepared to bid for the lots you are interested in. Now you are ready to go to your auction. The next sections address the atmosphere, the nature of the auction, details of the procedures you can expect to have to follow and suggests ways you might go about the purchase of your bargain lots.

The following checklist gives the key points you should watch out for at auction. Each one is discussed in depth below.

AUCTION CHECKLIST:
For the bargain hunter

1 Wise to attend yourself. ☐

2 Check the etiquette. ☐

3 Follow any registration procedure. ☐

4 Choose a good vantage point. ☐

5 Pay attention. ☐

6 Listen to the auctioneer's speech. ☐

7 Check for any amendments. ☐

8 Watch out for VAT. ☐

9 Make your first bid loud and clear. ☐

10 Subsequent bids should be obvious. ☐

11 Only bid enough to buy. ☐

12 Only bid up to your maximum. ☐

13 Watch competitive bidders. ☐

14 Try to read the auctioneer. ☐

15 Be aware the auctioneer rules the roost. ☐

16 Concentrate on what is happening
even if you have stopped bidding. ☐

17 Be aware of the lots you have bought. ☐

18 Sign the contract or memorandum
before you leave the room. ☐

19 Expect to pay a 10 per cent deposit
(subject to a stated minimum). ☐

20 An unsold lot could be a bargain –
move in quickly to negotiate. ☐

How to attend

Although you may expect most buyers to attend an auction in person, this is not necessary. Methods of bidding without attending are given below. But if you are to have the best opportunities of securing a bargain you would be wise to be in the room so that you can weigh up the atmosphere, judge the approach of the auctioneer and, particularly, to out-manoeuvre your opposing bidders.

What will it be like?

As we saw in chapter one, auctions are of various types but by the time you attend you will have had

LOT 203
10 Darefield Walk, Highgate, Birmingham, West Midlands
BY ORDER OF MORTGAGEES IN POSSESSION

A Leasehold Ground and First Floor Maisonette
TENURE Leasehold. Please refer to the Vendor's Solicitor for further details.
LOCATION The property is situated on the west side of Darwin Walk to the south of its junction with Alcester Street. Local amenities are available in Highgate itself and the facilities of Birmingham city centre are within reach.
DESCRIPTION The property comprises a self contained maisonette arranged over the ground and first floors of a purpose built block.
ACCOMMODATION
Ground Floor
Reception Room, Kitchen
First Floor
Three Bedrooms, Bathroom, Separate WC

A three-bed city flat that fell under the hammer for less than the price of a new car. Ridiculous but true. It sold for only £8,500.

every opportunity to judge the nature of the auction to which you will be going. Table 4.1 lists different types of auction, the number of lots, the size of audience and probable venue you can expect. A large and composite auction in a central city venue will have had extensive advertising and a large, high quality catalogue. You can expect a crowded room with between 200 and 1,000 potential bidders and a thoroughly organized room and reception laid out in theatre seating. With luck, you might even be offered free coffee and refreshments. There is still likely to be only a single auctioneer on the rostrum but he will probably be supported by two or three 'spotters' alongside who are there to help him pick bidders out of the large audience. Beside the auctioneer is likely to be his clerk who will record all bids as an aide-memoire during the sale. In some auctions, part of the room will be allocated as an area where contracts are signed after successful bids have been received. In other auctions there will be an area allocated for tables where solicitors, acting on behalf of owners, will be presiding ready to exchange contracts if their clients have been successful in selling.

> **KEY POINT:** *You will have the choice to sit or stand but do find a position from which you are able to watch your competing bidders.*

Table 4.1 Size of auctions

	Number of lots	Likely audience	Likely venue
Single lot	1	10–75	Hotel, Church Hall, Pub, Restaurant
Small composite	2–5	10–100	Hotel, Church Hall, Pub, Restaurant, Sale Room
Medium composite	5–50	50–200	Hotel
Large composite	50–100	200–500	Hotel/Conference Centre/Theatre

Make your first bid obvious

In such a crowd, you can expect quite a hubbub with people moving around the room. The auctioneer will have amplification equipment to assist him, but it is very probable that you will need to make a large and obvious gesture, or even to call out to attract the auctioneer's attention at your first bid for each of your chosen lots.

The size of the auction audience often comes down as the scale of the auction reduces. A composite auction, where the number of lots on offer is between approximately 50 and 100, is likely to attract an audience of between 200 and 500 people. The room and atmosphere are similar to that of larger auctions, but it will probably be easier for the bidder to attract the auctioneer's attention. Because of the size of the audience, it is possible for you to make your bids discreetly. Where auctions of this size occur outside London, it is more usual for the sellers' solicitors to attend the auction.

At smaller auctions, the audience is also frequently smaller (unless the lots offered are of overwhelming interest) with between 10 and 100 people attending. For a smaller auction, the venue chosen is often a smaller sale room or hired room in a public house or local hall, instead of a large hotel or conference centre. At this size, the proceedings are a little less formal. The auctioneer does not need spotters and the sellers' solicitor usually attends. The bidding is much more discrete and you will have more opportunity to see the quality and strength of any opposing bidders.

How to behave at auction

Listed below are the key points you need to know about auction room etiquette and behaviour:

1 The auctioneer and his staff welcome anyone who swells the crowd, who is dressed reasonably presentably, regardless of their intention to bid or not and who intends to behave reasonably quietly.

2 There is always a constant to-ing and fro-ing of people. You are welcome to arrive and leave whenever it suits you, although it is usual for the audience to avoid interfering with the enjoyment of the proceedings by other people while bidding on a lot is taking place.

3 Arriving late or leaving after the lot in which you are interested is not at all unusual, although it is unwise to miss the auctioneer's opening speech and announcements.

4 Auctioneers often seem to comment on vacant seats available at the front of the auction room, despite research showing that lots are no more expensive whether you are sitting at the front of the room or standing at the back. Don't hesitate to use empty seats if you are happy to do so, but it is a useful tactic to gain a vantage point from where you can observe opposing bidders.

5 Sitting or standing is left to the choice of the attenders. If you are intending to bid, you need to be in a position where you can see the auctioneer and he can see you easily.

Arrive early and make your final checks

6 Auction rooms usually open approximately one hour before the auction commences. Most of the audience turn up in the 20 minutes before proceedings start. Auctions often start approximately five minutes late, but do not rely on this. Amazingly, it is not unusual for 90 per cent or more of the audience never to bid. If you have questions to ask the auctioneer's staff or

solicitors before the auction, it is wise to arrive 30 minutes before the auction starts, if you are to avoid a crush. This will give you an opportunity to speak to solicitors, inspect local searches, deeds and leases and whatever else is available for your viewing.

7 On arrival, always check:
   • if there have been any additions or amendments to the lots and lot details;
   • if the lot in which you are interested has already been sold or withdrawn;
   • if the lots are to be offered in alphabetical or numerical order.

8 If the auctioneers have a registration procedure, it is polite to adopt it and complete appropriate forms at their request. You will not normally be asked for confidential information.

9 If the auctioneers publish in the catalogue or elsewhere any particular requirements, ensure you fulfil them in plenty of time.

10 If you are intending to bid, do not be shy about drawing the auctioneer's attention to your bid by an obvious gesture or by calling out loudly. Once you have attracted the auctioneer's attention, it is unlikely that you will need to attract his attention again for that particular lot. However, if it proves necessary, do not lose the opportunity to bid by being shy about repeating the obvious gesture or loud call.

11 Practices vary from auctioneer to auctioneer in the registration and identification of buyers. One of the more modern systems (said to have been first used at an auction of Beatles memorabilia) is the paddle system which is descibed in the next section of this chapter.

Auctioneer's Anecdote: A smoked salmon bomb!

On occasion, auctioneers are known to provide refreshments for their audience and a leading firm of London auctioneers decided to push the boat out with smoked salmon sandwiches which were particularly popular. At the end of the auction, they noticed a briefcase had been left behind in the refreshment area and feared it was a bomb. Curiosity overcame circumspection however and the briefcase was opened to reveal that it was absolutely full of smoked salmon sandwiches and a card identifying its owner. The auctioneer was delighted to note the owner's embarrassment when he telephoned him later to tell him that his briefcase had been retrieved.

How will the auctioneer know I am a bidder?

The paddle system is one method used to register prospective bidders. As the audience arrives, each person is invited (if they express interest in bidding) to complete a registration form (see Figure 4.1). This form will always include the name and address of the bidder or the name and address of the company or organization on whose behalf they are bidding. The information sheet is then exchanged for a numbered bidding paddle which is not necessarily used for bidding but which is shown to the auctioneer by the successful purchaser after the gavel has fallen.

This enables the auctioneer to identify the buyer immediately and to pass instructions for the preparation of contract. Other information useful to the auctioneer is frequently sought including the name of the solicitors acting for the bidder. It is not unusual for the form to be used by the auctioneer to collect statistical data, to find out where you saw the advertisement for the lot which interests you.

Auctioneers who do not use a registration system generally have more 'spotters' on their rostrum. These spotters identify the successful bidder with the help of the auctioneer and then approach him, asking him to complete a form which details the bidder's name, address and his solicitors. The form is collected so that the necessary contract or memoranda can be prepared. The same spotter returns later to the purchaser to take him over to the table for exchange of contracts.

Where the paddle system is used, it is usual for the bidder to be escorted over to the table for exchange of contracts immediately after the gavel has fallen. If a bidder wishes to bid on subsequent lots shortly after his successful purchase, he may need to defer attending the table for exchange.

DATE: . . . .   **NUMBER:** . . . .

TO ALL THOSE ATTENDING THE
LONGDEN & COOK COMMERCIAL AUCTION:

To assist in your identification and to maintain privacy, please complete the details below and return this sheet to one of our staff in exchange for a numbered bidding paddle.
When a Lot is sold to you, please advise the auctioneer of your number before going across to the solicitors' table to complete the documents.

1 (a) **Your full names**   . . . .
   (b) **Your address**   . . . .
                                   . . . .
   (c) **Your telephone number(s)** . . . .
2 (a) **Your Solicitors**   . . . .
   (b) **Their address**   . . . .
                                   . . . .
   (c) **The person acting**   . . . .
   (d) **Solicitors' phone number** . . . .

IF YOU ARE INTENDING to bid on someone else's behalf please indicate below:
3 (a) **That person's full name**   . . . .
   (b) **Their address**   . . . .
                                   . . . .
   (c) **Their telephone number** . . . .
4 **Do you wish to go on our Mailing List for future auction catalogues?**   Yes ☐   No ☐

I ACKNOWLEDGE RECEIPT of a bidding paddle or number sheet and acknowledge that by signing this form I agree to participate in this auction on the basis of the Conditions of Sale published in this Catalogue.

SIGNED: . . . .

Figure 4.1 Auctioneer's registration form

Exchanging contracts or memoranda

The full contract

In every case, buyers have to sign and exchange contracts or memoranda before they leave the auction room at the end of the sale. If they fail to do so, the auctioneer invariably has the right to sign the contract on their behalf. The contract is virtually identical to the contract which any purchaser signs to buy a property. It often follows a standard layout used by many solicitors throughout the country.

What the contract contains

- the names of the buyer and the seller;
- the price that is being paid (the final price of the successful bidder);
- the deposit to be paid;
- the completion date;
- whether or not vacant possession is given;
- details of the property and its tenure;
- the status by which the seller will convey the property;
- brief details of the title;
- covenants that affect the property being sold;
- fixtures and fittings that are included;
- the general conditions of the published Law Society conditions referring to the relevant edition;
- the interest rate payable if the sale is delayed;
- other specific items worthy of notice.

A sample contract can be seen in Appendix 1.

The memorandum

The memorandum is a much briefer contract which is usually printed in the auction catalogue. An example is shown in Figure 4.2. Where full contracts are not available for signing by buyers, then the memorandum in the catalogue is used. This details:

- the contract lot number and the property;
- the price and the deposit payable;
- the name of the purchaser, declaring them the highest bidder at the sale.

The memorandum is not normally detached from the copy of the auction catalogue, so that the details of the property and its lot number are linked to the

```
                    Auction
              15th November 2000
            Memorandum of Contract

Contract Lot No. .........................................
Property .................................................
Price: £ ...................   Deposit: £ .................
I/We
of                            do hereby acknowledge that I/we:
(1)   were the highest bidder(s) at the Sale by Auction this day of the lot detailed above.
(2)   was/were declared the Purchaser(s) thereof subject to the Particulars and Conditions
      and Special Conditions of Sale at the price detailed above.
(3)   have paid the deposit detailed above to the Auctioneers.
(4)   agree to complete the said purchase in all respects according to the Particulars,
      Conditions and Special Conditions of the Sale.

Purchase money ..................   £
Less Deposit paid ..............   £
Balance to be paid on completion ....  £

AS WITNESS my/our/hand(s) this   day of             19
                                 Signed ...................................
                                 (for and on behalf of/the Purchaser(s))
We hereby confirm this sale and acknowledge receipt as agents for the vendor
of the said deposit of £  .............   in accordance with the Particulars,
Conditions and Special Conditions of Sale.

                                 Signed ...................................
                                 (signed on behalf of the Vendor(s))
Abstract of Title to be sent to . ...................................
```

Figure 4.2 Memorandum of contract

memorandum. A small table in the memorandum details the purchase money, the deposit paid and the balance to be paid on completion.

In the case of both the memorandum and the contract, one copy is signed and dated by the purchaser. The other copy is signed and dated on behalf of the vendors. The two documents are then 'exchanged' with the one received by the purchaser acting as a receipt for the deposit.

> **KEY POINT:** *If you buy a property and exchange contracts, pass your copy of the contract or memorandum to your solicitor immediately.*

When a contract is created

It is an interesting feature of auction law that the moment of contract is the point at which the auctioneer bangs down his gavel. The exchange of contracts or memorandum that takes place afterwards is merely a recording of the existence of the contract. The auctioneer has the legal right to sign the contract on behalf of the vendor and also the right to sign on behalf of the purchaser provided the signature takes place in the environs of the auction room within a reasonable time of the sale having taken place. The right to sign on behalf of the vendor is frequently used, but it is most unusual for the auctioneer to sign on behalf of the purchaser. However, it does leave the auctioneer in a position where he can sign either part of a contract or memorandum prior to the exchange of the parts. This is a convenient arrangement where the owner of the property is not present at the sale or where the purchaser has sent in a written bid or is at the other end of a telephone.

> **KEY POINT:** *No purchaser or bidder should think they have an opportunity to renege on their bid, after the gavel has fallen, by leaving the room without completing their part of the memorandum or contract.*

Note: An example of an auction contract can be found in Appendix 1.

Financial, legal and tax traps – a last-minute check

Will the owner's solicitors be present?

Across the country, the practice of solicitors attending auction varies. It appears to be a more usual practice in the north than the south that solicitors acting on behalf of the sellers attend the auction. An enquiry to the auction firm will always give you the answer.

> **KEY POINT:** *If the answer is yes, the vendor's solicitors are attending, you should, nevertheless, arrange for your solicitor to check the title to the property well before the sale.*

Check for late information

If the vendor's solicitors are at the auction, they may have some late information or be able to show you the results of a local search. Your own solicitor may ask you to look at this essential item if he has not had the opportunity and if he thinks it will be available on the day. The questions from the search that need to be put to the local authority to check that there are no adverse plans affecting the property are reproduced in Appendix 2. The vendor's solicitors may be holding other documents that you would like to see again. It is a good idea to check whatever are available and ask if any changes have occurred. These may include:

- plans of the lot being sold;
- leases and their actual wording;
- local searches;
- title details;
- a copy of the contract or memorandum;
- requirements to pay VAT.

> **KEY POINT:** *Do not rely on your own researches unless you have either a satisfactory legal background or no alternative.*

It is not unknown for some bidders at auction to read through the catalogue as they arrive and recklessly decide to bid for a property unseen from the catalogue. If you are feckless enough to consider such a course, do at least check through whatever documents are available at the solicitor's table or at the auctioneer's clerk's table before you bid.

Auctioneer's Anecdote: Unseen is unsafe

It is not as unusual as you would think for bidders to buy lots unseen. There are investors who will tell you "I have always had my most successful deals where I never saw the property until after I bought it". There are those who have walked up to the auctioneer afterwards and said "I liked the look of that lot on the slide, so I bought it. Can you tell me exactly where it is?"

There was a man with £30,000 (at 1995 values) burning a hole in his pocket who bought 27 properties in one lot at that figure in the belief that he could not go wrong getting those properties for that price. He did! They had subsided, were subject to various closure and repair notices and 15 of them were about to be purchased for clearance at a very small site value.

Watch the legal traps

It is not the purpose of this book to be a legal treatise. Nevertheless, every buyer must be aware that the contract is created at the moment that the gavel comes down. The exchange of contracts or memoranda thereafter is only a documentation of the existence of that contract. As we have already seen, the auctioneer can sign on behalf of both sides certifying that the existing contract is satisfactorily documented by the written details.

All auctioneers are aware of the Sale of Land by Auction Act 1867 which prohibits vendor's bids being made by more than one method. In property auctions, the Sale of Goods Act 1979 is partially relevant, but more important are the Estate Agents Act 1979 and the Property Misdescriptions Act 1991. These Acts regulate the propriety and behaviour of the auctioneer and his employees and business colleagues. The Property Misdescriptions Act is intended especially to ensure that auctioneers' particulars are not misleading. Details of the Property Misdescription Act are given on pages 108–109.

More important to the purchaser are the Auctions (Bidding Agreements) Acts 1927 and 1969. The main purpose of these Acts (as far as the bidder is concerned) is to ensure that you do not come to any agreement not to bid against anyone else at an auction unless the existence of such an arrangement and the parties to it have been declared in writing to the auctioneer before the sale begins.

> **KEY POINT:** *The Act makes it a criminal offence for a potential bidder, who is in business as a dealer, to offer an inducement to anyone else not to bid.*

Conditional contracts

A limited number of property auctioneers uses a conditional contracts procedure which applies when the bidding just fails to reach the reserve price. The procedures do not apply if your final accepted bid is at or above the reserve price since then the normal contract exchange process will be used. The auctioneer will always indicate in the catalogue if the conditional contracts procedure will apply at the auction.

Vendors may decide not to accept your bid

The terms of the conditional contract normally provide for you to be committed to a purchase at your highest bid while the seller decides whether or not he wishes to accept a sale at the same sum below his reserve. The seller is usually given between 24 and 72 hours to decide. The terms of conditional contracts vary but are always published by the auctioneer. If you attend an auction where conditional contracts are used, you should read the terms particularly carefully. If the conditional procedure applies, it is unlikely that the auctioneer's gavel will fall, but the final bidder will be approached immediately after the lot has been withdrawn to sign the conditional contract.

> **KEY POINT:** *Where conditional contracts do apply, intending bidders should read the details specified in the catalogue or the auctioneer's terms carefully and, if necessary, take appropriate advice on them.*

How and when is the deposit paid?

Immediately the gavel has fallen, the purchaser is due to exchange his memorandum or contract and to pay over the deposit. Usually the payment is 10 per cent of the purchase price, subject to a specified minimum. The amount due is indicated in the auctioneer's catalogue, generally somewhere in the conditions of sale. It is not unusual for these terms to be displayed on the walls of the sale room as well as in the catalogue and it may also be referred to in the auctioneer's opening remarks.

Be ready to hand over your money

Most auctioneers will accept a normal cheque drawn upon a recognized bank or building society. Cash is only accepted by certain auctioneers; if you intend to pay this way, check before the sale. No auctioneer has yet indicated that he will accept payment by credit card.

Certain auctioneers require certified or guaranteed cheques or banker's drafts. Personal or building society cheques are not acceptable. This does create a slight problem, since you will need to arrange for the cheque or draft to be prepared before the auction and you will not know how much the purchase price is going to be and therefore, how much the cheque should be. The only way of covering this is to ensure that the amount specified on the draft is at least 10 per cent of the maximum bid proposed – and maybe a little higher to allow for a touch of indulgent bidding. It is normally sufficient for the payment order to be made out to the auctioneer's firm but, on occasion, the catalogue may specify different instructions. Where auctioneers have a practice of inviting the solicitors acting on behalf of the vendor to attend the sale, then sometimes (but not very often) the solicitors for the vendor ask for the cheque to be made payable in their name. In a few instances, where sales are being conducted for government or local authority departments or quangos, cheques are occasionally requested to be payable to them. Cheques are normally only payable to the vendor if it is a reputable and well-known body.

> **KEY POINT:** *The destination of this deposit cheque and the way in which the money is held, is very important to both parties to the transaction between contract and completion.*

LOT 211
53 Queen Street,
Desborough, Northamptonshire
BY ORDER OF MORTGAGEES IN POSSESSION

A Freehold Mid Terrace House

TENURE
Freehold.

LOCATION
Queen Street is located off Rushton Road, which in turn runs into Station Road. Local shops and amenities are within reach.

DESCRIPTION
The property comprises a mid terrace house arranged over ground and first floors beneath a pitched tile roof. The property benefits from a rear garden.

ACCOMMODATION

Ground Floor	First Floor
Two Reception Rooms	Three Bedrooms
Kitchen Area	
Bathroom with WC and wash basin	

A three-bed house in the shires for a very reasonable £16,500.

The conditions of sale usually indicate whether the deposit money, after the exchange of contracts, is held by:

- a stakeholder on behalf of the vendor;
- a stakeholder on behalf of the purchaser;
- a stakeholder on behalf of both sides;
- the vendor.

Insist on an indemnity bond

A stakeholder can be any person, but they must be acceptable to both parties. The auctioneers or solicitors often act as the stakeholder. If the money is held on behalf of the vendor, a purchaser should insist, before exchanging contracts, that the money is covered by an insurance bond, to be held by the auctioneers or the solicitors and require that the vendor is prohibited from having access to the money until completion. The bond will protect the

purchaser's money in the event of fraud or insolvency of the auctioneers or solicitors.

If the money is held on behalf of the purchaser, then there is no need to restrict control of the money further, although it is still wise to ensure that the money, whilst in the hands of professionals, is covered by a necessary insurance bond. Virtually all auctioneers and solicitors indicate the arrangements made. Once paid, the purchaser will not have access to the deposit unless the contract is cancelled.

Where the money is held by a stakeholder it is usually in the control of the auctioneers or solicitors who have been so nominated to hold it on behalf of both vendor and purchaser until completion. Again, it is wise that this money should be covered by an insurance bond and you should be satisfied that the amount is paid into an appropriate client account.

Who keeps the interest?

Where big deposit sums are payable or the period between purchase and completion is longer than usual and the amount of interest earned on the money in this period is significant, then it is important that everyone is clear who receives the interest. Normally, the interest is retained by:

- the auctioneers; or
- the solicitors; or occasionally
- the vendor; or very occasionally
- the purchaser (and then only by special agreement).

However, if the interest to be earned is large, discuss the matter with the auctioneers at least several days prior to the sale. You would be wise to make arrangements with the auctioneer's and vendor's solicitors for the interest to be credited to your benefit, making it a condition of your bidding that such an arrangement must be entered into. Alternatively, if you cannot make such arrangements, allow for loss of interest when calculating the amount of your final bid.

Bids by phone require deposit payments in advance

If you intend to bid by telephone, fax or letter then you will have to make arrangements with the auctioneer to pay the deposit before the sale. Unless you are well known to the auctioneer, he will invariably require you to pay the deposit by banker's draft, building society or personal cheque, which will have to be cleared before the sale begins. The amount will be equal to or higher than 10 per cent of your proposed maximum sum. It is wise to make such arrangements well in advance of the auction, giving the auctioneer at least a week's notice.

It is imperative that funds are available to cover any cheque issued for a deposit. If a cheque or financial instrument issued to cover the deposit fails to provide the necessary funds, the vendor will exercise his rights under the conditions of sale permitting him to:

- cancel the sale at his option; and
- take civil proceedings against the purchaser for any loss or costs.

The vendor is not required to re-offer the lot by auction, but can take any reasonable steps chosen to re-sell the lot. Before taking proceedings to recover any loss or costs the seller must show that reasonable endeavours have been made to re-sell at a proper price.

If a deposit cheque bounces, this could open up criminal proceedings. Such an offence does not remove the seller's rights to a civil claim.

CHECKLIST:
Paying the deposit

1 How much is payable? ☐
2 Who is it to be paid to? ☐
3 When is it required? ☐
4 Do they require cleared funds? ☐
5 Who receives the interest? ☐
6 Can the interest be paid into my account? ☐
7 Is the vendor prohibited from receiving the monies until completion? ☐
8 Is there an indemnity bond? ☐
9 Is there an insurance bond? ☐
10 Are the monies being paid into client accounts? ☐

Value Added Tax

In certain circumstances VAT is payable on property or land purchases. Where a property has been registered as subject to VAT, then the purchaser will have to pay at completion VAT at the going rate in addition to the purchase price. The purchaser will receive a VAT receipt and may be entitled to reclaim that tax or part of it. Nevertheless, the incidence of the payment may well affect cash flow, financing and, possibly, the legal vehicle in which the property is bought.

Almost invariably, the auction catalogue will disclose if VAT is payable. If not, the auctioneer should publish it in the amendment sheet. He may also mention it in his opening speech and will undoubtedly mention it at the time he offers the lot.

'SC' –
Self-contained

'P' –
This is normally used as an abbreviation for 'Vacant Possession' which can also be noted as 'V.P.'

'L' –
Leasehold

'F' –
Freehold

'RUP' –
Residential upper part

'Mais' –
Maisonette

LONDON

STRETTONS of E1 at New Connaught Rms, WC2, Apr 19

E1 — 18 Pevensey Hse, Ben Johnson Rd. S/C mais, 4 rms. L, P	**30,000**
50 Cephas Ave. End terr hse, 6 rms. Closing order. F, P	**53,000**
37 New Rd. Terr w/shop bdg. 2 floors. Let £2,068 pa. 2 floors, 388 & 410 sq ft with P. F	**55,000**
E3 — 104 Fairfoot Rd. Bdg plot. PP 2 flats. F, P	**15,000**
111 Grove Rd. Terr hse, 5 rms. F, P	**54,000**
13 Grafton Hse, Wellington Way. 2nd floor, S/C flat, 3 rms. L, P	**17,500**
E5 — 5/7 Chatsworth Rd. 2 adj shops, RUP 2 S/C flats, 4 & 5 rms. Let £3,120 PAX. Closing Order. F	**40,000**
4 Cricketfield Rd. S/C flat, 2 rms. L, P	**25,500**
19 Elderfield Rd. End terr hse, 9 rms. PP flat, mais, 2 garages. Closing order. F, P	**43,000**
30 Glenarm Rd. 2nd floor, S/C studio flat. L, P	**15,500**
103 Mount Pleasant Lane. S/C flat, 3 rms. L, P	**23,000**
E6 — 132 Charlemont Rd. RUP S/C flat, 2 rms. L, P	**20,500**
58 Dickens Rd. End terr hse, 3 bed. F, P	**35,000**
130 Masterman Rd. Terr hse, 2 bed. F, P	**36,500**
St Andrews Hall, Roman Rd. Derelict hall, site 0.10 a. Planning brief for 2 hses. F, P	**31,000**
E7 — 165 Capel Rd. Corner bdg, 6 rms, part used as clinic. PP 2 hses & garages on rear land. F, P	**66,500**
7 Neville Rd. End terr bdg as 3 S/C flats. 1 LGR, 1 studio flat & 1 x 3 rms with P. For completion. F	**36,500**
75 Pevensey Rd. Terr hse as 2 flats, 3 rms. F, P	**38,000**
7 Reginald Rd. Corner shop, rear rm. RUP, 3 rms. F, P	**35,000**
21 Shaftesbury Rd. Terr hse, 2 bed. F, P	**35,500**
E8 — 234 Dalston Lane. 4 storey hse, 10 rms, 2 store rms. F, P	**55,000**
376C Kingsland Rd. RUP S/C mais, 3 rms. L, P	**22,000**
113 Shacklewell Lane. Shop, rear rm. S/C mais, 3 rms. P	**28,500**
E10 — 287 High Rd. Shop, rear rm, basement, mais, 4 rms, garage. F, P	**60,000**
E12 — 32 Salisbury Rd. Terr hse, 3 bed. F, P	**36,500**
E13 — 198 Balaam St. S/C flat, 3 rms. L, P	**18,000**
163 Grange Rd. Terr hse, 6 rms. F, P	**34,500**
50 London Rd. S/C flat, 2 rms. L, P	**14,000**
31 Maud Rd. Terr hse as S/C flat, 3 rms & S/C mais, 3 rms. F, P	**41,000**
Tabernacle Ave. Site 0.16 a. Planning brief for development. F, P	**16,000**

Illustration 4. Estates Gazette auction results

Timing of VAT payments

VAT is almost always paid at completion of the purchase. Unless announced otherwise, the VAT will always be in addition to the price bid at the time the gavel falls.

How to find out if VAT is payable

Is VAT mentioned:

1. in the conditions of sale?
2. in the general preamble at the beginning of the catalogue?
3. in the description of the lot in the catalogue?
4. in any memoranda published in the catalogue?
5. in the auctioneer's amendment sheet?
6. in the auctioneer's opening speech?
7. at any time during the offering of the lot?
8. just before the gavel is brought down?
9. where the property on offer gives a rental income to the owner and VAT is paid by the tenants in addition to their rent?

> **KEY POINT:** *If VAT is not mentioned in any of these contexts, then you may rest assured that it is not payable in addition to the gavel price.*

How can I find out the reserve price?

Most owners are unwilling to sell their properties below a fixed figure. This is the amount which they indicate to the auctioneer as the reserve. The gavel is not brought down to create a contract for sale for any lot until there is a bid equal to or larger than the reserve figure. The auctioneer will of course encourage bidders to bid up to that price, so that he then has a sale. Usually he provides in the conditions of sale for the right to put in bids below the reserve amount on behalf of the owner who is selling.

> **KEY POINT:** *The reserve is a highly confidential amount and it is most unusual for it to be disclosed to the public or to any intending bidders.*

It is not unusual for public bodies to put the reserve in a sealed envelope which the auctioneer only opens as he goes onto the rostrum, although it is quite possible that he will have discussed an appropriate amount with his client beforehand. Some owners even refuse to disclose their final reserve to their own auctioneer and sit in the audience giving a pre-arranged signal when the bidding has reached a level at which the auctioneer can sell. This practice is discouraged by auctioneers because of the uncertainty it creates for them.

Reserves that are published

Only on a limited number of occasions – particularly where owners are thinking of selling at a low price – do auctioneers publish their reserve as part of their marketing campaign. This is done deliberately to create interest and the figure is usually published in the auction catalogue and often put into advertisements. It may be described as an 'upset price' (see Figure 4.3). This practice is frequently adopted where the instructions to sell have come from liquidators and receivers.

A published reserve puts you in the driving seat

To the auctioneer, having his reserve disclosed is rather like playing a poker hand face upwards on the table. Immediately the price at which he can sell is disclosed, then everyone in the audience is aware of whether the bids have reached a point at which the auctioneer can sell or not. He is not in a position to put pressure on people in the room to bid by going through the offering procedure on a 'mock' basis as if he were about to sell. This procedure is examined later in this chapter.

Without reserve

Very occasionally, lots are offered 'without reserve' and this literally means that if only one (even if it is excessively low) bid is received, the auctioneer has to sell. Anyone attending an auction where a property is offered at no reserve would be perfectly entitled to start the bidding at £1.

The vagaries of human nature are such that it is not at all unusual for properties offered with no reserve to attract a lot of attention and for bidders to get

Lot 20

VACANT OFFICE PREMISES OFFERED WITH A RESERVE OF £77,500

Situation:	A-Z B1 84, Off Waterloo Road, Middle Hillgate
Construction:	Brick and slate
Tenure:	Freehold
Accommodation:	The offices have been thoroughly refurbished.
Ground floor:	Entrance hall, 4 large offices, kitchen and storage.
First floor:	Two offices, large showroom fronting to Canal Street, toilet facilities.
Exterior:	Car parking at rear.
General:	The showroom area has an open ceiling revealing the original roof beams which have been polished and provide a most attractive feature. This building of character is a former public house which has recently undergone a comprehensive refurbishment. The offices are carpeted throughout and have double glazed windows, full gas fired central heating, suspended ceilings with recessed lighting on the ground floor.

Approximate Total Floor Area: 1950 sq ft
Viewing & Co-agents: Edwards & Co (N M Hunter), 20 Albert Square, Manchester, M2 5BE. Tel: 061-833 9991.

Vacant Possession: On completion

Solicitors: Gabbie & Co, 60 Talbot Road, Manchester, M16 0GB. Tel: 061-872 5363.

Figure 4.3 Auction catalogue illustrating an upset price. This was a property where the vendor had the building on the market for quite a long time before the auction, at an asking price noticeably higher than the upset price quoted. She felt that by publishing the upset price, it would be an indication to people who had previously been interested that the vendor would be willing to sell at a noticeably lower figure than had previously been asked in the market. As it happened the property offered still did not sell at the auction.

carried away but it is a brave owner who would offer his property on this basis thinking he will sell at a high sum. It is a practice used more often for properties for which there is little demand or where there are large liabilities for structural repairs or other costs.

> **KEY POINT:** *Properties offered without a reserve are not always the bargain which they may seem and should be approached with considerable care.*

A cautionary tale

Mr Black is after a cheap property that he can 'do up and rent out' to bring him a small income. He calculates that if he buys something under £5,000, refurbishes it for £10,000 and then rents it out at £4,000 a year, this would represent a really good investment.

Don't get carried away by 'no reserves'

He is delighted to see a property at a local auction at no reserve. It looks a little run-down in the picture but does not seem too bad and he dashes to the auction without doing any checking. Before Mr Black had even collected his wits at the auction, the bidding had started at only £5 for the lot which interested him and seemed to be going fast and furious until it slowed down at £2,700. He quickly jumped in with £2,800 and was delighted when the gavel fell on his first bid, particularly since he felt he had saved himself £2,200 already.

His solicitor's charges of £500 seemed rather expensive and he was even less pleased on seeing the property for the first time the day after the auction to discover that it suffered from subsidence, rising damp, was infected with woodworm and had suffered from an arson attack which had burnt out the back of the building. A surveyor estimated it would take around £35,000 to put it right.

The local council, having had their attention drawn to the property by the auction publicity, sent around their building inspector, who condemned it. Mr Black failed to respond to the request that he demolish it and they carried out the work for him submitting a bill for £3,200 including 15 per cent establishment expenses plus VAT.

Mr Black still owns an empty site which cost him over £7,600 and no-one wants to buy but upon which a lot of people seem to want to 'fly-tip' rubbish.

In Figure 4.4, the derelict nature of the property is obvious and, furthermore, was spelt out in the auctioneer's description. Defects in properties offered at no reserve are not always so obvious.

Disclosing when the reserve has been reached

Auctioneers will go to great lengths to prevent the audience from realizing which bids are made on behalf of the sellers and which bids have been made by people in the room. Therefore, there is usually no obvious indication when the auctioneer 'reaches' or 'passes' the reserve. Thereafter, certain auctioneers like to disclose that the bidding is higher than the reserve and will use such phrases as 'the property is in the market' or 'at this price I shall sell if I receive no higher bid' or simply indicate that the reserve has been reached. Other auctioneers only disclose this information on certain lots where they feel it will encourage the bidding.

> **KEY POINT:** *Many auctioneers never disclose that the reserve has been reached and it is only known when either the gavel falls for the sale or the gavel does not fall and the lot is withdrawn.*

Discovering the reserve price

If you are able to discover, by fair means or foul, the level of the reserve, you are in a stronger position than other bidders competing against you. To discover reserves, bidders must resort to their ingenuity. In most cases, the reserve figure will be known to the auctioneer and to some of his senior

---

Lot 26
23 Vale Street, Clayton
AT NO RESERVE
VACANT SEMI DETACHED HOUSE IN NEED OF COMPLETE RESTORATION

Situation: A-Z 2F 51. Off North Road, Ashton New Road (A662)
Tenure: Long leasehold subject to a ground rent of £4 pa.
Accommodation: *Ground floor:* Hall, lounge, kitchen. *First floor:* 3 bedrooms, bathroom/wc *Exterior:* Gardens front and rear, space for car
Viewing: Keys available from the auctioneers
Note: The property is boarded up. The entire property is in need of thorough overhauling and refurbishment.
Vacant Possession: On completion
Solicitors: Davies Wallis Foyster (Mr I Osborne) 37 Peter Street, M2 5GB

Figure 4.4 An auction lot offered at no reserve

and junior staff who may be led into disclosing the actual figure. Close acquaintanceship with the auctioneer might or might not help but, undoubtedly, a 'quick peek' at his auction catalogue (if he has an unguarded moment) could reveal the figure.

Can I tell what the reserve is from the starting price?

There is no fixed theory about the relationship between the price that the auctioneer first asks for, the figure at which he takes the first bid and the reserve price. It is worth considering the psychology of the auctioneer and weighing up his style and practice as the auction proceeds. There are several factors in his mind:

- On the papers in front of him for each lot, he will have the reserve 'writ large'. His note of the reserve figure will not only be in large numerals

Table 4.2 Opening bids, reserves and increments

Reserve	Likely opening increments with responsive bidding	Possible opening bid with unresponsive bidding	Possible opening bid
£10,000	£1,000	£6,000	£4,000
£20,000	£1,000	£15,000	£10,000
£30,000	£2,500	£20,000	£15,000
£50,000	£5,000	£30,000	£20,000
£100,000	£10,000	£60,000	£50,000
£200,000	£10,000	£150,000	£100,000
£300,000	£25,000	£200,000	£150,000

but also in a bright colour so he cannot miss it. He is striving to encourage the bidding to reach this reserve figure. As he starts off each lot, this amount will be uppermost in his mind as his target. It is not unusual that the first figure he mentions in seeking the opening bid could well be that reserve amount.

- The auctioneer likes to receive bids in the room and be seen to be taking them. On the other hand, if he has a considerable number of lots to sell and is in a hurry to complete the sale, he will wish to start the bidding not too far below the reserve. Table 4.2 illustrates possible opening bids and increments against given reserve prices.

- If the auction is going well, and the auctioneer is receiving responsive bidding from the floor, then he is likely to start the bidding closer to his reserve than otherwise. If there is very little response and not many bids forthcoming, he may try a starting bid that is particularly low to encourage enthusiasm from the audience. Unfortunately, there is no proven formula; but as you become used to your auctioneer's style you may be able to spot a pattern in his behaviour.

'The auction itself was run very well. I had been before so I knew they were good and entertaining – it's the best bit of free entertainment in Manchester.'
Don Lee, buyer of a residential property at auction.

5 Bidding and winning your bargain

'Buying at auction is very straightforward. If I could see houses that were being sold at comparable prices in comparable areas I would buy privately. But buying at auction is a way of ensuring I don't have to pay more than I need to pay. You want to make sure you acquire your property at a bargain level and auctions are the way.' Michael Roe, buyer of residential properties.

How does an auctioneer conduct an auction?

The auctioneer's opening speech

Bearing in mind that auctioneers are individualists, you can expect all their opening speeches to vary considerably. They do, however, frequently contain important information and it is wise to be at the auction before the start and before the auctioneer's introductory remarks. If you are only going to be interested in a lot towards the end of a long day of selling, ensure that you hear the opening speech, even if you then decide to take a break from listening to the sale of some of the earlier lots.

> **KEY POINT:** *Having decided to attend the auction, you should listen to the contents of the auctioneer's speech carefully.*

The speech will usually contain:

1. A polite welcome.
2. An indication of how the sale will be run with advice on any lots that have been withdrawn or that will be sold out of numerical or alphabetical order. For example, the auctioneer may decide to split a lot into two or put two lots together and sell them as one. Alternatively, he may decide to offer a lot as it stands and if it does not sell, then to split it into two. For some reason the vendors may decide that they want to vary the order of

sale and the auctioneer will indicate that he will sell lot 2 before lot 1 or make a variation such as lot 10 will only be offered at the end of the auction rather than after lot 9.

Announcements of changes

3. Details of any late amendments to the information published in the catalogue. (It is very common for auctioneers to issue amendment sheets which detail these variations.) Amendments may include corrections to addresses or descriptions or may be more fundamental. Quite often, the published details state the wrong terms or starting dates or the rents payable under leases. Even more frequently, review dates on leases seem to need variation.

4. Comment on the auctioneer's right to bid on behalf of vendors and on behalf of people who have left bids with him or his firm or his employees. The phrase in the speech may be:

   'On behalf of the auctioneers, I give notice that they reserve the right to bid, through me or otherwise on behalf of purchasers who have left bids with them, or on behalf of vendors, or as agents, or as principals for any lots.'

   You will see that this comment coupled with the conditions of sale leaves the auctioneer to take bids:
   - on behalf of people who are not present but who have made proxy bids;
   - made by people who are bidding by telephone;
   - on behalf of people who have already instructed him by letter, fax or similar instruction to bid up to a specific sum on a specific lot;
   - on behalf of the vendor;
   - on behalf of himself or his firm.

5. The procedures that follow during the auction for:
   - methods of bidding;

LOT 212
15 Simpson Avenue,
Higham Ferrers, Northamptonshire
BY ORDER OF MORTGAGEES IN POSSESSION

A Freehold Semi Detached House

TENURE
Freehold.

LOCATION
Simpson Avenue is located off Station Road (A6). The property itself is situated close to Simpson Avenue's juction with George Street. Local amenities are within reach.

DESCRIPTION
The property comprises a semi detached house arranged over ground and first floors beneath a pitched roof. The property benefits from a rear garden.

ACCOMMODATION

Ground Floor	First Floor
Two Reception Rooms	Three Bedrooms
Kitchen Area	Bathroom with WC and wash basin
	Shower Room

£16,000 is all you would have needed to collect the keys to this three-bed semi-detached property.

- obtaining the details of purchasers;
- the arrangements for signing and exchanging contracts or memoranda;
- the amount of the deposit and how it is to be paid.

6. The completion date of each lot.

Persuading, cajoling and bullying for the highest bid

Auctioneers come in all shapes and sizes and ages; their charisma and charm varies throughout the range, but almost invariably they are frustrated actors! There is no doubt the performance of a good auctioneer on the rostrum is the equivalent to that of a high quality professional actor on the stage. This performer on the rostrum sets out to use all his abilities to make the most of the competition engendered in the auction room and to persuade, cajole, lead or bully bidders into paying more than their common sense would suggest.

The auctioneer has the benefit that the entire audience must concentrate on him. Many newcomers to auctions fear that their slightest move might be interpreted as a bid and they will finish up buying a property they did not intend to take home.

> **KEY POINT:** *This fear is not justified and all auctioneers take care not to 'knock down' lots to individuals in the audience who make involuntary (or even voluntary non-bidding) gestures.*

What the auctioneer is thinking

The auctioneer runs the auction on three levels of consciousness. Uppermost in his mind will be the level of bidding at or above the reserve that he is striving to reach to effect a sale. For this reason, auctioneers often unconsciously seek to start the bidding at the reserve amount. If the bidding does not begin at this price, the auctioneer may ask for lower starting prices.

At the second level the auctioneer has a regular rhythm of patter relating to the bid that he has received and the next bid he is seeking. Auctioneers often have an almost monotonous mantra-like recitation of amounts.

At the third level he is hawkishly seeking movements or sounds in the audience which betray the existence of bidders.

Auctioneer's Anecdote: Bidders are like the opposite sex

Quote from the Manchester Evening News, 'Bidders are like the opposite sex. We can't do without them. Too often the low bidder is jeered, the tentative bidder chivvied and the reluctant bidder chided. Remember always, all bidders need encouragement and more encouragement until they thrive and smile and multiply and bid and bid and bid. Auctioneers should always ensure positively that the final bid they accept before the climactic bang of the gavel is a bid. No auctioneer earns merit from accepting as his last bid a smile, the response to a neighbour's joke, a nervous twitch or sneeze or a salutation across the sale room to a colleague.'

How large do the bids jump?

Having found a bidder or bidders, the auctioneer will aim to dictate the increments in the bidding. He will seek to make them as large as possible, probably in the range between two and a half per cent and five per cent of the bids. The increments may initially be in quite large amounts but as the price rises they will almost invariably reduce when the bidding slows down and the sale price nears.

Table 5.1 gives examples of increment sizes in line with bidding prices. Most auctioneers aim to encourage a regular rhythm of bidding by their audience. It is common for them to concentrate on only two bidders at a time moving on to other bidders only when one of the original pair drops out. Occasionally, auctioneers will take their bids in turn from three bidders. By following this practice of using their audience in pairs or trios he is able to ensure that the bidders are aware when it is their turn to participate.

The personal style of each auctioneer varies, but a typical offering and bidding scenario is as follows:

AUCTIONEER: I now wish to offer lot number six, a charming and desirable residence with vacant possession, 16 Acacia Road, Lewisham. Where may I start the bidding? £50,000?
(*Silence.*)

AUCTIONEER: Well, ladies and gentlemen, it is in your hands not mine as to where we start the bidding. Should it be £45,000?
(*Silence.*)

AUCTIONEER: Will £35,000 tempt someone to bid? Thank you sir, I have your bid (*as bidder number one waves his catalogue vigorously in the air*).

Table 5.1 Bidding ranges and increment sizes

Bidding range	Main increments	Intermediate increments	Possible final increments
£1,000–£20,000	£1,000	£500	£250
£20,000–£50,000	£2,500	£1,000	£500
£50,000–£100,000	£5,000	£2,500	£1,000
£100,000–£250,000	£10,000	£5,000	£2,500
£250,000–£500,000	£25,000	£10,000	£5,000
£500,000–£1,000,000	£100,000	£50,000	£25,000

AUCTIONEER: I am bid £35,000. Do I see £37,500? £37,500 anywhere?
(*Bidder number two coughs and raises a tentative finger in the air.*)

AUCTIONEER: £37,500 bid. £40,000 anywhere?
(*Bidder number one nods his head discreetly.*)

AUCTIONEER: £42,500?
(*Bidder number two shakes his head.*)
(*Bidder number three shouts £42,500!*)

AUCTIONEER: £42,500. £45,000 may I say?
(*Bidder number one nods his head.*)

AUCTIONEER: £47,500?
(*Bidder number three winks.*)

AUCTIONEER: £50,000?
(*Bidder number one looks away.*)
(*Bidder number three waves his catalogue.*)

AUCTIONEER: I have your bid, sir, at £47,500 which is your bid. £50,000 anywhere? Any further bid? I am bid £47,500. I am looking for £50,000. Have you all done? Has the bidding finished? At £47,500 for the first time. For the second time …
(*Bidder number four shouts out incomprehensibly.*)

AUCTIONEER: I have a new bidder at £50,000. £52,500 anywhere? Have you all finished at £50,000? Will a bid at £51,000 tempt anyone at this stage?
(*Bidder number one raises his finger in the air.*)

AUCTIONEER: I have £51,000. £52,000 may I say?
(*Bidder number four nods her head.*)

AUCTIONEER: I am bid £52,000. £53,000 anywhere? £53,000 may I say? Have you all now finished at this price? At £52,000 then for the first time, £52,000 for the second time (*pointing at bidder number four*). It is your bid, Madam, at £52,000. Any further bid? £53,000 anywhere?
(*The auctioneer lifts his gavel and holds it threateningly in the air and after a pause brings it down.*)

AUCTIONEER: Sold at £52,000.
(*Looking at bidder number four pointedly.*)

AUCTIONEER: May I see your paddle number, madam?
(*Bidder number four shows her paddle number.*)

AUCTIONEER: Sold to 142 at £52,000. And for my next lot …

Watch out for changes to the lot details

The auctioneer's firm will always indicate whether any lots have been sold prior to the sale and whether any lots have been withdrawn. They may have posters on the wall or at the entrance indicating lots sold prior. The information may also be recorded on amendment sheets that are issued.

Occasionally, lots are split or amalgamated for the purpose of a sale. It may be that the order of the sale has been changed or there are changes in the details of some of the lots. This is likely to be announced in the auctioneer's speech and detailed in any amendment sheets issued. A typical amendment sheet is shown in Figure 5.1.

How to make your bid

Use your own style

Any auctioneer will reminisce over the variety of styles adopted by bidders. Many of the stories may be apocryphal but tales are recounted of buyers who bid in mirrors, with their toes, their fingers, their nose, by winking or by proxy.

LOTS SOLD: 4, 5, 6, 8, 14, 15, 17, 25, 30, 32, 36

7   This property has recently had gas central heating installed and full rewiring.

12   The solicitors' correct address is 229 Burnage Lane.

13   This lot is freehold not leasehold as described in the catalogue.

25   The solicitors acting are Addleshaws, Dennis House, Marsden Street, Manchester. Tel: 0161-832 5994.

29   One of the lifts is in working order but the other is not.

30   2 bedrooms should read 3 bedrooms.

31   Special Conditions of Sale are available for inspection at the office of the auctioneers. The total weekly income is £696.15 and not as printed in the catalogue. The following is a schedule of occupiers' agreements as at 9.9.93.

Occupier	Weekly rent	Agreement date	Expiry date
World Book & Childcraft International	£140.00	01.10.99	31.12.00
TA Wise (t/a Tour inc Production Agency)	£46.15	04.08.99	05.09.00
Amjad Dar (t/a First Call)	£60.00	02.08.99	31.08.00
Elaine Chadwick	£140.00	01.06.99	30.09.00
Julian Stein	£50.00	01.06.99	30.09.00
Associated Homecare Limited	£220.00	18.08.99	17.02.01
Madman Movies Limited	£40.00	23.08.99	19.09.01

34   We have recently been advised that the tenant of the shop has not paid rent for 9 months. The purchaser will be required to pay the arrears of £1,800 outstanding over to the vendor at completion.

35   The solicitors acting are Alsop Wilkinson (Jill Worthington dealing), 11 St James Square, Manchester M2 6DR. Tel: 0161-834 7760.

Figure 5.1 An amendment sheet

Keep your eye on the auctioneer

Once he knows you are interested, then your movements can be a matter of your own style as long as they are sufficient to show your interest. It is wise during this period to keep looking directly at the auctioneer. Your bidding should always be confident. Act as if you attend auctions every other day. Make all your gestures strong and firm. Should the price become too high for you, then stop the movement and look away from the auctioneer. Many bidders specifically indicate with a shake of the head that they are no longer interested and occasionally some of those change their mind and start bidding again.

> **KEY POINT:** *There is no point in trying to unsettle or disturb the auctioneer, particularly since you need him 'on your side'. Much more important is the impression you create in the minds of competitors bidding against you.*

Auctioneer's Anecdote: The bidder is not always the decision-maker

Not surprisingly, husband and wife teams often sit together in auctions. Occasionally, a group of three or even four board members or partners may attend an auction together. In these cases, it is frequently very obvious to the auctioneer which member of the team is the decision-maker and, for some reason, it is most unusual for that decision-maker to be the actual bidder. The wife decides but the husband bids! The managing director decides but the company secretary bids! The auctioneer, on his rostrum, is frequently in a position to see these decisions being passed 'down the line' and is always intrigued to see the look of surprise on the husband's or company secretary's face when the auctioneer appears to take the bid off him before he has even made his gesture. No auctioneer would ever admit that he does not have a heightened sense of ESP.

Bidding by telephone

Many of us have seen the telephone bid used, particularly at the leading chattel auction sales on television. Most auctioneers of property are willing to make the telephone available for bidding, but this does have certain disadvantages to the buyer. You need to establish your credit with the auctioneer several days before the auction, and he will probably require you to send him a cheque before the auction representing the 10 per cent deposit of the maximum sum that you are willing to bid.

This has two disadvantages. First, the auctioneer is aware of the maximum you will pay and if he is unscrupulous may take advantage of this knowledge by increasing the reserve. Second, it prevents you from making any bids higher than 'the first number you thought of' at the time you dispatched the cheque. For some reason, perhaps because they disturb the auctioneer's rhythm of bidding, telephone bids always come over weakly in the room and seem to have less impact on opposing bidders. The audience may believe they are a ploy of the auctioneer to increase the number and level of bids.

Auctioneer's Anecdote: Long-distance bidding

A well-known firm of provincial auctioneers decided to run an auction in the provinces and in London at the same time. They installed an auctioneer and solicitors in each room and linked the rooms up with three telephone lines. Microphones at each end conveyed the proceedings in each room to loud-speakers in the other. The first eight lots were all sold in a room in the provinces and although one or two bids came through on the loud-speakers from the London end, the city bids were few and far between. As the bidding rose higher for the ninth lot, over the loud-speakers in the provinces were heard the bids taken by the second auctioneer in London from a bidder in that room. The lot was sold to the London buyer. This immediately provoked a strong murmur and comment from the provincial audience which the auctioneer in that room immediately picked up on and said 'You didn't really think there was anybody at the other end, did you?' to nods of assent all round the room.

Can I employ someone to bid for me?

Having read this guide, you will be well-equipped to tackle an auction yourself. But there is no reason why you should not seek out an auctioneer, solicitor or other professional experienced in the sale room to act on your behalf. It may be that the valuer who has assisted you in the earlier stages will be willing to join you in the room for an appropriate fee. He may charge a specific fee of between £150 and £300 or may charge at an hourly rate of between £80 and £200 per hour. You may want to discuss with him the tactics that you might both use to upset the opposition. But in the end, you will have to appreciate he can only bid up to the price you specify and that any different decision by you will need transmitting to him quickly if he is to enter a bid above your authorized amount. There are no other agencies that specialize in bidding on a purchaser's behalf.

Bidding by proxy

A final method of submitting your bids is to notify the auctioneer's firm by letter, fax or e-mail. As with the telephone bid, you will need to cover the 10 per cent deposit. Bidding by proxy has the same

disadvantages as the telephone bid, but if you resort to it then it is important that you instruct the auctioneer in writing to bid up to your chosen maximum price. All reputable auctioneers will accept this instruction, but again you have the disadvantage of not being able to vary your maximum price having gauged the atmosphere in the auction room. Also, the auctioneer is aware of the maximum figure that you are willing to pay and might adjust his increments accordingly.

> **KEY POINT:** *The best method is to attend the auction in person and, having obtained suitable advice, bid yourself.*

Bidding tactics to beat the competition

'I didn't start the bidding. There were one or two other bidders lower down. I let them have their say and then came in at the end. I bid twice and the second time it stopped, my bid being the highest bid. I thought the auctioneer might withdraw it because it was only slightly higher than we had bid before the auction. I thought it probably hadn't reached the reserve. But then the gavel came down and I knew it was ours.'

Michael Kirby, Chartered Surveyor.

Use a jump bid to put off the competition

Although you will hear the auctioneer dictating the bids he is seeking, if the bidding is well below the price you have decided to pay, you may elect to make a jump bid shouting out a figure which is higher than that for which the auctioneer has just asked. The auctioneer will not be too upset by your disturbance of his bidding rhythm and it may be that an opposing bidder will be put off their stride. You should set out to convince your opponents that you will cap their bids regardless of how high they go and so discourage them from putting in any more bids.

How to reduce the size of the auctioneer's increments

The auctioneer's aim is to dictate the increments in the bidding and to make them as large as possible.

LOT 250

23 Gordon Road,
Herne Bay, Kent

BY ORDER OF MORTGAGEES IN POSSESSION

A Freehold Mid Terrace House

TENURE
Freehold.

LOCATION
The coastal resort of Herne Bay is situated on the A299 within reach of the A2/M2 motorway. Gordon Road is located off King's Road close to the shopping amenities available along High Street. British Rail services run from Herne Bay Station.

DESCRIPTION
The property comprises a mid terrace house arranged over ground and first floors under a steep pitched roof with a single bay to the front elevation. There is a rear garden.

ACCOMMODATION

Ground Floor	First Floor
Two Reception Rooms	Four Bedrooms
Breakfast Room	Bathroom with WC
Kitchen	

A four-bed coastal home for £30,000.

He will have more opportunity to do this at the cheaper levels than in the middle range. Thus, with bidding at the £10,000 to £15,000 level, the auctioneer in his early stages may be able to take the bidding £10,000, £11,000, £12,000, £13,000, £14,000, £15,000. As he comes closer to his reserve and the prices get higher, you may find him reducing the increments to £500 to encourage the bidding and to indicate to his audience that he is coming closer to the reserve. The bidding might then proceed at £15,500, £16,000, £16,500, £17,000. Some auctioneers, having reached their reserve or being very close to it, might bring their increments down to £250 or even £100 or £50 a time. Knowledgeable auctioneers resist this knowing full well that by keeping the increments as large as possible they will obtain a final bid higher than they might otherwise achieve, thus obtaining more for their client.

The auctioneer's increment sizes may be:

Bidding range	Main increments	Intermediate increments	Possible final increments
£1,000–£20,000	£1,000	£500	£250
£20,000–£50,000	£2,500	£1,000	£500
£50,000–£100,000	£5,000	£2,500	£1,000
£100,000–£250,000	£10,000	£5,000	£2,500
£250,000–£500,000	£25,000	£10,000	£5,000
£500,000–£1,000,000	£100,000	£50,000	£25,000

A useful gambit is to try to reduce the size of the auctioneer's increments in the bidding figures at an early stage. An experienced auctioneer may be wise to this move and refuse to accept low increments but others will accept a reduction in the increment sought, if they are convinced you will give them a bid at that amount. By reducing the increments much earlier than the auctioneer would choose and making your opponents bid innumerable times, you will make them think that you have reached a high amount, enabling you to move in and catch the last bid at a lower level than it might otherwise reach. The following example illustrates this in practice:

Bidding the price down – in practice

AUCTIONEER: I now wish to offer lot number six. A charming and desirable residence with vacant possession, 16 Acacia Road, Lewisham. Where may I start the bidding? £50,000? *(Silence)*

AUCTIONEER: Well, ladies and gentlemen it is in your hands not mine as to where we start the bidding. Should it be £45,000? *(Silence.)*

AUCTIONEER: Will £35,000 tempt someone to bid? Thank you, sir, I have your bid *(as bidder number one waves her catalogue vigorously in the air).*

AUCTIONEER: I am bid £35,000. Do I see £37,500? £37,500 anywhere?

BIDDER NUMBER TWO: £35,500.

AUCTIONEER: I am looking for £37,500. Will you make it £37,500.

BIDDER NUMBER TWO: No. £35,500.

AUCTIONEER: Your bid at £35,500. I will accept £36,000? *(Bidder number one nods her head.)*

AUCTIONEER: £36,500. *(Bidder number two winks.)*

AUCTIONEER: £37,000? *(Bidder number one waves her finger.)*

AUCTIONEER: I am bid £37,000. I am seeking £37,500. Any further bid? £37,500 anywhere? Any further bids? At £37,000 then for the first time. For the second time. *(The auctioneer lifts his gavel and holds it threateningly in the air and, after a pause, brings it down.)* Sold at £37,000. May I see your paddle number, madam? *(The bidder shows her paddle number.)*

AUCTIONEER: Sold to 142 at £37,000. Now for my next lot …

How to reduce the increments even more …

Bidders have been known to bid in the 'and £100' style, quite specifically interjecting a rhythm of 'and £100 and £100 and £100'. If the auctioneer will wear it, our scenario would go as follows (the auctioneer has a reserve of £40,000):

'And 100' – in practice

AUCTIONEER: I now wish to offer lot number six, a charming and desirable residence with vacant possession, 16 Acacia Road, Lewisham. Where may I start the bidding? £50,000?
(*Silence.*)

AUCTIONEER: Well, ladies and gentlemen, it is in your hands not mine as to where we start the bidding. Should it be £45,000?
(*Silence.*)

AUCTIONEER: Will £35,000 tempt someone to bid? Thank you sir, I have your bid (*as bidder number one waves his catalogue vigorously in the air*).

AUCTIONEER: I am bid £35,000. Do I see £37,500? £37,500 anywhere?
(*Bidder number two coughs and raises a tentative finger in the air.*)

AUCTIONEER: £37,500 bid. £40,000 anywhere?
(*Bidder number one nods his head discreetly.*)

AUCTIONEER: I have £40,000.
(*Bidder number two shakes his head.*)

BIDDER NUMBER THREE: And £100.

AUCTIONEER: £40,100. £42,500, may I say?
(*Bidder number one nods his head.*)

AUCTIONEER: £42,500 I am bid.

BIDDER NUMBER THREE: And £100.

AUCTIONEER: £42,600. Do I see £45,000?
(*Bidder number one looks away.*)

AUCTIONEER: (*pointing at bidder number three*) I have your bid, madam, at £42,600 which is your bid. £45,000 anywhere? Any further bid? I am bid £42,600. I am looking for £45,000.
(*Pause.*)

AUCTIONEER: Can I perhaps tempt anyone at £43,000?
(*Pause.*)

AUCTIONEER: Have you all done?
(*Pause.*)

AUCTIONEER: Has the bidding finished?
(*Pause.*)

AUCTIONEER: Very well, then, at £42,600 for the first time (*pause*), for the second time …(*pause*), and for the final time at £42,600 …
(*The auctioneer lifts his gavel and holds it threateningly in the air and after a pause brings it down.*) Sold at £42,600.

(*looking at bidder number three pointedly*) May I see your paddle number, madam. (*Bidder number three shows her paddle number 142.*)

AUCTIONEER: Sold to 142 at £42,600. For my next lot ....

'PAX' –
An acronym for 'per annum exclusive'. Exclusive usually means that the rent is paid gross and that the tenant is responsible for outgoings such as council tax, water rates, insurance and similar. A similar acronym is FRI which stands for 'full repairing and insuring' which describes a lease where the tenant is responsible for all repairs and insurance for the property, in addition to paying the rent.

SHROPSHIRE

Thursday 11 February at 10-30 a.m. *at The May Fair Inter-Continental, Stratton St., London W1.*
ALLSOP & CO. (071-437 6977)
Market Drayton - 6 High Street. Shop Invest. arr. as grd fl sales, offices & storage, and 1st fl storage. Let at £14,500 p.a.x. f.r.l. with 5.5 yrs UT   F   w
Wellington - Chapel La. (formerly known as 99-105 New St.) Modern s'storey Sales Shop Invest. Frontage 44' x 21' shop depth. Let with 16 yrs UT rr £6,500 P.A.X. F   sold priv.

Thursday 11 February at 7.30 p.m. *at the Malt Shovel, Hadley Park Rd., Leegomery, Telford.*
BARBER & SON (0952 641155)
Hadley - 36 Castle St. Spacious double-fronted det. d-h. 4 beds. Offering scope for mod. & imp.   F   P   37,000
Telford - 8 Moorside, Preston-on-the-Weald Moors. S-d. cott. property in village location. Offering scope for mod. & imp.   F   P   20,250

Monday 15 February at 10.30 a.m. *at The International Convention Centre, Birmingham.*
ALLSOP & CO. (071-494 3686)
Whitchurch - Fenns Old Hall, Bronington. 3-storey Country Res. 6 rec. 11 beds. with range of outbdgs. set in 2.3a.   R   F   P   136,000

Illustration 5. Extract from Under the Hammer

Auctioneer's Anecdote: How to make big numbers sound small

An auctioneer selling a piece of land for a local authority had instructions that his reserve was any bid over £1,000,000. He wanted to take his increments in £100,000 jumps, so that because of the reserve, the minimum price at which he would sell would be £1.1m. From a psychological point of view, he wanted the increments in the bidding to appear as small as possible although he was determined that, at that stage, they would be not less than £100,000. He is reputed to have tested out on a variety of people whether £1.1m would sound less to a bidder than £1,100,000 or whether he should fall back on the 'and £100' formula discretely forgetting to mention that the £100 really related to the £100,000 that he was seeking. He decided that he would start the bidding at £600,000 so that the £100,000 increment pattern would be developed well before he reached his reserve. To the auctioneer's horror, having started the bidding at £600,000, and taken a second bid at £700,000, an astute builder 'jump bid' to £1,000,000 hoping to frighten off the opposition. The auctioneer could not sell at £1,000,000 and had lost his initiative in establishing the £100,000 increments. After the bid of £1,000,000 it looked as if the jump bid had succeeded, no other bidders were forthcoming and the silence was ominous. The auctioneer was in a quandary: he could not sell at £1,000,000 and he could not take a bid on behalf of the vendor since that would be in excess of his reserve. The room was silent for what seemed like an age, in an endeavour to regain the initiative the auctioneer changed the coloured slide which gave a second view of the piece of land that he was selling. With the tension broken, the bidding resumed (in £100,000 increments!), the professionals in the room were carried away and the land sold at £3.5m – which you must confess sounds much less than three million, five hundred thousand pounds!

Tricks the auctioneer will use against you

Watch out for the auctioneer bidding on behalf of the vendor

It is virtually always mentioned in the auctioneer's conditions of sale and often in his introductory speech that he reserves the right to bid on behalf of various parties. These parties always include the person selling the lot. It can sometimes happen that an auctioneer has only one bidder at some stage in his offering of a lot and where the level of bidding has not reached the reserve or upset price. As the auctioneer cannot sell below his reserve figure, he will use his right to take a bid on behalf of the vendor. This right is enshrined in the Sale of Land by Auction Act 1867 and is included in the auctioneer's conditions of sale.

How the auctioneer bids the price up – in practice

An example of how this works in practice follows (the auctioneer has a reserve of £45,000):

AUCTIONEER: On behalf of the auctioneers, I give notice that they reserve the right to bid, through me or otherwise on behalf of purchasers who have left bids with them, or on behalf of vendors, or as agents, or as principals for any lots.

AUCTIONEER: I now wish to offer lot number one, a charming and desirable residence with vacant possession at 10 West Road, Lewisham. Where may I start the bidding? £50,000?
(*Silence.*)

AUCTIONEER: Well, ladies and gentlemen, it is in your hands and not mine as to where we start the bidding. Should it be £45,000?
(*Silence.*)

AUCTIONEER: Will £35,000 tempt someone to bid? Thank you, sir, I have your bid (*as bidder number one waves his catalogue vigorously in the air*).

AUCTIONEER: I am bid £35,000. Do I see £37,500? £37,500 anywhere?
(*No one moves in the room.*)

AUCTIONEER: £37,500 I am bid.

Note: This is a bid which the auctioneer has interjected on behalf of the seller. The bidding level is well below the reserve of the lot but the auctioneer wishes to keep the momentum of the bidding going and has seen no signs of anyone else wanting to bid in the room and has therefore exercised his right to bid on behalf of the owner.

AUCTIONEER: £40,000 anywhere?
(*Bidder number one nods his head discreetly.*)

AUCTIONEER: £42,500?
(*No one moves in the room.*)

AUCTIONEER: I am bid £42,500.

Note: This is the second bid that the auctioneer has made on behalf of the seller because there is still no momentum in the bidding and the reserve has not been reached.

BIDDER NUMBER TWO: £45,000.

AUCTIONEER: £45,000 I am bid. £47,500 may I say?
(*Bidder number one nods his head.*)

AUCTIONEER: £50,000?
(*Bidder number three winks.*)

AUCTIONEER: £50,000, I have your bid sir. £52,500 anywhere? Any further bid? I am bid £50,000. I am looking for £52,500. Are you all done, has the bidding finished? I am bid £50,000 for the first time, for the second time.

Note: The auctioneer is now above his reserve. He cannot take a further bid on behalf of the owner/seller and is therefore about to bring his gavel down if there are no other bids from people in the room.

AUCTIONEER: Sold at £50,000 (*looking at the successful bidder pointedly*). May I see your paddle number, sir?
(*Bidder number three shows his paddle number as 142.*)

AUCTIONEER: Sold to 142 at £50,000 and for my next lot …

Watch out for bids that are 'off the chandelier'

In bidding parlance, in the better quality auction rooms, if the bidding has stopped more than one increment below the reserve, the auctioneer can then take a bid off the chandelier on behalf of the vendor. In slightly lower quality salerooms this is known as taking a bid off the wall! This right is a vital part of the auctioneer's armoury.

The auctioneer may continue to interject bids on behalf of the vendor in between genuine bids from the floor. He may therefore reach the point where his last bid, which was made on behalf of the vendor, is just one increment beneath the reserve. This will not stop the auctioneer then going through his first and second time patter to suggest that he is about to sell (despite being unable to do so because the bid was made on behalf of the vendor and it is below the reserve).

If he is competent, no one in the room should be able to judge from his demeanour, his body language or his tone of voice that a bid has been made by anyone other than someone in the room. If the auctioneer is not exceptionally competent, you may be able to judge that a bid was off the chandelier and there is no competition other than the vendor and so act accordingly. At that point, you may decide to bid no further, let the lot be withdrawn and bargain to buy it cheaply after the sale.

Stop bidding and make your offer after the auction

An interested bidder who wishes to follow this brinkmanship behaviour needs to be very sure that the opposing bid was taken *off the chandelier* before the lot was withdrawn and was not from an opposing bidder who made tiny movements that were only obvious to the auctioneer.

> **KEY POINT:** *If the last bid was made on behalf of the vendor and is below the reserve, the auctioneer will not bring down the gavel. Instead, he will announce that the lot has been withdrawn.*

A lot that gets withdrawn – in practice

The bidding for a lot that is withdrawn, might be as follows (the auctioneer has a reserve of £55,000):

AUCTIONEER: I now wish to offer lot number six, a charming and desirable residence with vacant

possession, 16 Acacia Road, Lewisham. Where may I start the bidding? £50,000?
(*Silence.*)

AUCTIONEER: Well, ladies and gentlemen, it is in your hands not mine where we start the bidding. Should it be £45,000?
(*Silence.*)

AUCTIONEER: Will £40,000 tempt someone to bid? Thank you sir, I have your bid (*as bidder number one waves his catalogue vigorously in the air*).

AUCTIONEER: I am bid £40,000. Do I see £42,500? £42,500 anywhere?
(*Bidder number two coughs and raises a tentative finger in the air.*)

AUCTIONEER: £42,500 bid. £45,000 anywhere? Do I hear £45,000?
(*Silence.*)

Note: The reserve is £55,000. The bidding appears to have stopped at £42,500. The auctioneer now chooses to interject a bid taken off the wall on behalf of the vendor.

AUCTIONEER: I am bid £45,000. £47,500?
(*Bidder number one winks.*)

AUCTIONEER: £50,000?
(*Bidder number two nods.*)

AUCTIONEER: I have a bid at £50,000. £52,500 anywhere? Any further bids.
(*Nobody moves.*)

AUCTIONEER: I am looking for £52,500. £52,500 I have.

Note: This is a bid made on behalf of the vendor.

AUCTIONEER: Have you all done? Has the bidding finished at £52,500. For the first time at £52,500, for the second time. £55,000 anywhere?
(*The auctioneer lifts his gavel and holds it threateningly in the air as if he is going to bring it down but does not do so.*)

AUCTIONEER: Any further bids? Well, ladies and gentlemen, I regret that we have not quite reached the reserve. The owner is looking for a slightly higher price than has been bid. I regret that I cannot sell the property at £52,500 and I

must therefore withdraw it from sale. If anybody would like to discuss a purchase of this lot after the auction with me, please do not hesitate to come up and see me.

Note: The property has been withdrawn. The last bid of £50,000 made from the floor was two increments below the reserve. The last bid was of £52,500, interjected by the auctioneer on behalf of the seller. No one bid thereafter. The reserve of £55,000 had not been reached and therefore the auctioneer could not sell from the rostrum.

What an auctioneer is not permitted to do

An experienced auctioneer will not:

1. Show by his demeanour that a bid has been taken off the wall.

2. Take a bid on behalf of the seller (off the wall) at the reserve price.

3. Take a bid on behalf of the seller from more than one source during the bidding for any lot.

What an auctioneer is permitted to do

An auctioneer is permitted to:

1. Take bids:
   - off the seller; or
   - off a single representative on the floor acting on behalf of the seller; or
   - himself on behalf of the seller.

2. Interject bids:
   - on behalf of the seller in between bids from potential buyers on the floor; or
   - made by the seller in between bids from potential buyers on the floor; or
   - from a single individual representing the vendor in between bids from potential buyers on the floor.

3. Interject bids on behalf of other potential buyers (in addition to those on behalf of the seller) up to the maximum amounts that they have specified in their proxy instructions.

4. Accept bids from individuals who are acting by proxy on behalf of potential buyers, where those instructions to bid have been given in writing or are being transmitted over the telephone.

Watch out for subtle changes in the auctioneer's behaviour

It is always worth analysing an auctioneer's pattern of performance in the early lots to see if you can detect subtle changes in the auctioneer's demeanour for lots that are sold, compared with those that are unsold, and for evidence in the auctioneer's behaviour that he has (or has not) reached his reserve. The anecdote below indicates one way in which an auctioneer's behaviour discloses a reserve price. However, there is much to be said for not trying to be too clever, but instead to be well satisfied with a purchase at or below your top figure where the gavel has come down on your bid. You then know for sure that the purchase is yours from that moment.

Auctioneer's Anecdote: A coded reserve

It is known amongst the dealers of one particular provincial town that a well-known auctioneer remains seated until he has reached his reserve and that he then stands up. This has been his practice for many years and the result is that, as soon as the auctioneer stands up, the knowledgeable bidders reduce the bidding increments to minimal amounts in the knowledge that they will be buying the property at, hopefully, very little more than the previous bidder.

Bids on behalf of the vendor

Once you are aware of the logic of the auctioneer's right to bid on behalf of the vendor, it should not disturb you, as owners of property will nearly always wish to specify the minimum sum at which they are willing to sell. Nevertheless, Parliament in 1867 was very concerned about auctioneers using 'puffers' in the audience to inflate artificially the price of the lot. Evidently, at that time, even property auctions had developed the sort of notoriety that mock auctions developed in the 1950s. The 1867 Sale of Land by Auction Act re-enforced the vendor's right to bid but was very insistent that he or she could not have 'two bites of the cherry'. Vendors can bid for themselves or someone in the audience can be appointed to bid on their behalf or the auctioneer can bid on their behalf but only one of these methods of bidding is permitted. Bids on behalf of, or by the vendor can

LOT 262
'Fieldview', Fernside Road, Toynton All Saints, Spilsby, Lincolnshire
BY ORDER OF MORTGAGEES IN POSSESSION

A Freehold Detached Cottage
TENURE Freehold.
LOCATION The village of Toynton All Saints is located just south of Spilsby and the A16. The town of Spilsby is located some 11 miles west of Skegness and 14 miles north of Boston. The amenities of Spilsby are within driving distance.
DESCRIPTION The property comprises a detached cottage arranged over ground and first floors under a tiled roof. The house is approached from an unmade road and benefits from front and rear gardens.
ACCOMMODATION
Ground Floor, Reception Room, Kitchen, Utility Room
First Floor, Three Bedrooms, Bathroom with WC

A three-bed home in the country for £18,000.

only be up to one bid below the reserve and will not be above the reserve price.

> **KEY POINT:** *No person attending an auction need fear that there are three or four individuals conveniently positioned in the audience to 'puff up' the price.*

Bidding with a vendor in the audience – in practice

The scenario for the bidding with the vendor in the audience might then go as follows (the auctioneer has a reserve of £54,000):

AUCTIONEER: I now wish to offer lot number six, a charming and desirable residence with vacant possession, 16 Acacia Road, Lewisham. Where may I start the bidding? £50,000? (*Silence.*)

AUCTIONEER: Well, ladies and gentlemen, it is in your hands not mine as to where we start the bidding. Should it be £45,000? (*Silence.*)

AUCTIONEER: Will £35,000 tempt someone to bid? Thank you sir, I have your bid (*as bidder number one waves his catalogue vigorously in the air*).

AUCTIONEER: I am bid £35,000. Do I see £37,500? £37,500 anywhere?
(*Bidder number two coughs and raises a tentative finger in the air.*)

AUCTIONEER: £37,500 bid. £40,000 anywhere?
(*Bidder number one nods his head discreetly.*)

AUCTIONEER: £42,500?
(*Bidder number two lifts his finger.*)

AUCTIONEER: £42,500. £45,000 may I say?
(*Bidder number one nods his head again.*)

AUCTIONEER: £45,000 bid. £47,500?
(*Auctioneer points in a general direction to his left and takes a bid off a member of the audience who is actually the vendor.*)

AUCTIONEER: £47,500 bid (*the bid made on behalf of the vendor*).

AUCTIONEER: £50,000 anywhere?
(*Bidder number one looks away.*)
(*Bidder number three waves her hand.*)

AUCTIONEER: I am bid £50,000. I am looking for £52,500. £52,500 anywhere? Have you all done? Has the bidding finished? At £50,000 then for the first time, for the second time …
(*Bidder number four shouts out incomprehensibly.*)

AUCTIONEER: I have a new bidder at £52,500. £55,000 anywhere? Have you all finished at £52,500? Will a bid at £53,000 tempt anyone at this stage?
(*No one moves. Auctioneer takes another bid off the vendor in the audience.*)

AUCTIONEER: I have £53,000 (*the bid made on behalf of the vendor*).

AUCTIONEER: £54,000 may I say?
(*Bidder number three nods her head.*)

AUCTIONEER: I am bid £54,000. £55,000 anywhere? £55,000 may I say? Have you all now finished at this price? (*Pause.*) At £54,000 then for the first time, £54,000 for the second time (*pointing at bidder number three*). It is your bid, madam, at £54,000. Any further bid? (*Pause.*) £55,000 anywhere? £55,000 do I see?

AUCTIONEER: Then for the last time …
(*The auctioneer lifts his gavel and holds it threateningly in the air and after a pause brings it down since the reserve of £54,000 has been bid by someone in the room.*)

Sold at £54,000.

(*Looking at bidder number three pointedly.*) May I see your paddle number, madam?
(*Bidder number three shows her paddle number.*)

AUCTIONEER: Sold to 142 at £54,000. My next lot is …

'I waited until the other bids had been made and then came in at the end. I only made one bid, and that was the last bid that succeeded. I was pleased to get it.'
Michael Roe, buyer of residential properties.

How to act and bid at the auction

If you are going to bid at auction for the first time the following checklist will help you:

1. Sit where you and the auctioneer can see each other clearly. Stay calm, acknowledge you are nervous (so is the auctioneer!).

2. Concentrate, listen and be aware of what is happening around you. Remember your homework and analyses of the lot(s), the auction, the auctioneer and other bidders.

3. Concentrate and listen harder when your lots come up.

4. Look the auctioneer in the eye.

5. Wait for a short pause in which to enter the bidding at or below your maximum figure.

6. Indicate your first bid at the price for which the auctioneer is asking by attracting his attention by a major movement (a wave of the catalogue, a paper, the hand or a bidding paddle).

Shout, wave and stand up if necessary!

7. If this fails, shout the figure of your bid and wave at the same time.

8. If necessary, stand up to attract his attention.

9. Make subsequent bids in the rhythm and pattern sought by the auctioneer. Violent movements should not be necessary. Subsequent bids can be

made by anything like:
- a raised finger;
- a nod of your head;
- a flick of the catalogue;
- raising the paddle;
- a wink or raised eyebrow.

10. If you wish to bid less than the increment asked for by the auctioneer, state your bid loudly. He may or may not accept it.

11. Keep looking the auctioneer in the eye until the lot is yours or unless you wish to stop bidding.

12. To stop bidding, withdraw your gaze and cease movements or speech. If you wish to be polite, indicate your lack of further interest by a shake of the head next time the auctioneer looks at you.

13. If you decide to come back into the bidding, go back to number 4!

14. If you decide to stop, still continue to analyse your competitors and the auctioneer, as the lot may be withdrawn and you may be competing against them later in negotiations by private treaty.

Do not:

1. Bid higher than the price you have fixed as your maximum.

2. Get carried away by the crowd and the auctioneer's enthusiasm (well, not by more than one bid anyway!).

3. Be shy about bidding – the auctioneer will love to have you doing it.

4. Be frightened by anyone else in the room into not bidding.

5. Accept payment from someone else in the room for not bidding.

6. Be frightened by tales of dealers' rings:
   - they don't usually exist in property auctions;
   - they can't force you into bidding higher than you fix as your maximum figure.

7. Be bullied by the auctioneer into paying more than your maximum or a greater increment than you choose (but do be realistic about your choice of increment in relation to the price level of the bidding).

8. Be shy about stopping when the bidding is higher than you choose to pay.

9. Buy a lot you have not researched just because it 'looks nice', 'seems cheap', 'is at no reserve', etc.

Auctioneer's Anecdote: The big bang

A London auctioneer, who is now a household name, recalls how in one of his first auction sales he was particularly nervous. A point that had been made to him in his training was the importance of timing. To ensure he did not dwell too long on any particular lot, he carefully removed his watch and placed it on the rostrum where he could clearly see it. On the very first lot, with the joy of passing his reserve and the enjoyment in working competitive bids, he promptly brought the hammer down with a large bang only to find that this had landed on his watch. So much for timing!

How quickly do the lots sell?

Auctioneers come in all shapes and sizes. They also offer lots at greatly different speeds. Many originally learned their rostrum techniques selling chattels and furniture and it is not unusual for chattels of moderate value to sell at 100 to 120 lots per hour. In the composite auction of property, the bidders are paying larger sums that are considerably more important to them. Although the bidding takes a little longer in a property auction, the numbers of bids are less than one sees for chattels because the increments are so much higher. Furthermore, in an auction of property there may be elements of the lot which the auctioneer chooses to highlight and the bidding can be slower.

Expect to see properties sell at 20 to 30 lots per hour

The auction catalogue may give an approximate guide of how long the auction will take. In a day-long sale, it is quite common for the catalogue to indicate starting times for various batches of lots. As the size of the auction reduces, the human nature of auctioneers leads them to draw out the proceedings. In a local pub or hotel where there are five or six lots to offer, the proceedings may take up to one hour. When all is said and done, vendors have to be convinced that the auctioneer has had a really good go at selling their property and has promoted it in its best light. This applies particularly where domestic owner-occupied properties are being offered and the rate of sales tends to be a little slower.

Auctioneers are usually consistent in their individual speed of selling. If you want to judge the rate at which an auctioneer sells, the best way of finding out is to attend one or two auctions in person. Even then, auction houses may put different auctioneers on the rostrum or have different qualities of properties to sell at different speeds. Furthermore, it generally takes longer to sell a lot than it does to offer and withdraw it. But, in a difficult market, the auctioneer is more likely to linger over trying to persuade bidders to add to their last price so that he can reach his reserve.

> **KEY POINT:** *Whoever the auctioneer and wherever the sale is taking place, you can guarantee that as the bidding gets closer to the end, it will always become slower.*

Will I always have the chance to make a bid?

If you are unable to make your offer at the early stages in the bidding, do not worry. Every auctioneer of merit will give you an opportunity to slip your bid in before the gavel comes down. Phrases such as 'going for the first time', 'going for the second time' or even the time honoured phrase of 'going, going, gone' are virtually always used. The auctioneer will invariably incorporate in his patter phrases which indicate that he is about to sell. What is more difficult to ascertain is whether he is going to withdraw rather than sell because he has failed to reach his reserve.

In the auction room, the auctioneer is God

You will always see in the auctioneer's conditions that the auctioneer reserves the right to regulate bidding and to refuse undesirable bids. Furthermore, the auctioneer also reserves the right to resolve any dispute over bidding. There have been one or two celebrated court cases where two bidders have been neck and neck and the unsuccessful buyer

has disputed the sale. But in each case it has been held that the auctioneer's decision is final.

> **KEY POINT:** *If a dispute arises, the auctioneer has absolute jurisdiction.*

It is unusual for an auctioneer to bring down the gavel before he has identified the actual bidder. A variety of phrases is used. The auctioneer may specifically indicate to the final bidder, looking him or her directly in the eyes, that they are the final bidder while going through the 'first time, second time' patter. The buyer may be identified by an article of their clothing or the colour of their clothing or their position in the room; 'the gentleman in the brown suit on the aisle', 'the lady on the back row', 'the couple in the front row in the matching raincoats'. The identity of the last bidder may be emphasized when the auctioneer refuses to take consecutive bids from the same individual where that person is raising their hand too enthusiastically.

Even if the gavel has fallen, the auctioneer is entitled to re-offer the property, in the event of a dispute, as long as he does it immediately. Where bidding paddles are used, then immediate identification of the buyer is easy and will enable any other bidder who feels that he was the buyer, to raise the question immediately.

This will not happen to you because you will have been bidding obviously and confidently and will have made the auctioneer very aware of your interest and determination to bid.

The auctioneer's code of conduct

The Royal Institution of Chartered Surveyors produced, during 1994 (and subsequently revised in 2001), a recommended code of conduct for auctioneers. It does not have the force of law nor even the force of the by-laws or regulations of this august body. Nevertheless, it is a set of guidelines which their members are expected to follow and which, in the future, may be incorporated in whole or in part in local government or central government regulations or legislation. It is available from the Royal Institution of Chartered Surveyors (tel: 020 7222 7000).

Specifically, the preamble to the guidance notes indicate they serve three purposes:

1. To act as an aide-memoire to points that should be considered by all members of the profession intending to conduct public auctions of real property in England and Wales.

2. To help the vendors of such property (being the clients of the auctioneer).

3. To provide guidance to members of the public (who may be potential purchasers) attending auctions about the background to and the procedures to be followed at auction.

The code is divided into the pre-auction, auction and post-auction periods and, apart from indicating many details of the recommended procedure for auctions, is intended to give considerable comfort and assistance to bidders and successful purchasers.

What happens if the lot is withdrawn or remains unsold?

'You can sometimes get a better deal at auction especially from lots that get withdrawn. Once you have reached your highest price you hope that the property hasn't reached the vendor's reserve and you can do a deal afterwards. You can get quite good deals that way.'

Michael Kirby, Chartered Surveyor.

Check before you attend that your lot is still for sale

There are many reasons for lots being withdrawn and on occasion vendors have been known to withdraw them without reason. It is always wise to check with the auctioneers, approximately 24 hours before the auction takes place, to see if the lot or lots which interest you are still going to be offered. This

'Rent Review Outstanding' –
This phrase indicates that a rent review that should have taken place in the past has not been agreed or implemented.

FREEHOLD SHOP INVESTMENTS
Reading, Berkshire   141 Crockhamwell Road, Woodley
Well located shop let to Forbuoys Plc. Producing £24,250 p.a. Rent review 1993.
Kingston upon Thames, Surrey   1 & 2 Station Building, Fife Road
BY ORDER OF LPA RECEIVERS
2 shops on corner site with ancillary accommodation above. Producing £35,500 p.a. Rent reviews 1993.
London N3   103/103a and 107/107a Ballards Lane, Finchley
2 shops. Producing £26,000 p.a. Rent reviews 1995. To be offered as 2 Lots.
Mitcham, Surrey   195, 197 & 199 London Road
3 attractive shops (including one restaurant), all with maisonettes above. To be offered in separate Lots. Currently producing £25,000 p.a. in total. One review outstanding. Further reviews from 1996.
Cheltenham, Gloucestershire   64 Bath Road
Shop with upper parts. Producing £5,000 p.a. 1993 rent review outstanding. Part Vacant Possession
Stroud, Gloucestershire   2 King Street
Attractive Listed shop producing £44,500 p.a. Rent review 1995. Let with guarantee from Lloyds Chemists plc.
Gants Hill, Essex   374–380 Cranbrook Road
One single and three double units. Producing £77,000 per annum. Tenants include Ritz, Beneficial Bank & 7 Eleven. Reviews 1993 & 1994.
London SW14   195 Upper Richmond Road West, East Sheen
Well located Shop with upper parts. Producing £14,000 p.a. Rent review 1996.
Crayford, Kent   14/14a High Street
Shop with ancillary offices. Producing £9,750 p.a. Rent review 1996.
Warrington, Cheshire   63 Bridge Street
Shop with upper parts. Producing £11,500 p.a. Rent review 1996. Let to Supasnaps Ltd.
Erdington, West Midland   120 High Street, Birmingham
First class location, let to Granada TV Rental Ltd. Currently producing £19,250 p.a. Rent review 1990.
Shirley, Hampshire   3/4 Gordon Buildings, High Street, Southampton
Town centre shop investment. Let to Currys Group Plc at £37,000 p.a. Rent reviews 1995.
London SE21   11 Herne Hill Road
Municipal office producing £6,000 p.a. together with vacant maisonette.

Illustration 6. Extract from an Allsop & Co auction advertisement

will certainly necessitate a telephone call. Some auctioneers maintain a pre-recorded message which gives the information on a special number. This will be shown in the auction catalogue.

Why lots get withdrawn

Since you may have spent money and time in researching a lot, it is perhaps most unreasonable for vendors to withdraw lots. Nevertheless, they can do this without any responsibility to you for your abortive costs. Their reasons may include:

The property has been sold before the auction

1. Sellers aim to dispose of their properties at a price which is acceptable to them. They are concerned more about an auctioneer's ability to market the property than his ability to sell the property on the auction day itself. The marketing may have been so successful that vendors receive an offer they are willing to accept. Some vendors are glad to sell at any price. Others do not want to lose the chance of a sale at a reasonable price as 'a bird in the hand is worth two in the bush'. It is not unusual for vendors to sell prior to the auction if they feel they have received a figure that exceeds considerably the amount which they expect to receive in the auction. If vendors did not think that the auction was the best way of obtaining a sale at the highest price, they would not decide to use this method in the first place. This thinking must influence their attitude to accepting or refusing pre-sale bids.

Incorrect details

2. A lot does not have to be sold to be withdrawn. Auction catalogues have to be prepared at speed and under pressure. While particulars are being prepared, information is frequently at a premium. Owners are not necessarily forthcoming with all the facts required for a catalogue and their solicitors may not be able to provide accurate information in a hurry. In many circumstances, therefore, the auctioneer's catalogue does not contain full details or contains inaccurate details. In these cases the firm may decide not to offer the property until the full

information can be made available. Alternatively, it may be the solicitor who decides that it is not possible to provide sufficient evidence on the title or background to the property for it to be safely included in a contract of sale in time for the auction. The solicitor may insist that the lot is withdrawn until everyone is sure the information is correct.

Change of mind

3. Owners of property quite often change their mind and decide not to sell a property or decide that the moment is not opportune. They may feel that the marketing prior to the auction has not produced the amount of interest they expect and that withdrawal at this stage is better than having the property offered and withdrawn at a disappointing bid.

These are just some of the reasons why lots may be withdrawn prior to auction. In each case, you have no entitlement to damages or compensation for your abortive costs, from either the vendor or the auctioneer.

Unsold lots

There have been recent discussions amongst auctioneers about how unsold lots should be treated. The code of conduct for auctioneers indicates very specifically that auctioneers should disclose in unequivocal terms when a lot has not been sold and should not bring the gavel down.

> **KEY POINT:** *A past practice amongst certain auctioneers of bringing down the gavel, even though the reserve price has not been reached, is now very strongly discouraged.*

This practice known as 'buying in' is most unlikely to be seen and heard in the sale room of any respectable auctioneer.

'For a house or a plot of land that is good you can be outbid if people get carried away. The professional who is buying property will not get carried away but the average punter can tend to get carried away quite easily.'
Michael Kirby, Chartered Surveyor.

6 After the auction – what happens next?

*'I bought another house at the end of 1999 and was
surprised when it was knocked down to me for £24,000
as I was expecting to pay up to £25,000. I did think at
one stage that I might not get the property although I
was prepared to bid £1,000 more than I paid for it. For
this second house, similar properties in the area are
costing almost twice as much. I was surprised it went for
what it did do. I was well pleased with it.'*

Don Lee, buyer of a residential property at auction.

What to do when you have got your lot

Is the property insured and secure?

The very first thing you must do is arrange for the
property to be adequately insured through your
insurance broker or company. You should then pass
the copy of the contract or memorandum that has
been signed by the vendor or his agent to your
solicitor so they can start preparing for completion.

Next, inspect the property again immediately and
arrange with the vendor to make it physically secure.
You may decide that the keys to the buildings have
been so widely distributed in the pre-auction period
that the locks should be changed and doors made
thoroughly secure. You must expect to have to meet
any security requirements imposed as a condition of
your insurance cover. It may be appropriate to
board up windows, remove any physical objects
lying around that could be used by vandals and have
any fences and other security arrangements
overhauled immediately. All these actions will need
the vendor's agreement which can be obtained
through either the auctioneers or their solicitors.

Speak to your finance house

Your finance should already be arranged. Whether it
is through a building society, a finance house,
merchant bank or bank, they must be told without
delay that you have been successful in your

purchase and be warned of the date you are
proposing to complete. Tell your finance house
which firm of solicitors you are using. Ask them to
liaise direct with your solicitors and provide the loan
in time for the completion date.

You will be expected to complete quickly

You will normally be expected to complete 28 days
after the auction. At that time, you will have to pay
the balance of the purchase monies, stamp duty and
any other costs that fall due. Occasionally, contracts
allow a shorter or longer time for completion,
which the special conditions of sale will have
revealed.

If VAT is charged on the purchase price, then this
must be paid in full at completion. You or your
solicitor should ensure that you obtain a VAT receipt
to reclaim the amount if your accountant advises
that this is appropriate.

It is usually prescribed in the conditions or special
conditions of sale that the conveyance is to be for
the entire lot as it was described and is to the
original buyer or bidder. If you wish to have the lot
conveyed in pieces and to people other than
yourself, you are unlikely to succeed in getting the
vendor to do this for you unless this was specially
arranged with the auctioneer and the vendor's
solicitors before the auction started.

If you wish to have the title to the property split
between different owners and this has not been pre-
arranged with the auctioneer and the vendor's
solicitors, then you will have to meet the extra costs
and delay in using your solicitor to prepare new and
separate conveyances of the individual pieces to the
separate buyers. The cost will increase your
solicitor's charges and may involve the separate
purchasers paying stamp duty on their own behalf,
if the sale prices are above the minimum figure at
which stamp duty is due.

What to do after the auction

1. Pass your copy of the contract or memorandum (signed by the seller or his agent) to your solicitor.

2. Arrange insurance.

3. Arrange security.

4. Revisit the property.

5. Tell your finance house you have bought the property.

6. Check for major misdescriptions of the lot (and discuss immediately with your solicitor, if there are any).

7. Meet the tenants (if any).

8. Arrange for future management and rent payments.

9. Prepare to complete 28 days after the auction.

10. Check your finances.

11. Recheck your cash flow.

12. Check the position on VAT.

13. Meet your accountants.

14. Confirm the date for completion with your solicitor, insurers and finance house.

15. Obtain a statement of funds due from your solicitor.

16. Pay and complete.

17. Collect a VAT receipt at completion (if appropriate).

18. Pay all your outstanding fees and costs.

19. Prepare to enjoy your new acquisition.

What happens if I decide not to complete?

Losing your deposit

When the gavel falls the contract is made. A condition of the contract is that the successful bidder exchanges contracts or memoranda and pays a deposit immediately. The conditions of sale indicate how much the deposit should be, but it is usually 10 per cent of the purchase price or £500 (whichever is the greater). The position is the same whether you buy at auction or by private treaty.

> **KEY POINT:** *It does not pay to change your mind after the gavel has fallen. If you renege on the contract, your deposit is forfeited, in full.*

You may lose more than your deposit

If you renege on the contract, the seller can take the deposit and is then entitled to resell the property. The resale might be at a lower price than the original. If the new proceeds (after deduction of all the new costs and expenses that the seller has been involved in) are less than the original price (minus the deposit) then the seller is entitled to charge you

LOT 278
Flat 4, The Dower House,
Hall Drive, Canwick, Lincoln, Lincolnshire
BY ORDER OF MORTGAGEES IN POSSESSION

A Leasehold First Floor Flat

TENURE
Leasehold. The property is held on a lease for a term of 125 years from 15th July 1988 (thus having approximately 119 years unexpired) at a ground rent of £1 per annum.

LOCATION
The village of Canwick is located to the south east of the Cathedral City of Lincoln on the B1188 to Branston. Hall Drive is approached from Canwick Hill. The flat while benefitting from a village location is also within 1/2 mile of the city centre and its extensive range of facilities and amenities.

The photograph is taken from the rear of the Dower House.

DESCRIPTION
The property comprises a first floor flat forming part of the former Dower House which is itself arranged over ground and first floors under a pitched slate clad roof. The flat is located at the rear of the Dower House with views over the communal garden.

ACCOMMODATION

Reception Room	Further Bedroom
Dining Room with stairs to galleried	Kitchen
Bedroom	Shower Room with wash basin
	Bathroom with WC

Who could resist this bargain of a flat in a Dower house for only £17,250?

his extra loss. However, if the net proceeds (less costs and expenses) are more than the original price (minus the deposit), then the seller does not have the right to proceed against you for more money, but he is not responsible to repay any part of the deposit.

> **KEY POINT:** *If the original sale price minus the deposit is less than the net proceeds on the resale, then the seller claims the shortfall from the original buyer.*

> **KEY POINT:** *If the original sale price minus the deposit is more than the net proceeds on the resale, then the seller keeps all of deposit as well as net proceeds.*

The following examples illustrate how it works.

How a seller claims for a shortfall

Example 1

Original sale price	£250,000
Deposit of 10% retained (£25,000)	
Resale at a lower price	£220,000
Less costs of resale	£10,000
Net proceeds of resale	£210,000
Original sale minus deposit	
£250,000–£25,000	£225,000
Resale minus costs	
£220,000–£10,000	£210,000
Shortfall claimed by seller from original buyer	£15,000

Seller also retains deposit of £25,000

Seller receives		
New sale proceeds		£220,000
Minus resale costs		£10,000
Net new sale proceeds		£210,000
Plus original deposit	£25,000	
Plus shortfall	£15,000	
		£40,000
Seller receives total of		£250,000

How a seller retains the deposit in full

Example 2

Original sale	£250,000
Deposit of 10% retained (£25,000)	
Resale at only a slightly lower price	£240,000
Less costs of resale	£10,000
Net proceeds of resale	£230,000
Seller receives	
New sale proceeds	£240,000
Minus resale costs	£10,000
Net new sale proceeds	£230,000
Plus deposit	£25,000
Seller receives total of	£255,000

Is there a get-out?

Misdescribing the property

You may discover, after a successsful bid, that there is a major misdescription of the lot in the catalogue or (less likely) by the seller or auctioneer. Auctioneers and vendors always aim to remove the right of buyers to withdraw from their purchase despite a major misdescription, but the Unfair Contract Terms Act 1977 can prevent such conditions from being enforced. In recent court cases, several judges have held that auctioneers have a duty of care to purchasers to describe lots accurately. This case law is distinct from the criminal offence which auctioneers and estate agents can commit under the Property Misdescriptions Act by giving misleading particulars.

CASE STUDY: How a purchaser cancelled a contract because of a misdescription

A builder decided that he had land which was surplus to his requirements in spite of owning it for almost 25 years. Just after the builder bought the land, he obtained planning consent for a development of 60 two-bedroomed flats. He did not start building; no work was carried out that was covered by the planning consent and five years after it was issued, the consent lapsed.

Six years after that, following pressure by environmental groups, the planning policy was changed for the district. Planning consent was now only available to build houses at low densities. A 60-flat development would no longer gain consent. Six months before the builder instructed the auctioneers, a new outline planning consent was granted for the land, allowing for a low-density development of 15 houses. The consent was granted and in existence at the time of the auction.

Misleading particulars can get you out of a contract

Unfortunately, due to staff errors at the builder's office and the auctioneers, the catalogue referred to the earlier consent for 60 flats and did not indicate the date of the consent or that it had lapsed. The successful bidder at the auction assumed, without checking, that the information in the auctioneer's catalogue was correct and based his highest bid on the feasibility of carrying out a high-density development.

Only after he had paid his 10 per cent deposit and exchanged contracts did he then research the planning position by contacting the local planning authority and discover to his horror that the land was only worth 50 per cent of what he had paid to use for the construction of 15 houses. The planning authority indicated the policy established for the district and said they would resist any application to renew the planning consent for a high-density development.

The purchaser took legal proceedings to have the contract cancelled maintaining, quite justifiably, that the auctioneer's catalogue contained a major misdescription that resulted in the bidder paying far more than the land was worth. The auctioneers pleaded in the case that the general conditions of sale excluded them from the responsibility to describe the property correctly and that the purchaser was not entitled to seek a recission of the contract.

The judge held that the conditions were in breach of the Unfair Contract Terms Act. He also held that there was a major difference in the value of the land with existing planning consent compared with that which had lapsed. He gave the decision that the purchaser was entitled to cancel the contract, to the return of his deposit and his costs in taking the action.

Had the Property Misdescriptions Act 1991 been in force, it is probable that if the purchaser or anyone else had chosen to complain to the local weights and measures office, the auctioneers would have been found guilty of a criminal offence by giving a misleading description, unless they could prove they had shown 'due diligence' in their research prior to the auction and the misleading particulars were in no way their fault.

How a purchaser failed to cancel a contract due to a misleading description

An industrial property was offered by auctioneers in Lincoln. In their catalogue they described the floor area as 3,980 sq ft. A successful bidder did not check this floor area before the auction but discovered the week afterwards that the floor area was only 3,880 sq ft. At the same time, he decided that the building was not quite what he wanted and that he would like to renege on the contract.

Minor discrepancies will not count

In the subsequent court case for rescission of the contract, he was unsuccessful because the judge decided that the difference in floor area was only small and not of a sufficiently significant amount to cancel the contract. The successful bidder had to proceed to completion and also had to meet the costs of the vendor.

> **KEY POINT:** *If there has been a major misdescription of the lot in the catalogue, it is very probable that you will be able to support a case to have the contract to buy cancelled (and your deposit returned) or the purchase price adjusted to take into account the diminution in value of the property between its real value and the value as originally described.*

Negotiate before you complete

If your research before the auction does not reveal a major misdescription, but after making the purchase you discover one exists, you should reveal the extent of the misdescription to your solicitor immediately. Ask his advice about having the contract set aside (cancelled) or seeking a reduction in the purchase price. These negotiations must be carried out before you reach completion of the purchase. Never consider completing the purchase subject to your right to claim an adjustment of the purchase price afterwards, in spite of the requirement that you complete at the end of 28 days. If an argument develops over whether a property has been misdescribed or not, you should not allow completion to occur until the argument has been resolved. If you do complete, then the vendor receives all the purchase price and is under no pressure to discuss the point. Furthermore, it will be up to the purchaser to decide whether or not to start an action. You are in a much stronger position if the vendor is waiting for his money and you leave the vendor in the position where he has to commence an action to complete the purchase.

If you wish claim to a misdescription:
- do it quickly;
- pursue the negotiations to a conclusion before completing;
- never complete, reserving the right to argue afterwards.

Wait until the auction is over to pick up a better bargain

After the auction, the bargain buyers move in. There is no reason why you should not be amongst them if the price you are willing to pay for certain lots proved to be less than the reserve and no one else stepped into the bidding to buy. If the bidding for any lot which interests you goes above the price that you are willing to pay and is withdrawn do not despair of buying it later. As soon as you stop bidding, listen and watch very carefully to try and assess the quality of any opposition there may be against you. It is possible that an opposing bidder, on seeing that a property has been withdrawn, will not be willing to repeat that bid after the excitement and urgency of the auction has passed.

Make your offer when the vendor is 'down'

It is probable that the property was withdrawn at a figure that is close to the vendor's reserve. Almost invariably the last bid that the auctioneer took on a withdrawn lot was made on behalf of the vendor and taken 'off the chandelier'. The seller may have fixed an optimistic reserve with high expectations and hope that the ambience of the sale room would encourage reckless bidding. In his despair of seeing the lot withdrawn after the auction, that is the time for you to move in and he may succumb to a lower bid from you.

> **KEY POINT:** *Do not hesitate if your lot is withdrawn to negotiate to buy it at your price afterwards.*

The auctioneer may nominate some of his staff to remain in the room and conduct negotiations on withdrawn lots. If so, he is likely to have mentioned this at the time he withdrew them. Even if he didn't, it is always worthwhile approaching senior staff to start negotiations immediately. They are as keen to sell as you are to buy. Remember, there may be other people in the room who are as experienced or more experienced than you, who will also be moving very quickly to see whether they can pick up withdrawn lots at cheaper prices. The auctioneer generally remains on or close to his rostrum after the auction. Do not hesitate to go up to the auctioneer and start negotiating straight away.

Find out the reserve, if you can

The auctioneer or his staff may be willing to disclose the reserve at this stage or it may be possible to read it on literature in front of them. If you can establish the reserve price, this will help you decide what private offer to make. If you make an offer and it is accepted, exchange contracts or memoranda straight away and pay your deposit so that the purchase is yours and no opportunist has the chance to acquire the property before you.

Buying immediately after the sale may not appeal to you because:
- you may feel you want to consider a little longer the price that you are willing to pay;
- you may feel you want to go and visit the lot again before you start negotiations to buy the property privately; by delaying, you run the risk that someone else may buy before you.

On the other hand, if you approach the auctioneers a week after the sale and the lot is still unsold, it is possible that the sellers will be beginning to lose their optimism and enthusiasm and be willing to consider a lower offer than they would have taken at the sale. Either way, there is no reason why you should not make an offer to the auction house and negotiate for any withdrawn lot at a reasonable time after the sale. Before you do so, check that the property is in the same condition as it was when you originally looked at it. After that, your bargaining can begin. It is probably the second oldest adage in the property profession that 'a buyer's first bid is never his final bid' and you should negotiate accordingly.

Auctioneer's Anecdote: The oldest adage in the property profession

There are only three matters that should really concern you in a property: 'position, position and position'.

How to buy a bargain from withdrawn lots by private treaty

1. Do not despair of buying at your price, however high the bidding went.

2. Listen and watch the auctioneer and other bidders immediately after you have stopped bidding.

3. Try to judge how much genuine opposition there is against you. Were there any other actual bids?

4. Try to assess the likely figure of reserve from the auctioneer's comments, actions and body language.

5. Remember the last bid and the amount at which the lot was withdrawn. This may be a future guide to your negotiations.

6. Speak to the auctioneer's staff immediately after the lot is withdrawn and find out if they are in a position to negotiate a post auction sale there and then.

7. If not, or if you are unsuccessful with the staff, move quickly up to the auctioneer on the rostrum after the auction and negotiate with him immediately.

8. Try to discover the reserve as a guide to your chances of success in that negotiation.

9. If negotiations fail at the auction, visit the property again, review your past research and reconsider your figure.

10. Try to negotiate again the next day.

11. If these negotiations fail, try again later – perhaps in a week. Vendor's resolve can and often does weaken as time goes by.

12. Be persistent in your attempts to negotiate a purchase.

13. In your negotiations, remember the auctioneer will act on the assumption that your first offer is lower than you are finally willing to pay. Do not disappoint him!

14. If you agree a post auction purchase, complete any outstanding research, pay your deposit and exchange contracts as quickly as you can.

Keep your solicitor on his toes

If you are successful in your negotiations then you and your solicitor need to be just as speedy as if you were negotiating a purchase before the sale. If you agree a private treaty purchase after the sale, make sure your solicitor does not go to sleep on the paperwork, research and enquiries. It may be that his research and enquiries are complete and that he is satisfied with the title. In this case, consider exchanging contracts or memoranda at the auctioneer's office rather than waiting for your solicitor to do it with his opposite number acting on behalf of the seller. You will have to pay the 10 per cent deposit to the auctioneers or the vendor's solicitor at the agent's instruction.

> **KEY POINT:** *If you buy through private treaty negotiation after the auction, the procedures are exactly the same as when you exchange contracts before the sale or at the auction itself.*

The best bargains can be found even later

Some of the best property bargains are bought not at the auction itself, but much later. By keeping a close eye on auction results, it is possible to spot which properties were withdrawn and did not sell immediately afterwards and then move in to pick them up at a bargain price. It is a technique used by many entrepreneurs and dealers but there is no reason why anyone cannot find their home in this way.

> **KEY POINT:** *It pays to research auction results for withdrawn lots.*

Auctioneer's Anecdote: How to make £90,000 from one bargain

A well-known dealer who frequents London auctions relies almost entirely on buying lots after the sale. A well-known firm prepared their details in a hurry and the vendor was too busy to check the draft that they sent him. The owner's solicitors had no physical knowledge of the property. Only half the accommodation of the building was listed in the catalogue. The dealer was aware of this but no one else seemed to notice it. The vendor fixed a high reserve for the property. The dealer was unwilling to bid up to that reserve and the lot was withdrawn. The vendor was dis-spirited by the lack of interest in the auction and a week later he told the auctioneer he would accept a price 20 per cent less than his reserve for a quick sale. Coincidentally, on the very same day, the dealer checked through the list of unsold lots and noticed it was still available. He rang the auctioneer and was told of the price reduction. He bought the property for £140,000. Shortly after completion, he obtained planning consent to split the property into two individual units, carried out the moderate amount of building work necessary at approximately £20,000 and then sold off the front and back portions of the property at £130,000 and £120,000 respectively making a handsome profit of £90,000. The deal started that buyer on a property career which has made him a multi-millionaire and he is still an avid searcher through the lists of withdrawn lots.

How to find your bargain property

Property Auction News

The best source for finding out when and where property auctions are taking place every month, together with detail of prices achieved for curious and interesting lots. Excellent comment, tips, advice and inside information.

Under the Hammer

The best source of withdrawn lots is *Under the Hammer*. It is published fortnightly and available on subscription only. As well as listing auctions for the next fortnight it also gives details of prices realised at auctions in the past fortnight. It divides its results into geographical areas and is generally circulated to property professionals, auctioneers and valuers.

Private subscriptions to a home address can be arranged. Frequently, the auctioneers indicate in this list the prices at which withdrawn properties can be purchased. It also publishes prices at which properties have been sold prior privately, either before or just after each auction. For later research, *Under the Hammer* also publishes an annual digest of results in book form for each geographical area. These digests are divided into categories of property. A sample page of *Under the Hammer* illustrating withdrawn lots is shown in Figure 6.1.

The Estates Gazette

Although the *Estates Gazette* is a good source of property information and lists prices realised at auctions, analysing them on a geographical basis county by county, it does not show any details of lots withdrawn.

Property Week

This publication, at present, carries a smaller auction information page than other similar publications and only publishes results as news items. It is therefore not easy to pick up withdrawn lots from this publication.

Faxwise Plc

Faxwise report on every London property auction by fax. The results are available at a cost on the evening of the auction by using a premium rate number. This service is only at present in the process of being extended to cover the whole of the country rather than the London auctions where it started. A sample of their output is shown in Figure 2.10 on page 23. The penultimate column lists the price at which lots have sold. Lots which did not sell are shown in brackets, indicating the highest bid. The price at which the property is available is indicated in the last column. A recent extension to their service has been the provision of an on-line spoken commentary direct from certain auctions. Details of these can be obtained from Faxwise.

Local and national news items

You can only discover by reading them which local newspapers feature auction news. Some national newspapers such as the *Financial Times* and the *Daily Telegraph* occasionally carry auction news but it is not as comprehensive as the journals such as *The Estates Gazette*. It is unusual for any articles to refer to unsold lots.

UNDER THE HAMMER
RESULTS

ABBREVIATIONS

adj.—adjoining   **cr.**—corner   **d-h.**— dwelling house   **det.**—detached   **F** freehold   **f.g.r.**—freehold ground rent   **f.r.l.**—full repairing lease   **g.**— gross, landlord paying rates   **grd.**—ground   **L.**— leasehold   **l.g.r.**— leasehold ground rent   **lic.**— licensed   **Mod.**— modern   **mth.**—monthly tenancy   **n.**—net, tenants pay rates   A ground rent thus marked is net payable after deducting receivable ground rent.   **n.o.**—not offered.   **nr.**—near   **OPP**—outline planning permission   **P.**—possession   **PL.**—part let   **P.P.** - Planning Permission   **pt.** -part   **sold priv.**—sold privately   **p.a.**—per annum.   **P.A.X.** Per Annum Exclusive.   **rev.**—reversion   **rr.**—rack rental   **rsv** — reserve price   **RUP.**—residential upper part.   **R.**- repossessed   **s.d.** semi-detached   **sold priv.** — sold privately   **s.y.**— square yards   **sq.ft.** — square feet.   **UT.**—unexpired term   **w.**—withdrawn   **wk.**—weekly rent   **yrs.**—years   **Av.**—available at

---

BRISTOL & KINGSWOOD

Thursday 11 February at 2-30 p.m. at *The Sachas Hotel, Tib St., off Market St., Manchester.*
LONGDEN & COOK COMMERCIAL (061-236 1114)
Bristol - Rent charges 375 collections. Total income
£3,987.68 p.a.   w

Wednesday 17 February at 2-30 p.m. at *Le Meridien Hotel, Piccadilly, London W1*
ERDMAN LEWIS (071-629 8191)
Bristol - 125 Cheltenham Rd. Grd fl Office Prems. on A38
   Long leasehold   L   P   sold priv.

AVON, SOMERSET, GLOS. & WILTS.

Tuesday 2 February at 6-30 p.m. at *The Town Hall, Melksham, Wiltshire.*
ALDER KING (0225 707788)
East Coulston, Wilts. - pt. of Barrack Farm. 10.649 acres
   level pasture land   F   P   20,000
do.   pt. of Barrack Farm. 118.346 acres level pasture
   land severed by Railway line   F   P   102,000
do.   pt. of Barrack Farm. Det. derelict listed Cottage,
   2 beds & s-storey annex, tog. with Bdg. Plot for a
   single d-h. & a Bdg Plot for a pr. of Cotts   F   P   w
Trowbridge, nr. - Newhouse Farm, Semington, Wilts. 4 bed
   det. farmho. in need of rep. & mod. 2 attic beds
   Small gdns. Domestic bdgs. Gge. & farm bdgs.
   Paddock, bdgs, yard and land pt. pasture/arable
   ext. to 31.22 acres   F   P   155,000
do.   pt. of Newhouse Farm. 3.24 acres permanent pasture
   land adj. A361   F   P   5,300
do.   pt. of Newhouse Farm. 6.33 acres permanent pasture
   land with access off Brickfield Farm La. F   P   12,000
do.   pt. of Newhouse Farm. 2.31 acres permanent pasture
   accom. pony paddock land access A361 F   P   4,200
do.   pt. of Newhouse Farm. 2.94 acres permanent pasture
   accom. pony paddock land access off A361   F   P   5,800
do.   pt. of Newhouse Farm. 16.07 acres permanent pasture
   land adj. A361   F   P   20,000
do.   pt. of Newhouse Farm. 8.28 acres permanent pasture
   paddock adj. Mill La. access off A361   F   P   13,500

Thursday 11 February at 10-30 a.m. at *The May Fair Inter-Continental, Stratton St., London W1.*
ALLSOP & CO. (071-437 6977)
Cinderford - Holly Hill Park Ind'l Est., Holly Hill Rd., Gos.
   Modern Ind'l Est. comprising 12 s-storey Ind'l units. 2 vacant.
   Total 14,000 sq ft arr. in a terr. of 8 & 2 prs s-d units.
   Ample pkg. rr £46,444.80 P.A.X. various 3 yr leases
                                                          w

Thursday 11 February at 2.00 p.m. at *Kensington Town Hall.*
WINKWORTH AUCTIONS (081-686 6667)
Heytesbury, Nr. Warminster - 32 Little London.
   4 bdm. d-h. Needs updating. R.   F   P   35,000

Tuesday 16 February at *The Star Hotel, Wells.*
BLACK HORSE AGENCIES ALDER KING (0749 673002)
East of Wells - South Lodge, Frome Rd. Large det. d-h. in need of
   renov. Large gdns. Driveway. (G. P. £55-60K) P
do.   Mendip House. 4 bed. modern det. d-h. set in large
   gdns. Driveway, Gge. (Guide P. £80-85,000) P   sold priv.
do.   Firbank. 4 bed. modern det. d-h. with est. gdns. & views
   to golf course. Det. Gge. (Guide P. £70-75,000) P   sold priv.
do.   1 Frome Road Cottages. Vic'n s-d cott. with gdn.
   and outbdgs. 2 beds. (Guide P. £30-35,000) P   sold priv.
do.   2 Frome Road Cottages. Vic'n s-d cott. with gdn.
   and outbdgs. 2 beds. (Guide P. £30-35,000) P   sold priv.
do.   Mendip View. Very large det. prop. with Pot. Set in
   its own grds. 6 beds. 2 s-storey outbdgs. Car pkg.
   (Guide Price £90,000)   sold priv.
do.   West Villa Lodge. Spacious det. period d-h. in need
   of imp. 4 beds. Gdns. (Guide Price £45-50,000) P   sold priv.
do.   Tor View. Investment prop. currently let.
   (Guide Price £225-250,000)   F   sold priv.
do.   Paddock approx 2.88a. Easy access from East/West
   Horrington. (Guide Price £7-10,000) P   sold priv.
do.   Westfield. Large 3-storey det. prop. set in large grounds.
   Pot. as Offices, Nursing Home or conv. to Flats. Subj.
   to PP. 4 rec. 10 beds. (G.P. £155-160,000)P   sold priv.
do.   Greenmount. Stone built det. bung. 3 beds. Gge.
   Gdns. (Guide Price £30-35,000)   P   sold priv.
do.   Access to Bath Rd. 18 acres open pasture field and
   wooded valley. (Guide Price £10-15,000) P   sold priv.

Wednesday 17 February at 2-30 p.m. at *Le Meridien Hotel, Piccadilly, London W1.*
ERDMAN LEWIS (071-629 8191)
Midsomer Norton - 103 High St. Retail Invest. Grd fl Ret.
   & ancillary accomm. tog. with 1st fl storage. Review
   1996   rr £27,500 p.a.x. F   w

Thursday 18 February at 3.00 p.m. at *the Rougemont Hotel, Queen St., Exeter.*
CONNELL PROPERTY AUCTIONS (0793 480028
Bath - Lower Ground Floor Flat, 12 Grosvenor Place. Lower
   grd. fl. flat conv. in need of refurb., forming part of Grade II
   listed Georgian town house. 2 beds.
   L. residue of 999 yrs. R.   L   P   unsold
Weston-super-Mare - 11a Nithsdale Rd. S-c. 1st fl. flat. 1 bed
   L. residue of 999 yrs. R.   L   P   unsold
Bruton, Somerset - Harlequin Arcade, 26 High St. Comm.
   Invest with part possession comprising 5 Ret. units of which
   Units 1 & 4 are let 15 yrs. rr £4,000 p.a. Basement conv.
   to res. flat. L. 999 yrs from 1984 G. r. £20 p.a.
   Accomm: Unit 1 180 sq.ft. Unit 2 283 sq. ft. Unit 3 183 sq. ft.
                 Unit 4 148 sq. ft Unit 5 1168 sq. ft.
   1st fl. storage space 2,450 sq. ft.   R   F   unsold

Thursday 18 February at 12 noon at *The Kensington Hilton International Hotel, Holland Park Ave., London W11.*
BARNARD MARCUS (081-741 9001)
Bedminster - Reliance House, Whitehouse St. 4-storey Factory/
   Warehouse Prems approx 19,000 sq ft   F   P   w
Weston-super-Mare - Holm Cottage, Beach Rd. 2 bed. s-d
   2-storey cott. Rear gdn   R   F   P   28,500
Salisbury, Wilts. - Flat 2, 173 Wilton Rd. Grd fl s.c. Flat
   in det. d-h. 94 yrs UT   R   L   P   n.o.
Gloucester - Flat 1, 35 Midland Rd. Long lease 1 bed.
   s.c. B'ment Flat within 3-storey terr. d-h. R   L   P   12,000

Results Continued Overleaf

7 The insider's guide to an auction house

'I would definitely buy another property at auction and have no hesitation recommending others to buy at auction provided they understand the risks and have no worries.'
  Don Lee, buyer of a residential property at auction.

The auctioneer's timetable – sale day is A-day

This chapter gives you an inside view of what happens in an auction house in the two months before the auction and the month afterwards. The number of weeks and days before or after A-day (auction day) are indicated in the left hand margin.

In a busy auction house where composite auctions are organized on a monthly basis, the auction team will be organizing a regular round of two to three auctions at a time. Each auction has its own three monthly programme overlapping the others. The organization of an auction may be in the hands of one individual or a team. A standard auction programme spans three months from the preparation period through to post-auction. To ensure the programme runs smoothly, the auctioneer has built-in standards, routines and procedures. Even so, each programme has its periods of relative quiet and frantic activity. Some days proceed smoothly with routine administration, inspection and preparation of the catalogue while others are frantic, making arrangements and negotiating with vendors, buyers and potential bidders.

At the same time, the accountancy team will be concerned with keeping records of sales, ensuring bills are rendered for entry fees and sales commissions, collecting in amounts due and being positive that deposit and purchaser's cheques are dealt with in accordance with professional rules and held in appropriately secure and insured accounts.

In a firm that holds auctions less frequently the programme will be similar.

Entry fees

9–10 weeks before A-day

It is a universal practice for auctioneers to separate their charges into two elements. These are an entry fee when instructed and a separate fee when contracts are exchanged.

The entry fee charged depends on a number of factors:

1. **Situation of the auction house**
    A major London firm may charge three times the entry fee that a local provincial firm will charge for the same service.

2. **Advertising**
    The extent of promotion and marketing necessary varies considerably from lot to lot and area to area. Firms may recommend supplementary advertising in addition to that covered by their normal entry fee where special lots justify it.

3. **Quality of the catalogue**
    The catalogue may be in an expensive, glossy and coloured style produced at an enormous cost which the auctioneers seek to cover by entry fees. Alternatively, it may be of lesser quality at cheaper cost justifying a smaller entry fee.

4. **Size of mailing list**
    Many of the principal auction houses maintain a mailing list of over 10,000 names which may be expanded further for especially attractive lots. Other firms may only maintain mailing lists of between 300 and 3,000 names which can be serviced at a cheaper cost and which justify a smaller entry fee.

> **KEY POINT:** *Entry fees can vary from £250 to £2,500 (excluding supplementary advertising). (See page 100.)*

Similarly, commissions on sales vary. They are frequently quoted as a percentage of the sale price obtained in a range from 1.5 per cent to 6 per cent. Auction houses generally specify a minimum sale fee. Some firms specify as low as £400, a norm for provincial firms is around £600, while in London it can be around £1,500.

Under the Estate Agents Act 1979 and subsequent regulations, auctioneers are required to provide details of their charges. Failure to do this puts them in a very weak position when claiming fees after a sale has taken place. A sample of an auctioneer's auction terms is shown in Figure 7.1 and analysed in more detail in chapter 8.

At this stage, the ball is firmly in the court of the seller to return the entry form and fee promptly and to provide the fullest and most accurate details possible of the property that is to be sold. The auctioneer may provide an auction details sheet similar to the one in Figure 7.2. Often those basic details will need amplification depending upon the nature of the property being sold. For example, the details of the tenancies may be extensive for a commercial investment. The accommodation may be more than can be covered in the space available on the form. Nevertheless, the form does provide the vendor with an aide-memoire to the vital details required.

Wise auctioneers forcefully encourage vendors to disclose known defects in properties such as outstanding repair or sanitary notices, major arrears of rent, structural failings now existing or which ought to have been remedied in the past. Auctioneer's always stress that properties should be described 'warts and all'.

Most auctioneers have a deadline date for the entry of lots in a particular auction but quite frequently they can be persuaded to adjust this date by two or three days.

The inspection and the preparations
8 to 9 weeks before A-day

Sellers need to help the auctioneer at this stage to make it easy for them to inspect the property. They need to provide:
- keys that fit and enable access to all portions of the building;
- letters of authority for production to tenants to allow entry;
- an accurate description of how to reach the property;
- plans showing the extent of the boundaries with details of any easements;
- full details and telephone numbers that may be necessary for access or to cover emergencies;
- details of burglar alarm provisions and how they may be switched on and off.

During the following week, the auctioneer's team:
- inspects the properties;
- organizes photographs;
- prepares catalogue details;
- obtains plans and copies of planning consents (see Figure 7.3);
- gains details of building regulation consents;
- obtains copies of leases (see Appendix 4);
- collates any other items necessary for the catalogue.

The catalogue details
8 weeks before A-day

With the details organized, the catalogue is now prepared in draft, the auctioneers taking great care that they are not in breach of the Property Misdescriptions Act 1991. They may ask the vendor, their solicitors, co-agents and anyone else who has provided information to co-operate in ensuring that the catalogue details are correct.

During this period, if they have not already been instructed by the vendors, the solicitors who are acting on their behalf are warned of the proposed sale, asked to check the catalogue details, check the property details in it, apply for a local search and prepare a contract for sale. They need at least four weeks' warning and prefer more if possible.

Final copy
7 weeks before A-day

This is a hectic period when all the details have been collated and approved and are merged into the copy ready for submission to the printers. At this stage, the photographs, plans and other material are chosen and redrawn, edited, cropped or changed in scale to fit the style of the catalogue and the nature of the property being offered.

AUCTIONEER'S AUCTION TERMS

1   Following the receipt of instructions and the full entry fee as communicated, the Auctioneers will take all reasonable steps to include the property described in these instructions (hereinafter referred to as 'the property') in their next suitable and available composite public auction (hereinafter referred to as 'the auction').

2   Entry fees which are to cover the costs of advertising and promotion are non-returnable and are due as a debt from the owner/agent to the Auctioneers upon the signing of the instructions.

3   By signing this instruction form, the owner/agent gives the Auctioneers absolute irrevocable authority to act as sole selling agents to negotiate and enter into a contract for sale of the property:

    a   from the date hereof until the auction at a price authorised by the owner/agent;

    b   at the auction at the highest genuine bid at or above the reserve price;

    c   at any time up to 8 weeks after the auction at the reserve price;

and by so signing this instruction form the owner/agent warrants to the Auctioneers that he has the authority to give such absolute it-revocable authority.

4   Upon unconditional exchange of any such contract for sale entered into the Auctioneers shall become immediately entitled to 3% plus VAT of the contract price for the sale of the property or the minimum sale fee plus VAT whichever is the greater from the owner/agent and the Auctioneers and their duly authorised agents shall be entitled to deduct that sale fee plus VAT from any deposits received on, before or after exchange of any such contract for sale from the intending purchaser without further authority.

5   The balance of any such deposits will be held to an insurance bonded clients' account up to completion of such contract for sale, but any interest earned on such deposits held by the Auctioneers shall be held to their credit and not to the credit of the owner/agent and shall at all times be the absolute property of the Auctioneers.

6   Should any such contract for sale be exchanged but not completed the Auctioneers shall become immediately entitled to a commission payment from the owner/agent of 1.5% of the contract price, or 511% of the minimum sale fee whichever is the greater, plus VAT, without deduction.

7   The owner/agent hereby confirms his understanding that the effect of appointing the Auctioneers as sole selling agents as set our above is inter alia to prevent the owner/agent whether by himself, his servants or agents or otherwise whatsoever

    a   from negotiating or entering into a contract for sale of the property from the dare hereof until 12 weeks after the date of the auction otherwise than through the Auctioneers;

    b   from negotiating or entering into a contract for sale of the property from the date hereof at any time with a person introduced to him by the Auctioneers other than through the Auctioneers.

S   The owner/agent further confirms that he has been provided with and read the Auctioneer's information for Vendors.

9   If in breach of the Auctioneers' rights as sole agents a contract for sale of the property is negotiated otherwise than through the Auctioneers and such contract for sale in entered into or exchanged at any time up to 12 weeks after the date of the auction, or at any time with a person introduced to the owner/agent by the Auctioneers, the Auctioneers shall on exchange of such contract become immediately entitled to payment from the owner/agent of liquidated damages equal to

    a   where the contract price is revealed by the owner/agent to the Auctioneers 3% of the contract price, or the minimum sale fee, whichever is the greater, plus VAT;

    b   where the contract price is not revealed to the Auctioneers and a reserve price has been fixed for the property. 3% of 110% of such reserve price, or the minimum sale fee, whichever is the greater, plus VAT;

    c   where the contract price is not revealed to the Auctioneers and no reserve price has been fixed for the property 3% of the Auctioneers' estimate of the market value of the property, or the minimum sale fee, whichever is the greater, plus VAT.

10   If the property is withdrawn by the owner/agent other than by reason of a sale made pursuant hereto before the auction, the Auctioneers shall on such withdrawal become immediately entitled to a commission payment from the owner/agent equal to:

    a   where a reserve price for the property has been fixed. 15% of the reserve price or 50% of the minimum sale fee, whichever is the greater, plus VAT;

    b   where no reserve price for the property has been fixed 1.5% of the Auctioneers estimate of the market value of the property or 50% of the minimum sale fee, whichever is the greater, plus VAT;

save that should a contract for sale of the property thereafter be negotiated otherwise than through the Auctioneers and such contract for sale be entered into or exchanged at any time up to 12 weeks after the date of the auction (or at any time with a person introduced to the owner/agent by or contacted by, the Auctioneers) the Auctioneers shall be entitled to claim liquidated damages under Clause 8 hereof in lieu of their claim to a commission payment under this clause, and should a claim for commission payment under this clause have already been made by the Auctioneers and paid by the owner/agent they will nevertheless be entitled to claim from the owner/agent the difference between the sum paid hereunder and the sum they are entitled to under Clause 9 above.

Figure 7.1
Auctioneer's auction
terms

11		The minimum sale fee described in there auction terms shall be £1000 plus VAT.
12		The reserve price will be notified to the Auctioneers by the owner/agent either verbally or in writing at least 3 working days before the date of the auction. If it is not, or in the event of the owner/agent fining a reserve price which in the opinion of the Auctioneers is too high, then the Auctioneers may at their discretion choose not to offer the property at the auction. In such an instance the owner/agent will not have any claim whatsoever against the Auctioneers and will still be liable for the entry fee whether paid in advance or not. In the event of the owner/agent notifying the Auctioneers of the reserve price which in the opinion of the Auctioneers is lower than they themselves would recommend then in the absence of a suitable explanation from the owner/agent as to why such reserve price is suggested the Auctioneers may within 14 days of such notification notify the owner/agent that such reserve price is lower than the Auctioneers would recommend and shall not be regarded as the reserve once for the purpose of Clauses 9 and 10 herein.

13   The Auctioneers require the owner/agent:

    a   to instruct solicitors to act on his behalf:-

          i   to deduce full and proper title to the property;

          ii   to provide full contract of sale documents together with any additional and special conditions necessary;

          iii   to attend at the auction to render details of the title, and provide a copy of an tip-to-date local search if available;

          iv   to exchange contracts if so required by the Auctioneers;

          v   to indicate that all deposits paid may be received and held as agents for the owner/agent in accordance with the terms hereof;

          vi   to take full responsibility for the preparation and use of the memorandum of contract in the brochure if it is used by the owner/agent or by the Auctioneers.

    b   to indemnify the Auctioneers and their agents against any claims made because of faulty title or information provided by the owner/agent or any other failures by the owner/agent or his solicitors or other agents.

14		For the avoidance of doubt the Auctioneers will be entitled to receive value added tax in accordance with the law in addition to all commissions and entry fees payable.
15		The Auctioneers will use their best endeavours to obtain a signed memorandum and deposit from the successful bidder at the auction but cannot beheld responsible to the owner/agent if the successful bidder will not comply with these requirements. In the event of a failure of a successful bidder to supply his name and address, and, if appropriate, the name and address of the person or company on whose behalf be has been bidding, the Auctioneers are authorised to resubmit the property for sale at their total discretion at any time during the course of the name or future auction sessions within 12 weeks thereof.
16		The Auctioneers have the owner/agent's authority to refuse to accept any bids in the Auctioneers' absolute discretion. Even though this shall only be done in the best interests of the owner/agent, exercise of the discretion shall not in any way render the Auctioneers liable to the owner/agent.
17		The Auctioneers are authorized to accept payment of deposits by cheque.

© Howard R Gooddie

Figure 7.1
Auctioneer's auction
terms (continued)

Each catalogue contains the following information for each lot:

- address;
- nature of property;
- tenure;
- summary of fundamental terms of any leases;
- brief description of accommodation;
- viewing arrangements;
- any co-agents.

Human nature being what it is, it is inevitable at this stage that certain responses have not been received from vendors or their solicitors or co-agents who will need chasing up.

Printing and first advertising

5 to 7 weeks before A-day

The final copy is read, checked and approved.

Printers' programmes vary but auctioneers look to their printers to organize the catalogue being printed, collated and returned to their office within 6 to 10 working days. During this period, the auctioneer's office is not quiet since the advertising programme has to be organized, the first advertisements submitted and For Sale boards organized. The mailing list, which is on constant update, is run off ready for the despatch of the catalogues immediately they are received from the

AUCTION DETAILS SHEET

Property Address: _____

Description (eg tenanted house, vacant semi, commercial investment) _____

Route to Property: _____

Construction Materials:

Tenure: Freehold/Leasehold (Please delete as appropriate)

Chief or Ground Rent: (Please delete as appropriate)

Tenants' Names:

Rent or Rents Receivable:

Outgoings Payable:

Period of Lease:

Rent Reviews: **Rent Review Formula:**

Approximate Site Area:

Accommodation: **Ground Floor:**
                First Floor:
                Exterior:
                Additional:

Viewing Arrangements:

Any Co-Agents:

General Comments:

Solicitors: **Name of Firm:** _____
           Address: _____
                         _____

           Person Dealing: _____ **Phone No.** _____

Reserve Price:

BLUE - Retained by Vendor   **GREEN - Auctioneer**   **WHITE - Auction Co-ordinator**

Figure 7.2
Auction details sheet

Town and Country Planning Act 1971 (as amended)

PLANNING PERMISSION

Name and address of applicant   Name and address of agent (if any)

    Mr & Mrs Turner,   Jenkins Technical Services,
    28 Kings Road,   The Business Centre,
    Kilbyfield,   Kay Street,
    Kilner,   BURY,
    KL1 7BC.   BL9 6BU.

Part 1 - Particulars of application

Date of application: Application no.

          14th April, 1999   17/28/307

Particulars and location of development:

                             Two storey rear extension to
    Residential Home, Kings Road, Kilner.

Part II - Particulars of decision
The Rossendale Borough Council hereby give notice in pursuance of the Town and
Country Planning Act (as amended) that **permission has been granted** for the carrying
out of the development referred to in Part 1 hereof in accordance with the
application and plans submitted <u>subject to the following conditions</u>:-

1. The development must be begun not later than the expiration of five years
beginning with the date of this permission.

2. Car parking, servicing and manoeuvring facilities shall be provided within the
application site, and thereafter laid out and surfaced to the satisfaction of the
local planning authority before any building which is hereby permitted is first
occupied for the purposes of this permission, or at such other time as may
subsequently be agreed, in writing, with that authority.

3. Samples of the proposed reconstructed stone to be used for the construction of all
external walls shall be submitted to and approved by the local planning authority
before any development is commenced.

<u>The reasons for the conditions are:</u>

1. Required to be imposed pursuant to section 41 of the Town and Country Planning Act
1971 (as amended).

2. In order to ensure that sufficient car parking and servicing space is provided
within the application site thus ensuring that visiting vehicles are not encouraged
to park on the carriageway of adjoining highways thereby causing obstruction to same.

3. For the avoidance of doubt

Engineering and Planning Department,

Stubbylee Hall,   ENGINEER AND PLANNING OFFICER

BACUP, Lancashire, OL13 0DE.   Date: **15 JUN 1999**

IMPORTANT NOTICE
This is an approval under
PLANNING ONLY

<u>**(See overleaf for general information and guidance on post-decision procedures)**</u>

Figure 7.3
planning
consent

GENERAL INFORMATION FOR APPLICANTS INCLUDING GUIDANCE ON POST-DECISION PROCEDURES

1. If the applicant is aggrieved by the decision of the local planning authority to refuse permission or approval for the proposed development, or to grant permission or approval subject to conditions, he may appeal to the Secretary of State for the Environment in accordance with Section 36 of the Town and Country Planning Act, 1971 (as amended), within six months of receipt of this notice. (Appeals must be made on a form which is obtainable from the Department of the Environment, Tollgate House, Houlton Street, Bristol, BS2 9DJ). The Secretary of State has power to allow a longer period for the giving of a notice of appeal but he will normally be prepared to exercise this power unless there are special circumstances which excuse the delay in giving notice of appeal. The Secretary of State is not required to entertain an appeal if it appears to him that permission for the proposed development could not have been granted by the local planning authority, or could not have been so granted otherwise than subject to the conditions imposed by them, having regard to the statutory requirements.

2. If permission to develop land is refused or granted subject to conditions, whether by the local planning authority or by the Secretary of State for the Environment, and the owner of the land claims that the land has become incapable of reasonably beneficial use in its existing state and cannot be rendered capable of reasonably beneficial use of carrying out of an development which has been or would be permitted, he may serve on the Council of the district in which the land is situated a purchase notice requiring that Council to purchase his interest in the land in accordance with the provisions of Part IX of the Town and Country PLanning Act 1971 (as amended).

3. In certain circumstances, a claim may be made against the local planning authority for compensation, where permission is refused or granted subject to conditions by the Secretary of State on appeal or on a reference of the application to him. The circumstances in which such compensation is payable are set out in section 169 of the Town and Country Planning Act, 1971 (as amended).

4. (Applicable only to cases where planning permission or reserved matters approval has been granted). This permission refers only to that required under the Town and Country Planning Acts and does not include and consent or approval under any other enactment, byelaw, order or regulation; not will it operate as a listed building consent in respect of any works described in the permission for the alteration or extension of a listed building. Such works should be the subject of a separate application for listed building consent in that behalf. In particular the applicant should take note that it may also be necessary to seek building regulation approval to carry out the works described in plans accompanying this application pursuant to the provisions of the Building Regulations 1976. The applicant should take further note that it is necessary for him to ensure that all relevant permissions or consents are obtained including, where applicable, order to divert or stop up public footpaths, before any development is commenced.

5. In cases involving the erection of a building, or any extension to an existing building, the applicant should take note that the provisions of Section 31 of the County of Lancashire Act 1984 will, as appropriate, apply to any concurrent or subsequent submission for Building Regulation approval for such development insofar as the provision, or, as the case may be, the retention of adequate means of access to the building (or any extension thereto), or to any neighbouring building, for the fire brigade is concerned.

Figure 7.3 planning consent (continued)

printers. These catalogues may be sent out by a mailing house if this method of mailing is used. Addresses from enquirers responding to the advertisements are added to the mailing list.

Computer programs are ideally suited to deal with the registration of enquiries, their assessment, analysis and organization, whether received by telephone, letter, fax or answerphone. Some auctioneers maintain free mailing lists; others maintain annual subscription lists at costs from £20 to £100 per annum and a limited few run dedicated telephone numbers where the caller pays. Figure 7.4 shows how an auctioneer's mailing list is structured.

The mailing of the catalogue should allow you to have at least four clear weeks in which to assess the lots in the auction and organize your research and enquiries. The catalogue is also dispatched to all vendors, vendors' solicitors, landlords, tenants and anyone else (other than all those already registered on the mailing list) whom the auctioneers feel will be interested in the property. Owners of land or buildings which adjoin lots may well be interested in expansion of their ownership by buying next door and will receive a copy. Because of their potential as buyers they are frequently targeted in auctioneers' mailing shots.

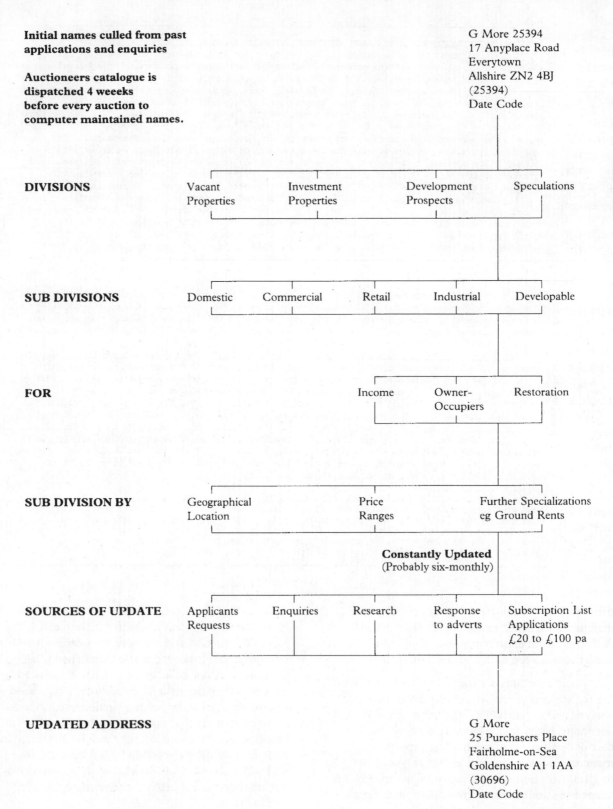

Initial names culled from past applications and enquiries

Auctioneers catalogue is dispatched 4 weeeks before every auction to computer maintained names.

G More 25394
17 Anyplace Road
Everytown
Allshire ZN2 4BJ
(25394)
Date Code

DIVISIONS — Vacant Properties | Investment Properties | Development Prospects | Speculations

SUB DIVISIONS — Domestic | Commercial | Retail | Industrial | Developable

FOR — Income | Owner-Occupiers | Restoration

SUB DIVISION BY — Geographical Location | Price Ranges | Further Specializations eg Ground Rents

Constantly Updated
(Probably six-monthly)

SOURCES OF UPDATE — Applicants Requests | Enquiries | Research | Response to adverts | Subscription List Applications £20 to £100 pa

UPDATED ADDRESS

G More
25 Purchasers Place
Fairholme-on-Sea
Goldenshire A1 1AA
(30696)
Date Code

Figure 7.4 An auctioneer's mailing list structure

Co-agents (other firms of estate agents who may have been employed by either the auctioneers or the vendor to promote the sale of the property at the same time as the auctioneers) have to be given a good supply of catalogues to issue from their offices.

Enquiries frequently include requests for guideline prices. These figures are usually a pessimistic and an optimistic estimate by the auctioneers (agreed in conjunction with the vendors) of the prices that might be realized for the lots. They are only guidelines but they need to be available from the moment the first enquiries start coming in. On occasion, auctioneers publish them in their advertisements or in the catalogue. The fixing of guidelines (and the philosophy behind them) is explained in more detail on page 111.

Enquiries and offers before the auction

During the next 30 days, the auctioneer's office deal with all the initial enquiries and, shortly after the catalogues go out, start to receive offers from potential buyers who would like to negotiate the purchase prior to the auction. Negotiating to buy a lot before auction is common. Many potential buyers feel confident enough to risk negotiating before the auction. This cuts out the competition by preventing others from making a bid on auction day. By initiating negotiations, you gamble disclosing your hand to the auctioneers before the sale. You have to judge whether the gamble is worthwhile depending on how badly you want to buy the lot and beat the competition. You must be sure how much you are prepared to pay and to negotiate quickly. If your offer is successful you will be expected to exchange contracts before (and probably several days before) the auction. You will need to pay the 10 per cent deposit when contracts are exchanged.

KEY POINT: *Only after contracts have been exchanged on a sale prior to the auction will the seller withdraw the lot from being offered on the auction day.*

Sellers will make up their own minds, in consultation with the auction team, whether to accept offers before auction. In the light of the interest shown, they may be encouraged to revise the reserve in an upward direction, rather than accept a figure prior to auction. Auctioneers have mixed feelings about offers prior to the auction. They are encouraged by the response to the advertisements but they are often tempted to encourage vendors to accept on the 'bird in the hand' philosophy. Nevertheless, their judgement is put to the test in advising the seller about the merits of accepting or rejecting a prior bid rather than risking having to withdraw the property on the day.

Auctioneer's Anecdote: 'I cannot possibly make it on the day'

It is an acknowledged fact in auctioneers' circles that all people, without fail, when making offers before the auction state categorically that they 'will not be able to attend on auction day'! Their reasons frequently emphasize human beings' originality.

Enquiries are notoriously difficult to analyse. Some enquirers do not disclose their hand at all and merely ask for catalogues to be sent to them. Other enquirers disclose the interest they have in types of property in general or sometimes in specific lots. These enquiries frequently stretch to asking the auction house what price a particular lot might reach. The enquirer's response to the guidelines that are then quoted can give the auctioneers some opportunity to define the strength and quality of the applicant's interest at that stage.

Vendors frequently want to know the amount of interest that has been shown in their lots. The number of applicants wishing to view particular properties can indicate the degree of interest. Nevertheless, every auctioneer will tell stories of properties that fail to sell, despite tremendous interest and other lots that sell with considerable competitive bidding, despite little interest being shown before the auction. Although many buyers deny it, it is common to see individuals who have been unsuccessful in buying prior to the auction day, attend and bid. However, no wise auctioneer relies on this happening.

KEY POINT: *In the light of interest shown and offers received, guidelines and reserves are frequently reviewed.*

Immediately before the auction

3 to 5 days before A-day

During this period, pressure needs to be exerted on buyers (and frequently on buyers' and sellers' solicitors) to exchange contracts on any sales that are agreed prior to the auction. If such contracts have not been exchanged by the day of the sale, then the lot is offered.

An amendment sheet is prepared giving any changes to the details and describing the lots and the order of selling. Steps are taken to advise interested parties and enquirers where lots are sold prior to the auction.

At this point, reserves are agreed with sellers in the light of the amount of interest shown in the properties and offers received. Many auctioneers require the reserves to be confirmed in writing by the vendors (to be received before the auction commences). Government bodies frequently detail their reserves in a confidential letter to the auctioneer, only to be opened just before the auction starts.

1 day to go

Last minute negotiations and revisions of reserves and guidelines continue while the auctioneer and his staff prepare for the auction and organize their support material and equipment. The auctioneer checks the last details in the amendment sheet and prepares his auction brief, schedule of reserves and his speech.

The auction

A-day

The auction passes in a flurry of hectic activity. What happens on the day is explained in chapters 4 and 5. The work of the staff does not finish with the auction. Immediately after it, negotiations with potential buyers start on withdrawn lots. These potential buyers fall into three categories:

1. Bidders or intending bidders who were not willing to bid at prices equal to the reserve. They will be hoping to buy the property after the auction at their maximum figure or may be having second thoughts and hoping that by

LOT 293
44 Tivoli Road,
West Norwood, London SE27
BY ORDER OF MORTGAGEES IN POSSESSION

A Freehold Semi Detached House

TENURE
Freehold.

LOCATION
The property is situated on the east side of Tivoli Road to the north of its junction with Crown Dale (A214). Local amenities are available along Beulah Hill and the facilities of Streatham are within reach. British Rail services run from West Norwood Station.

DESCRIPTION
The property comprises a semi detached house arranged over ground and first floors under a steep pitched slate clad roof.

ACCOMMODATION

Ground Floor	First Floor
Two Bedrooms	Reception Room
Bathroom with wash basin	Kitchen
Separate WC	

£30,000 is all it took to acquire the keys to this two-bed south London home.

negotiating a little higher they will be successful. Alternatively, they may sense that the owner of the property is willing to reduce the price, having been disheartened by the lack of success at the auction.

2. Bargain hunters who are looking to pick up cheap lots.

3. Potential buyers who were perhaps not sufficiently researched or prepared or did not have their finance in place to buy at the auction but who hope that their arrangements can be completed shortly.

All three types of potential buyer will be encouraging the auctioneer to disclose his reserve. If they succeed in persuading the auctioneer to reveal the reserve, they will start negotiating from that figure having discovered the price at which the vendor is willing to sell.

The schedule of the results has to be prepared for immediate transmission to relevant publishers such as the *Estates Gazette, Under the Hammer* and

Faxwise. Cheques are collected, banked and 'express' cleared as appropriate. Press releases are submitted to the *Estates Gazette*, *Property Week*, and whichever local newspapers and financial press the auctioneers feel might be willing to publish their results.

Immediately after the auction

The week after A-day

If a number of lots has been withdrawn, this period is particularly hectic with continuing negotiations for sales. These negotiations do not stop the routine work being carried out of preparing and issuing bills for the auctioneer's fees, transferring the deposits and payments for fees, and updating the records for filing and preservation. All vendors, regardless of whether they have attended the sale or not (and the majority don't), are advised of the results of the sale as far as their lots are concerned. The solicitors for both sellers and purchasers need to be contacted. The boards erected under the advertising programme need to be updated with SOLD slips where appropriate and subsequently removed.

Auctioneer's Anecdote:

For one provincial auctioneer, a SOLD indication is insufficient on his boards which can be seen adorned round his town with a blurred gavel against the words 'Going, Going, Gone'!

After the auction

2 to 4 weeks after A-day

Now the final tidying takes place. The sales of any remaining lots (those withdrawn and unsold) are still promoted. The final fee notes are rendered as the remaining pre- and post-auction private treaty sales are completed. Sellers who have been unfortunate enough not to sell their lots are approached to see if they wish to offer them in a subsequent auction. Completion of all the sales should then take place approximately one month after the auction.

THE AUCTIONEER'S PROGRAMME

9 to 10 weeks before A-day	Receive lots, confirm terms. Demand and collect entry fees.
8 to 9 weeks before A-day	Obtain full details from vendors. Inspect, photograph and catalogue.
8 weeks before A-day	Draft catalogue, check details and arrangements with vendors and solicitors.
5 to 7 weeks before A-day	Final copy prepared and submitted to printers. Guidelines agreed with vendors. Solicitors apply for local searches and organise draft conditions and contracts. Catalogues printed, for sale boards erected, adverts prepared, mailing list run off, enquiries recorded.
4 weeks to A-day	Catalogue mailed. Details of auction published.
4 weeks to 5 days	Enquiries dealt with, viewings arranged and made, offers prior to auction negotiated and solicitors instructed on contracts.
3 to 5 days before A-day	Press for exchange of pre-auction contracts, agree reserves with vendors.
1 day to go	Last preparations for auction room.
A-day	Auction takes place, deposits banked.
The week after A-day	Negotiate on unsold lots, arrange invoices, transfer fees, publish results.
2 to 4 weeks after A-day	Liaise with solicitors leading up to completion, hand over balance of deposits, remove for sale boards.

8 Thinking of selling your property?

There may come a time when you wish to sell your property. This chapter takes you step by step through the key points, ensuring a smooth passage to a successful sale at auction.

To auction or not?

The traditional property, which auctioneers encourage vendors to sell by auction, is one where the lot is so unique that the auctioneers expect an exceptional demand and the final valuation is difficult to judge. However, many sellers find auctions a quick and successful method of selling almost any type of property. The types of property which are offered at auction fall into three groups.

1. The exceptional property seeking an exceptional price

The types of property that can benefit from the ambience of the auction room and where competition can be brought out into the open and fostered are:

- the thatched cottage overlooking the trout stream;
- the retail investment let at a good rent to a company of impeccable covenant;
- the mews home in an area of exceptional demand;
- the plot of building land which all the local builders are convinced they can sell at high prices exceptionally quickly.

Surprisingly, these lots probably make up less than 5 per cent of what is being offered in the sale room at the beginning of the 21st century.

2. Properties forming the main auction market

Vendors have discovered that the auction room is also a successful place from which to market the more run-of-the-mill property. They benefit from having the competition out in the open following good advertising and widespread exposure to the market. The exceptional circumstances where a contract exists when the gavel falls is a very worthwhile benefit. No wonder more than 55,000 properties a year are offered for sale in the auction rooms of England.

3. Properties for a quick disposal

The third type of property sold by auction is that which a vendor is seeking to dispose of quickly. It may be that the seller has been trying to sell the property by private treaty for a long time and has now reached the end of the line. Such disposals are often provoked by pressure from financiers or follow repossession or liquidation.

> **KEY POINT:** *Many bargains exist where properties need to be disposed of quickly.*

Seek the auctioneer's advice

All auctioneers are willing to discuss the advantages and disadvantages of auction. If you are looking to sell, they will be able to advise you if the sale room is the place to offer your property or not, depending upon your circumstances.

Advantages of selling by auction

1. The contract exists immediately the gavel falls.
2. Auctions have extensive and exciting marketing and advertising.
3. The marketing period is short.
4. Purchasers can see the competition that exists.
5. Competitive bidding results in a sale at market price.
6. The seller and purchaser know where they stand immediately – there is no renegotiation or gazumping.
7. The national average success rate from offering of properties for sale by auction was just under 75 per cent in 1999.

The types of auction houses

Auctioneer's offices

With over 80 auctioneers offering their services throughout the country, choosing the firm to use may not be easy. The range of firms to choose from falls into the following groups.

- Firms around London that specialize in the property offered.

- Firms in London that cover a wide range of properties both in general, composite auctions and in specialized ones. Consider where your buyers are likely to be based. Local firms are best for locally based bidders. City firms are best if your lot will appeal to major investors or speculators. Do you want a local or a national market?

- Firms based in London that conduct auctions throughout the UK. (Those that do not have an office relatively close to your property should be rejected unless they cater for an important specialization.)

- Firms based in the larger towns throughout the country that run regular composite auctions.

- Local firms that run smaller auctions frequently on demand.

How to choose your auction house

1. Find a newspaper that advertises auctions in your area or your specialization and collect the various catalogues.

2. Subscribe to *Property Auction News* for a full listing of forthcoming sales and collect auction catalogues (see page 8 for details).

Do your research thoroughly

3. Research the catalogues and the advertisements and prepare a shortlist of the firms. Select those that offer plenty of property similar to yours or that appear to have a niche in the style of property you are offering.

4. Research the advertisements and publicity which the auction houses offer to help you decide the style and media choice appropriate for your lot. For example, if you are selling a major commercial investment nationwide, advertising in the *Estates Gazette* is imperative. On the other hand, for a desirable cottage in the country your publicity is better placed in local newspapers and magazines that have plenty of articles on country affairs. The golden rule is to plump for the media and auction houses that will give you maximum exposure amongst your likely bidders.

5. Which firm is most successful in selling property like yours? Your own experience from visiting auctions and word of mouth is probably the best guide. If you are looking at success rates from sales, rely more on your own experience than on published figures in news items which frequently tend to be 'hyped'. Don't forget to take into account sales prior to and after the auctions.

Pick an efficient firm

6. When approaching firms, make a note of how efficient they are. Were you dealt with promptly, courteously and efficiently? Remember, when you ask for catalogues or information, you are using the same services as a potential bidder.

7. Don't base your decision on the auctioneer who quotes the highest likely selling price or guidelines. He can only give you his impression of the market and at the first meeting may deliberately be a little optimistic. What really matters to you is how high actual bidders can be encouraged to go on auction day, not an auctioneer's valuation.

Don't go for the cheapest

8. Don't be persuaded to employ an auction house that quotes a low commission or entry fee. An extra £250 in commission can be easily paid for by an auctioneer who is sufficiently good on the rostrum or in his pre-auction publicity to gain just one extra bid. Auctioneers that regularly use large bidding increments in the sale room can procure a final bid far in excess of the gain a reduced rate of commission brings.

CHECKLIST:
How to choose your auction house

1 Analyse catalogues. ☐

2 Visit some auctions. ☐

3 Which firms offer your type of property in plenty? ☐

4 Which auction house has the right style of publicity and media choice to suit your lot? ☐

5 Which auctioneer is most successful in selling properties like yours? ☐

6 Which firm deals with you most efficiently? ☐

7 Which auction firms have a specialization that may be an advantage to you? ☐

8 Do you want a local or a national market? ☐

9 Where are your buyers likely to be based? – Local firms are best for locally based bidders. ☐

10 Don't base your decision on the auctioneer who quotes the highest likely selling price or guidelines. ☐

11 Don't be swayed by a low commission or entry fee. ☐

12 Which auctioneer has the charisma to charm bidders 'out of the trees'? ☐

13 Which auctioneer insists on large increments at the end of the bidding? ☐

Agreeing the auctioneer's terms

All auctioneers publish agency terms, but those terms vary from firm to firm. It is usual for auctioneers to charge an entry fee. They may recommend supplementary advertising and promotional elements which are specified at the beginning. Thereafter, there are various other features of the terms to note:

When are the fees payable?

The entry fee is usually due at the time of instruction. Sales fees are due in the following circumstances.

1. When contracts are exchanged or at completion.

Fees may be due if you do not complete

2. The auctioneer may be entitled to a fee or a reduced fee where contracts are exchanged but completion does not follow.

3. A fee or reduced fee may be payable where the property is withdrawn by the vendor before the auction. The amount is usually calculated on either the reserve price fixed or the figure that the auctioneer reasonably judges to be a realistic reserve.

4. A fee or reduced fee is normally payable if the seller withdraws the property from the sale, either because it has been sold elsewhere or merely on a whim.

5. Most auctioneers require a fee to be paid where a lot is sold before, at or even after the auction during a specified period. The auctioneer's terms usually provide a formula for calculating the fee if a sale price is not disclosed by the vendor and the property sells by private treaty, not through the auction house.

What type of agency?

Most auctioneers provide a sole agency agreement specifying how long they have the right to sell the property. Under these terms, the owner is responsible for paying the auctioneer the entry and sale fees laid down, however the lot is sold during that period. These fees are payable, even if the property is sold by another agent or by the owner direct. On occasion, auctioneers agree to joint sole agency terms where they act in tandem with another agent. The agents agree between each other how the entry and sale fees are to be split.

> **KEY POINT:** *Under sole agency, the seller has to pay a fee however the property is sold during the period specified.*

It is very unusual for auctioneers to accept an agency agreement where the owner is not liable to pay them a fee if the property has been sold privately or through another agency.

Right to collect the fee

It is normal for auctioneers to reserve the right to collect their sale fee from the deposit that is paid after the exchange of contracts or memoranda. It is usual for auctioneers to claim the right to retain any interest earned on deposits while they are held in their accounts.

What level of fees can a seller expect to pay?

Entry fees and sale fees vary depending upon the quality of the catalogue, the amount of advertising and the extent of the services which are provided by the auctioneer. The major auction houses can charge up to £2,500 entry fee for each lot. For this amount, the vendor can expect to see his property extensively advertised and included in a high quality catalogue. Sale fees are normally between 1.5 per cent and 3 per cent of the price at which the property is sold, subject to a minimum fee which may be between £250 and £2,500. On occasion, auctioneers may recommend additional expenditure on specialized advertising, if they feel such an approach justifies it. Table 8.1 illustrates the range of fees payable.

> **KEY POINT:** *The Estate Agents Act 1979 and its subsequent regulations requires estate agents to specify their terms in writing to all vendors.*

The legal clauses to watch out for

The terms might include the following clauses:

Payment in advance

1   Following the receipt of instructions and the full entry fee as communicated, the Auctioneers will take all reasonable steps to include the property described in these instructions (hereinafter referred to as 'the property') in their next suitable and available composite auction (hereinafter referred to as 'the auction').

LOT 308
16 Viewland Road, Plumstead, London SE18
BY ORDER OF MORTGAGEES IN POSSESSION

A Freehold End of Terrace House

TENURE
Freehold.

LOCATION
The property is situated on the north side of Viewland Road to the west of its junction with Riverdale Road. Local amenities are available along Plumstead High Street and the open spaces of Winns Common are within reach.

DESCRIPTION
The property comprises an end of terrace house arranged over lower ground, ground and first floors under a steep pitched tile clad roof. The house benefits from a rear garden and has views to the rear over south east London.

ACCOMMODATION

Lower Ground Floor	Ground Floor
Reception Room	Bedroom
Kitchen Area	Bathroom with WC and wash basin
	First Floor
	Two Bedrooms

A two-bed south London home that could have been yours for only £33,500.

The auction house is confirming that their entry fee is payable in advance. This sample term has been culled from a document issued by a company which runs composite public auctions. A number of lots is offered in one place on one day. The number of lots may range from 2 to 302 or more.

Non-returnable fees

2   Entry fees which are to cover the costs of advertising and promotion are non-returnable and are due as a debt from the owner/agent to the Auctioneers upon the signing of the instructions.

This term again confirms the entry fee is due in advance and that no part of it is returnable. Some auctioneers do allow all or part of the entry fee to be used in payment of the sale fee due, if the lot is sold.

Table 8.1 Auctioneer's fees

Sale price	Entry fee	Minimum fee	Sales fee at: 1.5%	2%	2.5%	3%	VAT	Total cost	Comment
Up to £20,000	£400	£600	–	–	–	–	£175	£1,175	
Up to £25,000	£400	£600	–	–	–	–	£175	£1,175	
	£400	–	–	–	£625	–	£179	£1,179	
	£400	–	–	–	–	£750	£201	£1,351	
Up to £30,000	£400	£600	–	–	–	–	£175	£1,175	
	£400	–	£600	–	–	–	£175	£1,175	
	£400	–	–	–	£750	–	£201	£1,351	
	£400	–	–	–	–	£900	£228	£1,528	
Up to £50,000	£400	–	£750	–	–	–	£201	£1,351	
	£400	–	–	£1,000	–	–	£245	£1,645	
	£400	–	–	–	£1,250	–	£289	£1,939	
	£400	–	–	–	–	£1,500	£332	£2,232	
Up to £75,000	£400	–	£1,125	–	–	–	£267	£1,791	
	£400	–	–	£1,500	–	–	£332	£2,232	
	£400	–	–	–	£1,875	–	£398	£2,673	
	£400	–	–	–	–	£2,250	£464	£3,114	
Up to £110,000	£400	–	£1,500	–	–	–	£332	£2,232	
	£400	–	–	£2,000	–	–	£420	£2,820	
	£400	–	–	–	£2,500	–	£508	£3,408	
	£400	–	–	–	–	£3,000	£595	£3,995	
Up to £150,000	£400	–	£2,250	–	–	–	£464	£3,114	Supplementary advertising usual at and above a selling price of £150,000
	£400	–	–	£3,000	–	–	£595	£3,995	
	£400	–	–	£3,000	–	–	£595	£3,995	
	£400	–	–	–	£3,750	–	£726	£4,876	
	£400	–	–	–	–	£4,500	£858	£5,758	
Up to £200,000	£400	–	£3,000	–	–	–	£595	£3,995	
	£400	–	–	£4,000	–	–	£770	£5,170	
	£400	–	–	–	£5,000	–	£945	£6,345	
	£400	–	–	–	–	£6,000	£1,120	£7,520	
Up to £250,000	£400	–	£3,750	–	–	–	£726	£4,876	
	£400	–	–	£5,000	–	–	£945	£6,345	
	£400	–	–	–	£6,250	–	£1,164	£7,814	
	£400	–	–	–	–	£7,500	£1,383	£9,283	
Up to £500,000	£400	–	£7,500	–	–	–	£1,383	£9,283	
	£400	–	–	£10,000	–	–	£1,820	£12,220	
	£400	–	–	–	£12,500	–	£2,258	£15,158	
	£400	–	–	–	–	£15,000	£2,695	£18,095	
Up to £750,000	£400	–	£11,250	–	–	–	£2,039	£13,689	
	£400	–	–	£15,000	–	–	£2,695	£18,095	
	£400	–	–	–	£18,750	–	£3,351	£22,501	
	£400	–	–	–	–	£2,250	£4,008	£26,908	
Up to £1,000,000	£400	–	£15,000	–	–	–	£2,625	£17,625	
	£400	–	–	£20,000	–	–	£3,570	£23,970	
	£400	–	–	–	£25,000	–	£4,445	£29,845	
	£400	–	–	–	–	£30,000	£5,320	£35,720	

Authority to sell

3   By signing this instruction form, the owner/agent gives the Auctioneers absolute irrevocable authority to act as sole selling agents to negotiate and enter into a contract for sale of the property:

(a)   from the date hereof until the auction at a price authorized by the owner/agent;

(b)   at the auction at the highest genuine bid at or above the reserve price;

(c)   at any time up to 8 weeks after the auction at the reserve price;

and by so signing this instruction form the owner/agent warrants to the Auctioneers that he has the authority to give such absolute irrevocable authority.

This term emphasizes a sole agency has been entered into and that the person instructing has authority to sell the property. Not only are the auctioneers given authority to negotiate a sale but also to enter into a contract for its sale on behalf of the vendors in the following circumstances:

• in the event of a pre-auction sale at a price the owner agrees; or

• to a genuine bidder at the reserve or above it on auction day; or

• at any time up to 8 weeks after the auction at the reserve price.

Since the vendor will be commited to a sale entered into by his sole agent, it is necessary that the auctioneer's authority is irrevocable. Both the auctioneer and the vendor need to be positive that the latter has not entered into a contract at a price which the owner does not like and, therefore, the terms very specifically define the price at which the auctioneers can sell. Section 3a underlines the fact that the auction house will have to obtain the vendor's specific authorisation to the price before the sale. Section 3b emphasises the procedure which takes place in the auction itself where the auctioneer is aware that he can only enter into a contract by bringing down the gavel at the highest bid providing it is at or above the reserve. Section 3c, apart from giving the auction house a reasonable time to sell after the auction, stresses that during this time the owner accepts that he is willing to sell at the reserve. Although the terms of agency specifies this final point in the procedure, it is not unusual for the auctioneer and the vendor to discuss the price at which the property can be sold after the auction.

The seller may be willing to vary this agreement and advise his or her agents that a lesser price than the reserve will be acceptable.

Some sellers are willing to extend the 8 week period, others seek to reduce it, but since it is very common for sales to be negotiated after the auction, auctioneers always feel that it is only fair that they should have the opportunity to sell after the auction so that they can capitalize on the way in which they have marketed the property before the auction.

Right to collect fee

4   Upon unconditional exchange of any such contract for sale entered into the Auctioneers shall become immediately entitled to 3% plus VAT, of the contract price for sale of the property or the minimum sale fee plus VAT whichever is the greater from the owner/agent and the Auctioneers and their duly authorized agents shall be entitled to deduct that sale fee plus VAT from any deposits received on, before or after exchange of any such contract for sale from the intending purchaser without further authority.

It is usual for the auction house to become entitled to its fee immediately contracts have been exchanged. Where their auctioneers belong to the recognized bodies such as the Royal Institution of Chartered Surveyors and the Society of Valuers & Auctioneers, their members are specifically prohibited from deducting fees from the client's money without written permission. This term eliminates the need for specific separate permission to be obtained for each lot sold.

Deposit arrangements

5   The balance of any such deposits will be held in an insurance bonded clients' account up to completion of such contract for sale, but any interest earned on such deposits held by the Auctioneers shall be held to their credit and not to the credit of the owner/agent and shall at all times be the absolute property of the Auctioneers.

The position concerning deposits and their ownership is explained on page 116. This auction term assumes that the conditions of sale will provide for the deposit to be held by the auctioneer on behalf of the vendor. The term will need changing if the conditions of sale are varied. If the deposit is held by the auctioneers or others as stakeholder or on behalf of the purchaser in the period between contract and completion then the purchaser may be entitled to the interest on the deposit. This clause gives comfort to the vendor that the deposit monies will be placed in a clients' account which is subject to regulation and that the security of that money is covered by an insurance bond.

Fees due if completion does not happen

6   Should any such contract for sale be exchanged but not completed the Auctioneers shall become immediately entitled to a commission payment from the owner/agent of 1.5% of the contract price or 50% of the minimum sale fee whichever is the greater, plus VAT, without deduction.

Approximately 1 in every 100 auction lots sold does not proceed to completion despite the fact that the purchaser has paid a 10 per cent deposit at the exchange of contracts. How that deposit is treated between vendor and purchaser in the event of non-completion of the sale is explained on page 116. The auctioneer in this term is pointing out to the vendor that his fee will be reduced by half but will still be due and payable in such circumstances.

Auctioneer's right to commission

7   The owner/agent hereby confirms his understanding that the effect of appointing the Auctioneers as sole selling agents as set out above is inter alia to prevent the owner/agent whether by himself, his servants or agents or otherwise whatsoever

   (a)   from negotiating or entering into a contract for sale of the property from the date hereof until 12 weeks after the date of the auction otherwise than through the Auctioneers;

   (b)   from negotiating or entering into a contract for sale of the property from the date hereof at any time with a person introduced to him by the Auctioneers other than through the Auctioneers.

This term complements the sole selling nature of this agreement, emphasizes the term outlined at 3 above and strengthens the auctioneer's entitlement to commission on a sale however it occurs:

- between the time at which the auctioneer is appointed and 12 weeks after the date of the auction to anyone however they have been introduced and negotiated with; or

- at any time after the initial instruction to anyone with whom the auction house has been in contact.

LOT 360
69 Tickford Street,
Newport Pagnell, Buckinghamshire
BY ORDER OF MORTGAGEES IN POSSESSION

A Freehold End of Terrace House

TENURE
Freehold.

LOCATION
Tickford Street (A509) is the continuation of London Road. The property itself is situated close to its junction with Chicheley Street. Local shops and amenities are available along High Street.

DESCRIPTION
The property comprises an end of terrace house arranged over ground and first floors beneath a pitched tile roof. The property benefits from a rear garden.

ACCOMMODATION

Ground Floor	First Floor
Reception Room	Two Bedrooms
Kitchen	Bathroom with WC and wash basin

£23,500 is all it would have taken to acquire this two-bed end of terrace house.

In this clause the auctioneers have extended the 8-week period referred to in clause 3c to 12 weeks. In clause 3, the auctioneers as sole selling agents are giving 8 weeks in which to negotiate a contract for sale of the property. Once negotiations have been completed, it is not unusual for the solicitors acting on behalf of both sides to take up to 4 weeks to exchange contracts. For this reason, clause 7 specifies a period extended by 4 weeks to allow for this step in the transaction to take place.

Auction terms

8   The owner/agent further confirms that he has been provided with and read the Auctioneers' 'Information for Vendors' catalogue.

The Estate Agents Act 1979 requires that specific wording shall be incorporated in agency terms. Rather than put it in this portion of the auction terms, the auctioneers in this instance have chosen to incorporate it in a separate auction information catalogue. The terms of the Estate Agents Act 1979 governing provision of information and explanation of terms used are reproduced in Appendix 6.

Entitlement to fees if the price is kept secret

9   If in breach of the Auctioneers' rights as sole agents a contract for sale of the property is negotiated otherwise than through the Auctioneers and such contract for sale is entered into or exchanged at any time up to 12 weeks after the date of the auction, or at any time with a person introduced to the owner/agent by the Auctioneers, the Auctioneers shall on exchange of such contract become immediately entitled to payment from the owner/agent of liquidated damages equal to:

(a)   where the contract price is revealed by the owner/agent to the Auctioneers 3% of the contract price, or the minimum sale fee, whichever is the greater, plus VAT;

(b)   where the contract price is not revealed to the Auctioneers and no reserve price has been fixed for the property 3% of 110% of such reserve price, or the minimum sale fee, whichever is the greater plus VAT;

(c)   where the contract price is not revealed to the Auctioneers and no reserve price has been fixed for the property 3% of the Auctioneers' estimate of the market value of the property, or the minimum sale fee, whichever is the greater, plus VAT.

Not only does this term reiterate the sole agency agreement which has already been referred to in sections 3 and 7 above, it also sets out to cover the auctioneer's entitlement to commission where the contract price has not been revealed. In such circumstances, the auctioneer becomes entitled to his fee at the rate agreed based on 110 per cent of the reserve price or, if that has not been fixed, at the relevant percentage of the Auctioneer's estimate of the market value of the property. Any minimum commission agreed in the terms is retained for the purpose of this computation.

Right to fees for properties withdrawn before auction

10   If the property is withdrawn by the owner/agent other than by reason of a sale made pursuant hereto before the auction, the Auctioneers shall on such withdrawal become immediately entitled to a commission payment from the owner/agent equal to:

(a)   where a reserve price for the property has been fixed, 1.5% of the reserve price or 50% of the minimum sale fee, whichever is the greater, plus VAT;

(b)   where no reserve price for the property has been fixed 1.5% of the Auctioneers' estimate of the market value of the property or 50% of the minimum sale fee, whichever is the greater, plus VAT; save that should a contract for sale of the property thereafter be negotiated otherwise than through the Auctioneers and such contract for sale be entered into or exchanged at any time up to 12 weeks after the date of the auction (or at any time with a person introduced to the owner/agent by or contracted by, the Auctioneers) the Auctioneers shall be entitled to claim liquidated damages under Clause 8 hereof in lieu of their claim to a commission payment under this clause, and should a claim for commission payment under this clause have already been made by the Auctioneers and paid by the owner/agent they will nevertheless be entitled to claim from the owner/agent the difference between the sum paid hereunder and the sum they are entitled to under Clause 9 above.

In this term the auction house preserves a right to 50% of its standard fee if the property has been withdrawn by the owner prior to the auction for reasons other than because of a prior sale. There is provision for the calculation of the fee if no reserve has been settled, again based on the auctioneer's estimate of the market value of the property and the minimum sale fee has been preserved.

The balance of the auctioneer's entitlement to commission which has already been covered in Clause 7 of the terms is reiterated once more in this Clause 10, so that a vendor cannot avoid paying the auction house a full commission in the event of a sale by withdrawing the property from the auction before the auction day and before contracts have been exchanged elsewhere.

A minimum fee

11   The minimum sale fee described in these auction terms shall be £1,000 plus VAT.

Agreeing the reserve

12   The reserve price will be notified to the Auctioneers by the owner/agent either verbally or in writing at least 3 working days before the date of the auction. If it is not, or in the event of the owner/agent fixing a reserve price which in the opinion of the Auctioneers is too high, then the Auctioneers may at their discretion choose not to offer the property at the auction. In such

'outline planning permission' –

Local authorities will agree in principle that a piece of land can be developed. Outline planning permission normally specifies the type of property that can be built on the plot. However, this does not entitle you to begin building straight away. The planning committee will want to see more detailed plans of the property before granting 'full permission'. Even then, they may specify that they want to approve some of the materials used, such as the type of brick, or other matters that affect the appearance of the property to ensure it is in keeping with it is in keeping with its surrounding environment.

ABBREVIATIONS

adj.—adjoining **cr.**—corner **d-h.**— dwelling house **det.**— detached **F.**—freehold **f.g.r.**—freehold ground rent **f.r.l.**—full repairing lease **g.**— gross, landlord paying rates **grd**—ground **L.**— leasehold **l.g.r.**— leasehold ground rent **lic.**— licensed **Mod.**— modern **mth.**—monthly tenancy. **n.**—net, tenants pay rates A ground rent thus marked is net payable after deducting receivable ground rent. **n.o.**—not offered **nr.**—near **OPP.**—outline planning permission. **P.**—possession. **P.A.X.** · per annum exclusive **PL.**—part let **PP**—planning permission. **pt.**—part **pvt.**—sold privately. **p.a.**—per annum **rev.**—reversion **rr.**—rack rental **rsv.**— reserve price **RUP.**—residential upper part. **R.** —repossessed. **s.d.**—semi-detached. **sold priv.**— sold privately. **s.y.**— square yards. **sq.ft.**— square feet. **UT.**—unexpired term **w.**—withdrawn. **wk.**—weekly rent. **yrs.**—years **Av.**—available at

WEST YORKSHIRE

Monday 1 March at 6.00 p.m. *at the Auctioneers' Offices, 12 Horton St., Halifax.*
BREARLEY-GREENS (0422-330088)
Shelf - Brow Lane. Single res. bldg. plot with OPP
    sit. close to village centre with road frontage
                                     F P

Thursday 4 March at 12-30 p.m. *at The Salamanda Suite, The National Exhibition Centre, Birmingham.*
GENERAL ACCIDENT PROPERTY SERVICES (0705 872312)
Cleckheaton · 25 Westfield Lane, Scholes. 2 bed. s-d. d-h.
    Gdns. Storage outbdgs. (G.p. £18-20K) R F P
Leeds · 5 Bawn Vale, Farnley. 4 bed. s-d. d-h. Gdns.
    (Guide price £23-25,000)   R P

Thursday 4 March at 7.00 p.m. *at Nont Sarah's Hotel, New Hey Rd., Scammonden.*
ROBERT E.A. NEWTON (0484 666680)
Scammonden - New Hey Rd. Approx. 15a. grassland within
    ring fence, good road frontage   F P
do. Approx. 11a. grassland within ring fence, good road
    frontage.   F P
do. Agricultural Bdg and Land. Large s-storey brick built
    Agr. Bdg., 2 loose boxes & adj. grass paddock apx 1a
    Mains elec. & spring water supply   F P

Thursday 11 March at 2.30 pm *at The Hotel Metropole, King St., Leeds 1.*
EDDISONS AUCTIONS (0532 430101)
West Ardsley - 4 & 6 Batley Road, Hill Top. Pair of stone s-d.
    cotts with gdn let on reg. ten's plus gge let sep
    No. 4 - 1 bed + boxroom/child's room. Let at £20 pw
    No.6 - 1 bdm. Let at £19.50 pw
              Both effective from 15.2.91. F
Halifax · 2 Pear Tree Cottages, Norwood Grn. 1 bdm. stone
    cott. let on reg. ten. prod. £85 pcm from 1.1.1992. F

Illustration 7. Extract from Under the Hammer

an instance the owner/agent will not have any claim whatsoever against the Auctioneers and will still be liable for the entry fee whether paid in advance or not. In the event of the owner/agent notifying the Auctioneers of the reserve price which in the opinion of the Auctioneers is lower than they themselves would recommend then in the absence of a suitable explanation from the owner/agent as to why such reserve price is suggested the Auctioneers may within 14 days of such notification notify the owner/agent that such reserve price is lower than the Auctioneers would recommend and shall not be regarded as the reserve price for the purpose of Clauses 9 and 10 herein.

Auctioneers always discuss reserves with owners both after they have carried out their initial inspection of the property and during the period up to the auction as the effectiveness of the marketing campaign is assessed, as interest is shown or as any offers are received. It is usual for the reserve to be fixed at a compromise figure between the auctioneer's views of the value of the property and the owners' desire to obtain what they feel is a reasonable sum. In this example, the auctioneer is willing to accept reserve prices both verbally and in writing although it is more usual for prices to be agreed in writing. Thereafter, the auctioneer reserves the right to refuse to offer the property if in his view the reserve is too high.

The balance of the term prevents the owner specifying a particularly low reserve price prior to withdrawing the property from the auction to reduce the commission which he might otherwise have to pay under clauses 9 and 10.

Requirements to instruct a solicitor

13 The Auctioneers require the owner/agent:
    (a)   to instruct solicitors to act on his behalf:
        i   to deduce full and proper title to the property;
        ii to provide full contract of sale documents together with any additional and special conditions necessary;
        iii to attend at the auction to render details of the title, and provide a copy of an up-to-date local search if available;
        iv to exchange contracts if so required by the Auctioneers;
        v to indicate that all deposits paid may be received and held as agents for the owner/agent in accordance with the terms hereof;
        vi to take full responsibility for the preparation and use of the memorandum of contract in the catalogue if it is used by the owner/agent or by the Auctioneers.
    (b)   to indemnify the Auctioneers and their agents against any claims made because of faulty title or information provided by the owner/agent or any other failures by the owner/agent or his solicitors or other agents.

This term emphasizes to the vendor that the auctioneer needs the full co-operation of the vendor's solicitor. In part, it also acts as an aide-memoire for the solicitors, about the work they are required to do. The indemnity required under 13b stresses to the seller the importance of correct information being given to the auctioneer. It is also intended to be used as a defence against any actions the auctioneer's firm might suffer under the Property Misrepresentation Act 1991, if misleading details are published in the auction catalogue.

VAT

14 For the avoidance of doubt the Auctioneers will be entitled to receive value added tax in accordance with the law in addition to all commissions and entry fees payable.

Auctioneer's right to re-offer the property

15 The Auctioneers will use their best endeavours to obtain a signed memorandum and deposit from the successful bidder at the auction but cannot be held responsible to the owner/agent if the successful bidder will not comply with these requirements. In the event of a failure of a successful bidder to supply his name and address and, if appropriate, the name and address of the person or company on whose behalf he has been bidding, the Auctioneers are authorized to re-submit the property for sale at their total discretion at any time during the course of the same or future auction sessions within 12 weeks thereof.

This clause is self-evident. It is unusual for bidders to disappear once the gavel has fallen on their successful bid. This probably occurs only once in every 500 lots. Obviously, the bidder does not stay long enough for the auctioneer to discover why he will not proceed! This clause gives the auctioneer the right to re-offer the property (which he will generally wish to do) immediately he discovers the successful bidder did not (or will not) exchange contracts or has fled the sale room. When the property is re-offered it will generally not reach the same price as before, even though the auctioneer is still prevented from selling below the reserve. This term protects the position of the auction house in such an instance.

Right to refuse bids

16 The Auctioneers have the owner/agent's authority to refuse to accept any bids in the Auctioneer's absolute discretion. Even though this shall only be done in the best interests of the owner/agent, exercise of the discretion shall not in any way render the Auctioneers liable to the owner/agent.

Usually, auctioneers welcome all bids in the room. A pro-active response from the audience adds excitement, interest and increases the ambience of the sale. Nevertheless, on occasion, auctioneers may choose not to accept bids from certain individuals who have failed to fulfil responsibilities in the room before or who have committed other indiscretions not acceptable to the auctioneer and this term protects the auctioneer's entitlement.

Payment

17 The Auctioneers are authorized to accept payment of deposits by cheque.

Very occasionally, deposit cheques are not honoured. This term protects the decision of the auctioneer to accept cheques as deposits and also serves as a reminder to the seller that in the auction room, cheques will be taken to cover the 10 per cent or minimum deposit at the time of exchange.

Auctioneer's Anecdote: A camera-shy buyer

Several years ago a provincial auctioneer had to offer the title of the Lord of the Manor of Treffos. Because the manorial estate included the village of Llanfaipwllgwyngyllgogerychwyrndrobwllllantysiliogogogoch there was considerable media and public interest. The auctioneers intended to work this interest for maximum publicity. Two television companies had their cameramen present. Arc lights were installed. The auctioneer carried out two preliminary interviews with each of the television companies to set the scene and spelt out the nature of the lot to a clutch of journalists. As the lot came up, the arc lights went on and the cameras started rolling. Several discreet bids were made by

members of the audience. As the cameras frantically panned over the room to find them, the lot was finally knocked down at £12,000 to a bidder who was behind a pillar at the back of the room but whose bidding arm was visible to the auctioneer. The auctioneer halted the sale, stepped down off the rostrum and invited the new Lord of the Manor to come forward to receive his congratulations on succeeding into the title, intending to create the 'photo opportunity' which he had offered to TV and newspapers. He did not know at that time that the successful bidder had already run out of the room, dropping a £500 deposit in cash on the reception desk and mouthed to the auctions co-ordinator (to whom he was known) 'I will be back later'. The photo opportunity never occurred, the auctioneer never obtained the publicity which he had sought and various news hawks were too late in realizing what had happened to catch the new Lord on his way out of the room and out of the hotel. It was only after reassurance from his auctions co-ordinator that he did not need to re-offer the lot that a rather chastened auctioneer returned to the rostrum to continue the sale whilst the cameramen packed up around the bidders. The purchaser did return several hours later, signed and exchanged contracts and subsequently completed. It was only one enterprising and patient journalist who lingered behind long enough to eventually be able to 'scoop' the news the next day.

Responsibilities of the seller

These terms show that it is usual for the vendors:

1. To certify that they have authority to offer the lot for sale.

2. To give irrevocable authority to the auctioneer to negotiate and enter into a contract for sale of the property.

3. To pay the entry fee and commission on the terms laid down.

4. To undertake to fix the reserve price and confirm it in writing at least 3 days before the auction.

5. To instruct solicitors to act on their behalf to deduce title to the property and to provide full

contract of sale documents with any additional special conditions necessary. The vendor is normally required to indemnify the auctioneers against any claims made because of faulty title or information that they or their solicitors may have rendered.

6. To undertake to provide full and correct details of the property to be sold indemnifying the auctioneer against misdescriptions.

Getting the catalogue details right

It is always important that the particulars of the catalogue are right for the sake of the purchaser. No-one wishes to see him misinformed. However, it is equally important to the vendor, since incorrect details may give the purchaser the right to withdraw from the contract and claim the return of their deposit. To the auction house, however, it is even more important that the particulars are right. This is vital not only because of their reputation, but also because the publishing of misleading particulars is now a criminal offence under the Property Misdescriptions Act 1991 with a maximum fine of £5,000 and the ultimate punishment of preventing the firm or its staff ever acting as estate agents again.

Catalogue items that must not mislead

The Property Misdescriptions Act 1991 specifies the following categories in which catalogues must not be misleading.

1. Location or address.

2. Aspect, view, outlook or environment.

3. Availability and nature of services, facilities or amenities.

4. Proximity to any services, places, facilities or amenities.

5. Accommodation, measurements or sizes.

6. Fixtures and fittings.

7. Physical or structural characteristics, form of construction or condition.

8. Fitness for any purpose or strength of any buildings or other structures on land or of land itself.

9. Treatments, processes, repairs or improvements or the effects thereof.

10. Conformity or compliance with any scheme, standard, test or regulations or the existence of any guarantee.

11. Survey, inspection, investigation, valuation or appraisal by any person or the results thereof.

12. The grant or giving of any award or prize for design or construction.

13. History, including the age, ownership or use of land or any building or fixture and the date of any alterations thereto.

14. Person by whom any building, (or part of any building), fixture or component was designed, constructed, built, produced, treated, processed, repaired, reconditioned or tested.

15. The length of time during which land has been available for sale either generally or by or through a particular person.

16. Price (other than the price at which accommodation or facilities are available and are to be provided by means of the creation or disposal of an interest in land in the circumstances specified in section 23(1)(a) and (b) of the Consumer Protection Act 1987(a) or Article 16(1)(a) and (b) of the Consumer Protection (NI) Order 1987(b) (which relate to the creation or disposal of certain interests in new dwellings)) and previous price.

17. Tenure or estate.

18. Length of any lease or of the unexpired term of any lease and the terms and conditions of a lease (and, in relation to land in Northern Ireland, any fee farm grant creating the relationship of landlord and tenant shall be treated as a lease).

19. Amount of any ground-rent, rent or premium and frequency of any review.

20. Amount of any rent-charge.

21. Where all or any part of any land is let to a tenant or is subject to a licence, particulars of the tenancy or licence, including any rent, premium or other payment due and frequency of any review.

22. Amount of any service or maintenance charge or liability for common repairs.

23. Council tax payable in respect of a dwelling within the meaning of section 3, or in Scotland section 72, of the Local Government Finance Act 1992(a) or the basis or any part of the basis on which that tax is calculated.

24. Rates payable in respect of a non-domestic hereditament within the meaning of section 64 of the Local Government Finance Act 1988(b) or, in Scotland, in respect of lands and heritages shown on a valuation roll or the basis or any part of the basis on which those rates are calculated.

25. Rates payable in respect of a hereditament within the meaning of the Rates (Northern Ireland) Order 1977(c) or the basis or any part of the basis on which those rates are calculated.

26. Existence or nature of any planning permission or proposals for development, construction or change of use.

27. In relation to land in England and Wales, the passing or rejection of any plans of proposed building work in accordance with section 16 of the Building Act 1984(d) and the giving of any completion certificate in accordance with regulation 15 of the Building Regulations 1991(e).

28. In relation to land in Scotland, the granting of a warrant under section 6 of the Building (Scotland) Act 1959(f) or the granting of a certificate of completion under section 9 of that Act.

29. In relation to land in Northern Ireland, the passing or rejection of any plans of proposed building work in accordance with Article 13 of the Building Regulations (Northern Ireland) Order 1979(g) and the giving of any completion certificate in accordance with building regulations made under that Order.

30. Application of any statutory provision which restricts the use of land or which requires it to be preserved or maintained in a specified manner.

31. Existence or nature of any restrictive covenants, or of any restrictions on resale, restrictions on use, or pre-emption rights and, in relation to land in Scotland (in addition to the matters mentioned previously in this paragraph) the existence or nature of any reservations or real conditions.

32. Easements, servitudes or wayleaves.

33. Existence and extent of any public or private right of way.

> **KEY POINT:** *Since the owner/agent has already indemnified the auctioneers in his terms against claims made because of faulty information (see clause 13b of the auctioneer's terms on page 106) he has a heavy responsibility to ensure the details of the property in the catalogue are totally correct and not misleading.*

Instructing your solicitor

The vendor should instruct his solicitor that he is including his property or properties in a sale at the same time as the auctioneer is approached. It is important that the vendor knows how much the solicitor will charge. Table 8.2 gives examples of solicitor's conveyancing fees. The solicitor needs plentiful warning after the confirmation of instructions to:

- obtain the deeds and investigate the title;

- obtain the auction catalogue and the auctioneer's standard conditions;

- draft the contract and any additional special conditions.

The solicitor will raise pre-contract searches and go through the pre-contract enquiries with the seller so that information for the prospective bidder is available. Solicitors frequently prepare an auction information pack to include title details, searches and replies to enquiries so that they can be provided to solicitors who make approaches on behalf of potential bidders. Particularly, the solicitor needs to be instructed to liaise with the auctioneer to ensure that the particulars published in the auction catalogue are not misleading. The solicitor needs to be informed of the auction timetable so that he can act with the necessary speed.

Table 8.2 Solicitor's fees for acting on behalf of the vendor

Sale at auction (excluding disbursements)	Fee range
Up to £50,000	£350–£450
£50,001 to £150,000	£450–£650
£150,001 to £250,000	£600–£800
£250,001 to £50,000	£800–£2,000
£500,001 to £750,000	£1,500–£2,500
Over £750,000	0.3%–0.5%

Note: Fees include cost of attending the auction and assume that a sale occurs.

SOLICITOR'S CHECKLIST:
Acting for a Buyer

1 After confirming instructions, obtain deeds and investigate title. ☐

2 Obtain auction catalogue and/or auctioneers' standard conditions. ☐

3 Inspect site if appropriate. ☐

4 Draft contract in light of 1, 2 and 3 above. ☐

5 Raise pre-contract searches you would make if acting for a buyer, eg local search, British Coal search. ☐

6 Go through pre-contract enquiries with the seller so the information to a prospective bidder is available. ☐

7 Prepare an auction information pack to include title details, searches and replies to enquiries. ☐

8 Re-check the contract in the light of searches and replies to pre-contract enquiries and also check the auction catalogue particulars are correct. If not send auctioneer's amendments. ☐

9 Deal with pre-auction enquiries as promptly as possible to sustain prospective bidders' interest. ☐

10 Attend auction or appoint agents on your behalf and ensure you attend at least half an hour beforehand with an information pack (see point 7) so you can deal with enquiries. ☐

11 Make sure the auctioneer draws bidders' attention to amendments. ☐

12 After the lot is sold, ensure you receive the purchaser's details from the auctioneers to insert in both parts of the contract. ☐

13 Obtain the purchaser's signature to the contract and a cheque for the deposit and obtain details of purchaser's solicitors and ask the purchaser to deliver your part of the contract to them as soon as possible. Explain that you will send all the information a solicitor needs and also tell them what the completion date is, even if that is clear on the front of the contract. ☐

14 Liaise with purchaser's solicitors, as normal, up to completion. ☐

Checklist supplied by Vaudrey Osborne & Mellor, Solicitors, Manchester.

Agreeing the figures

The second greatest ability needed for an auctioneer is to be an accurate valuer. But with all the skill in the world it is impossible to judge what is in the mind of bidders on sale day. On that day, the cliché that valuation is an art not a science is put to the test. The auctioneer/valuer has all his skills, training and experience behind him. The auction house has access to all the records of prices obtained for comparable properties, but in the end the judgement of value is still very subjective. Even the most competent auctioneer/valuer can find his confidence severely dented in the sale room. Especially, when lots that he advises may only just reach their reserve, either go on to sell at high prices after runaway competitive bidding, or have to be withdrawn at bids considerably less than he recommended as a value or reserve.

KEY POINT: *Nevertheless, it is a vital part of the marketing prior to auction and of the auction itself that the guidelines and reserve are astutely judged.*

The guidelines

Right at the beginning, owners frequently have strong views about the price at which they will sell. The valuer, after inspection, may have similar or totally divergent views. The divergence may be so great that the vendor decides not to include the lot in the sale, but hopefully those views can be reconciled so the property can be included. At this stage, there can be a spread between the top and bottom guidelines which may help towards that compromise. The bottom guideline should be a rather pessimistic estimate of the figure at which the property might sell whilst the top guideline represents a slightly optimistic view. That pessimism and optimism has to be balanced with the need to encourage interest in the property initially and to persuade bidders to attend the auction subsequently.

Don't make the guidelines too low or too high

Too low a bottom guideline will encourage many potential buyers to attend the auction who will be unhappy if they have wasted their time because the reserve was noticeably higher. In contrast, guidelines that are too high will frighten would-be bidders away who otherwise might have been successful on auction day.

> **KEY POINT:** *It is usual for the bottom guideline to be relatively close to the figure that the auctioneer and vendor are contemplating fixing as a reserve.*

Varying the guidelines

As the marketing for the auction develops, the auction house should be in a position to start judging the amount of interest in the lots. Exceptional interest may be shown in particular properties and offers may be received. If none of those offers are accepted, the interest – or lack of it – should prompt the auctioneer and the seller to reconsider their guidelines. This is, of course, not possible if the guidelines are being published in the catalogue itself. In other circumstances such fine-tuning may prove worthwhile and may enable the spread between the guidelines to be reduced. Table 8.3 illustrates initial guidelines, fine-tuned guidelines and the likely reserve.

Table 8.3 Guideline ranges

Likely reserve	Initial guidelines	Fine-tuned guidelines
£5,000	£4,500–£6,000	£4,500–£5,500
£7,000	£6,500–£8,000	£6,500–£7,500
£10,000	£9,000–£12,000	£9,500–£10,500
£20,000	£19,000–£24,000	£19,500–£21,000
£30,000	£28,000–£35,000	£29,500–£31,500
£50,000	£45,000–£55,000	£49,000–£52,000
£75,000	£70,000–£80,000	£74,000–£79,000
£100,000	Around £100,000	£95,000–£105,000
£150,000	£140,000–£160,000	£145,000–£155,000
£200,000	£180,000–£220,000	£195,000–£210,000

The reserve

Accurate advice on this figure from the auction house is vital. Far too often vendors are inclined to fix an amount which is high on the principle 'you can always bring it down afterwards'. Such an approach is totally unrealistic in the auction scene. If the reserve is realistic, then the final fine-tuned guidelines will be at a level to encourage would-be-bidders to attend. If, during the auction, it becomes obvious to bidders that they are likely to be successful, then they are often encouraged to bid again and a little higher than wisdom would suggest. A high reserve and no sale kills the interest. The market for the property is depressed. The vendor is no longer in a strong position when the auctioneer has to start negotiating a private treaty sale after the pressure in the auction room has been removed.

Agree your reserve before the auction day

Vendors must come to a decision on the minimum figure that they will accept and agree this with the auctioneer well before auction day.

Sellers frequently suggest that they sit in an obvious position in the sale room and give a nod to the auctioneer if the bidding has reached a price at which they find acceptable. In the context of a properly run auction, such an arrangement is not possible.

All the vendors are doing is putting off the decision until the last moment. They are misleading themselves if they believe they can assess the amount of genuine interest in the room at the precise moment the bids are taking place. The auctioneer needs the reserve fixed so that he can judiciously use bids taken off the chandelier made on behalf of the vendors to encourage bidders in the room and to maintain the rhythm of the sale. If the vendors insist on only giving authority by a nod in the room, they run a considerable risk of instructing the auctioneer to accept a bid which was made by the auctioneer on the vendor's behalf. This could happen especially if the bidding does not reach the reserve.

> **KEY POINT:** *The vendor and auctioneer will be wise to agree their reserve three or four days before the sale and certainly before the auctioneer goes onto the rostrum.*

> **KEY POINT:** *The vendor must remember, when settling the reserve with the auctioneer, that if a bid is received in the sale room at that amount or above, the lot will be sold without further reference to the vendor.*

The post-auction price

When the auction has taken place and the euphoria has died away, the owners of any unsold lot are in a weak negotiating position. It is then too late to indicate that they would have accepted one of the bids in the room.

Lower your sights on price

The vendor must realise that when a bidder leaves, their enthusiasm to buy the property has waned. Because the lot did not sell, the bidders reconsider their judgement and revise their views. The auction house will be in a position to contact all the people who registered interest at the auction, but may not be in a position to pinpoint the highest bidder. The vendor and the auctioneer must then wait until a bidder indicates a renewal of interest. The balance of the bargaining positions has been reversed.

> **KEY POINT:** *A vendor should not expect the highest bidder necessarily to repeat his bid at the same amount in the post-auction negotiations.*

Nevertheless, the auction experience has enabled both the seller and the auctioneer to review their opinions of value. At this time the vendor should think about accepting a price lower than the reserve. In fact, the vendor should have thought about having a lower reserve on the day, but it is now too late because this is the time when bargain hunters, dealers and entrepreneurs look to purchase withdrawn lots at bargain basement prices. Table 8.4 illustrates possible post-auction prices for withdrawn lots.

Table 8.4 Post-auction prices for withdrawn lots

	Fine-tuned guidelines	Actual reserve	Post-auction price
£4,500–£6,000	£4,500–£5,500	£4,500	£3,500
£6,500–£8,000	£6,500–£7,500	£7,000	£5,500
£9,000–£12,000	£9,500–£10,500	£9,500	£8,000
£19,000–£24,000	£19,500–£21,000	£20,000	£17,500
£28,000–£35,000	£29,500–£31,500	£30,000	£27,000
£45,000–£55,000	£49,000–£52,000	£50,000	£45,000
£70,000–£80,000	£74,000–£79,000	£75,000	£65,000
Around £100,000	£95,000–£105,000	£100,000	£90,000
£140,000–£160,000	£145,000–£155,000	£145,000	£130,000
£180,000–£220,000	£195,000–£210,000	£195,000	£175,000

> **KEY POINT:** *The vendor and auctioneers should aim for a reserve price strategy which gives them a high chance of selling on the auction day.*

Disclosing personal interest

The Estate Agents Act

The Estate Agents (Undesirable Practices) Order 1991 Statutory Instrument 1991 No. 861 lists various undesirable practices in the view of the Department of Trade and Industry that could be entered into by estate agents. In particular, in section two of this Statutory Instrument, the parliamentary under-secretary of state indicates:

For the purposes of section 3(1)(d) of the Act the following practices in relation to estate agency work are hereby declared undesirable that is to say as regards – (a) the disclosure of personal interest, any failure to disclose that interest is described in Schedule 1 to this order; ...

Schedule 1 reads as follows:

Disclosure of Personal Interest

Failure by an estate agent;

1 To make disclosure his personal interests as required by section 2(1) of the Act promptly and in writing.
2 To disclose to his client promptly and in writing that: (a) he himself has, or is seeking to acquire, beneficial interest in the land or in the proceeds of sale of any interest in the land; or ...

Although in this context the clause appears only to affect estate agents, the definition of 'estate agents' for the purpose of the Estate Agents Act is particularly broad. The legislation also includes persons who are connected to estate agents. Vendors must be certain that they do not fall within these definitions or if they do, that the interest is disclosed in the auction catalogue.

Section 21(i) provides for those engaged in estate agency work to disclose their personal interest and reads:

A person who is engaged in estate agency work (in this section referred to as an 'Estate Agent') and has a personal interest in any land shall not enter into

negotiations with any person with respect to the acquisition or disposal by that person of any interest in that land until the estate agent has disclosed to that person the nature and extent of his personal interest.

Section 32 defines those that are regarded as being connected to an estate agent and required to disclose their connection.

32- (1) In this Act 'associate' includes a business associate and otherwise has the meaning given by the following provisions of this section.

(2) A person is an associate of another if he is the spouse or a relative of that other or of a business associate of that other

(3) In subsection (2) above 'relative' means brother, sister, uncle, aunt, nephew, niece, lineal ancestor or linear descendant, and references to a spouse include a former spouse and a reputed spouse; and for the purposes of this subsection a relationship shall be established as if an illegitimate child or step-child of a person had been a child born to him in wedlock.

(4) A body corporate is an associate of another body corporate

   (a) if the same person is a controller of both, or a person is a controller of one and persons who are his associates, or he and persons who are his associates, are controllers of the other; or
   (b) if a group of two or more persons is a controller of each company, and the groups either consist of the same persons or could be regarded as consisting of the same persons by treating (in one or more cases) a member of either group as replaced by a person of whom he is an associate.

(5) An unincorporated association is an associate of another unincorporated association if any person

   (a) is an officer of both associations;
   (b) has the management or control of the activities of both associations; or
   (c) is an officer of one association and has the management or control of the activities of the other association.

(6) A partnership is an associate of another partnership if -

   (a) any person is a member of both partnerships; or
   (b) a person who is a member of one partnership is an associate of a member of the other partnership; or

(c) a member of one partnership has an associate who is also an associate of a member of the other partnership.

> **KEY POINT:** *Vendors must appreciate that if they are an 'associate' of the auctioneer the exact extent of their association must be detailed in the auction catalogue and the auctioneer must be encouraged to draw attention to that note before the lot is offered on auction day.*

When should a vendor accept an offer before the auction?

Having made the decision to include a property in an auction, the vendor should not be dissuaded from this course too easily. It must be assumed that the decision was correct in the first place. Nevertheless, there are various factors to consider if a prior offer is received.

How great is the interest?

The auction house will have been monitoring the extent of interest shown by the public in every lot. This does not mean that they will be aware of every single enquirer who has a specific interest in your property since the enquirers often do not disclose it. However, the auction house should be aware of the number of people who have chosen to make a detailed inspection of property.

> **KEY POINT:** *Prior interest cannot be guaranteed to produce bidders on sale day.*

How big is the offer?

Offers can be tempting. For attractive lots they may be well above the upper guideline. For less attractive lots they may be only close to the bottom guideline but at a figure which the vendor will find acceptable. If the amount of interest shown on the property has been very limited, then the auctioneer and the seller must consider whether it is better to accept the offer than to risk selling at a reduced figure with difficult negotiations after the sale. On the other hand, the figure may be one which is acceptable to the vendor and the auctioneer can vouch that there has been very little other interest in the lot.

> **KEY POINT:** *Any prior offer at or close to the reserve price must be considered very favourably. Obviously the vendor should consider very carefully the advice put forward by the auctioneer or his firm.*

Exchanging contracts

When a vendor has accepted a prior offer, the auctioneer will insist that contracts or memoranda are exchanged with the buyer before the auction. Many auctioneers have a deadline for exchange of such contracts two or three days before the auction, so that they have time to announce the sale has taken place and to save any other would-be-bidders attending the auction, seeking to purchase the lot that has already been sold.

> **KEY POINT:** *If contracts or memoranda have not been exchanged before the auctioneer walks onto the rostrum, the property should still be offered whatever undertakings have been given by the prior buyer.*

LOT 468

Raised Ground Floor Flat, 26 Ryecroft Road, Hither Green, London SE13

BY ORDER OF MORTGAGEES IN POSSESSION

A Leasehold Raised Ground Floor Studio Flat

TENURE Leasehold. The property is held on a lease for a term of 99 years from 25th December 1988 (thus having approximately 94 years unexpired) at a current ground rent of £50 per annum.

LOCATION The property is situated on the north side of Ryecroft Road at the corner of its junction with Hither Green Lane, The amenities of Lewisham are within reach and British Rail services run from Hither Green Station.

DESCRIPTION The property comprises a studio flat situated on the raised ground floor of an end of terrace house arranged over raised ground, lower ground and two upper floors under a steep pitched slate clad roof.

ACCOMMODATION
Studio Room, Kitchen
Shower Room with WC and wash basin

A studio flat in south London for only £9,000.

How should the vendor behave at the auction?

Some vendors attend the auction of their lots, others do not. These are a set of guidelines if you choose to attend the auction:

- **Do not bid yourself unless agreed beforehand with the auctioneer.** The auctioneer will wish to judge if it is necessary to make bids on your behalf to maintain the momentum and rhythm of the bidding. If you bid as well, you may upset the strategy he is setting up since he may not recognise you and may believe you are a genuine bidder. Secondly, you are committing an offence under the Sale of Land by Auction Act 1867 which requires bids on behalf of the vendor to come from only one source. If you bid in addition to the auctioneer bidding on your behalf, the sale will be invalidated.

- **Do not wait to fix the reserve until the last minute.** The auctioneer may have between 50 and 200 lots to offer on the day. Different auctioneers may be on the rostrum at differing times. They need to have their documentation and strategies prepared well in advance. Your reserve should be confirmed in writing to the auction house at least three to four days before the sale. Imagine the chaos if all the vendors in a large auction chose to communicate the reserves in the final minutes before the sale began!

- **Do not change your mind about the reserve price.** Remember, if the bidding does not go well the auctioneer will make bids on your behalf. Do not suddenly change your mind, as the auction proceeds about the amount you will accept. You cannot try to change the reserve or communicate to the auctioneer from the audience that he should accept the highest bid he has received once the auction is under way.

- **Watch the audience and listen carefully to the auctioneer.** By watching the audience, you will know how much interest there is from bidders. Listen carefully to the auctioneer towards the end of the bidding so that you are positive either that the lot has been sold or that it has been withdrawn. If the property is withdrawn, by knowing the prices bid and the

amount of interest from bidders you will be in a better position to discuss a reduced asking price after the sale.

CHECKLIST:
What vendors should do at auction

1. Fix the reserve and notify the auction house well in advance. ☐

2. Do not try to talk to the auctioneer just before the auction, communicate through another member of staff. ☐

3. Do not interfere publically in the proceedings. ☐

4. Do not bid yourself unless agreed with the auctioneer beforehand. You could invalidate the sale. ☐

5. Remember, some bids (including the last one if your lot was withdrawn) may have been taken off the wall. ☐

6. Listen to the proceedings and bids carefully. Try to gauge the feeling in the room. ☐

7. Note if the gavel falls marking the sale of your lot or if the lot has been withdrawn. ☐

8. Do not expect to receive the deposit yourself. ☐

9. Leave the paperwork to the auction house or your solicitor. ☐

10. Do not celebrate prematurely but do not hesitate to congratulate your auctioneer and the staff. ☐

11. If your lot has been withdrawn, try to agree an early new selling price with the auction staff. ☐

What happens afterwards?

Your lot has been sold

If you were at the auction, you will be aware of the price at which the gavel fell. If you were not at the auction, the auctioneer will notify you soon after the sale of your success. Contracts or memoranda will have been exchanged in the sale room between the purchaser and your solicitor. If your solicitor attended the auction, he will leave the room with a copy of the contract or memoranda signed by the purchaser. If your solicitor was not present then the auctioneer will send the documents to him.

The purchaser will have paid a deposit of 10 per cent of the purchase price of the property (if VAT was due in addition, he will not have paid 10 per cent of this; VAT is only payable at completion). If the conditions of sale describe a minimum deposit of more than 10 per cent then that amount will have been paid.

> **KEY POINT:** *The money or cheque will have been collected by your solicitor or by the auction house depending upon what has been agreed in the auctioneer's terms. The terms should ensure that the money is retained in a clients' account and covered by suitable insurance bonding.*

Usually the deposit will be held on your behalf and the auctioneer will be entitled to charge his sale fee against it immediately. If the deposit is being held by your solicitor or the auctioneers, then the money will be passed to them, put on deposit if appropriate and covered by insurance bonding. If the conditions of sale provide for the money to be held on behalf of the purchaser, then appropriate arrangements will be made in a similar manner by the auctioneers or the solicitors. If the conditions of sale made special provisions for holding the deposit then the auctioneers or your solicitor will ensure that the necessary conditions are fulfilled.

> **KEY POINT:** *The onus is now on your solicitor to liaise with the solicitor acting on behalf of the successful bidder. Any wise seller will maintain close contact with his solicitor to check that everything is moving smoothly to completion.*

You are unlikely to need to contact the auctioneers again except perhaps to thank them for their services. If any hiccups do occur, then speak to the auctioneers who may be able to help. A receipt for

the auctioneer's sale fee and the balance of the deposit received (if the auction house was holding it) will be passed over to your solicitor in plenty of time for completion.

What happens if your lot is withdrawn?

If you are at the auction, you will know that the property has been withdrawn. If you were not, your auctioneer is likely to contact you within two or three days to discuss the next steps. Your auction house may already be negotiating with potential buyers who are seeking to purchase the lot afterwards. You need to discuss with the auction house, very soon after the auction, the price at which you are now willing to sell. You are in a weak bargaining position in any negotiations the auctioneers may be having with potential buyers. It may be that during those negotiations, or even before any start, you will need to agree the figure at which the property can now be sold.

> **KEY POINT:** *The first two or three days after an auction, where there has been a lot of withdrawn lots, frequently see frenetic negotiations.*

If your property is withdrawn you will normally have given the auctioneer authority to disclose your reserve and to sell at that reserve. If you are unwilling to sell at that reserve you should ensure your auctioneer is told immediately after the auction.

Should you put your lot in another auction?

This is a matter to be discussed with your auction house. Many auction houses are willing to offer a concessionary entry fee for lots that are offered for sale in a subsequent auction if there is not too long an interval between the two sales. A revision of the guidelines and the reserve will need to be discussed. The auctioneer should be in a position to discuss the wisdom of re-offering in the light of the vendor's new expectations on price.

> **KEY POINT:** *It is most unusual for a property to be offered a second time by the same auction house at the same reserve unless there has been a change in the market value levels in the interim.*

When does the vendor get paid?

Conditions of sale usually state that completion will take place 28 days after the auction. In normal circumstances, your solicitor should ensure that completion takes place on that day and that the balance of the proceeds is paid over to the vendor very quickly thereafter. If there are disputes between contract and completion, these may cause delays. Very occasionally, purchasers are not in funds to complete on time and can use bureaucratic and systematic delays to hinder completion. If the vendor's solicitor doubts the willingness of the purchaser to complete on the day set out for completion, a notice to complete can be served on the purchaser. The auctioneer is likely to have passed over the balance of the deposit (after deducting sale fees) in plenty of time. The vendor will not normally be able to collect this amount until completion has taken place. Any delays can be kept to a minimum if the vendor liaises frequently with his solicitor. Most contracts allow for interest to be charged on the amount outstanding after 28 days from the date contracts are exchanged, if completion has not occurred.

How much does a vendor receive out of the purchase price?

The vendor's net proceeds from the sale of a property that reached £80,000 at auction is given in Table 8.5. This example assumes that VAT is chargeable on the

LOT 190

Flat 46, Pullman Court, Streatham Hill, Streatham, London SW2

BY ORDER OF MORTGAGEES IN POSSESSION

A Leasehold Studio Flat

TENURE
Leasehold. The property is held on a lease for a term of 125 years from 25th December 1976 (thus having approximately 108 years unexpired) at a current ground rent of £10 per annum.

LOCATION
The property is situated on the east side of Streatham Hill to the south of its junction with Christchurch Road (A205). Local amenities are available along Streatham High Road and British Rail services run from Streatham Hill Station.

DESCRIPTION
The property comprises a self-contained studio flat situated on the second floor of a purpose built block arranged over ground and four upper floors. The flat benefits from a passenger lift, residents parking and communal gardens.

ACCOMMODATION
Studio Room
Kitchen
Bathroom with WC and wash basin

Who said you could not afford a London residence? £11,000 was all it took to obtain this studio flat.

Table 8.5 The vendor's net proceeds for a property selling for £80,000

Purchase price		£80,000
Plus VAT received		£14,000
Total proceeds		**£94,000**
Less:		
VAT payable	£14,000	
Credit to purchaser for tenants advance payments	£2,000	
Auctioneer's entry and sale fees and VAT	£3,220	
Solicitor's fees and VAT for attending at auction (if appropriate)	£294	
Solicitor's fees and VAT for dealing with contract and conveyance	£353	
Local search fees	£25	
Repayment of grants and charges	£1,200	
Planning application fees	£500	
Building regulation application fees	£250	
Covenant buyout	£3,000	
Contractors bill for making the property secure	£250	
Champagne	£25	
	£25,117	
Net proceeds		**£68,883**

Table 8.6 Vendor's net proceeds for properties selling from £350.

| The purchase price | Auctioneers' fees | | | Solicitors attending auction incl VAT | Solicitors' fees | Plus VAT | Vendors' expenses | Possible net proceeds |
	Entry fee (minimum £400)	Commission at 3% (minimum £600)	Plus VAT					
£350	£400	£600	£175	–	£200	£35	£150	(£1,210)
£500	£400	£600	£175	–	£200	£35	£150	(£1,060)
£1,000	£400	£600	£175	–	£200	£35	£150	(£560)
£3,000	£400	£600	£175	£176	£200	£35	£150	£1,264
£5,000	£400	£600	£175	£176	£200	£35	£150	£3,264
£8,500	£400	£600	£175	£176	£200	£35	£150	£6,764
£12,000	£400	£600	£175	£176	£250	£44	£250	£10,105
£20,000	£400	£600	£175	£176	£250	£44	£250	£18,105
£30,000	£400	£900	£228	£176	£300	£53	£250	£27,693
£50,000	£400	£1,500	£332	£294	£300	£53	£250	£46,872
£100,000	£400	£3,000	£595	£294	£550	£96	£350	£94,715
£150,000	£400	£4,500	£858	£294	£600	£105	£350	£142,893
£250,000	£400	£7,500	£1,383	£470	£1,000	£175	£450	£238,622
£500,000	£400	£15,000	£2,695	£470	£2,000	£350	£550	£478,535
£1,000,000	£400	£30,000	£5,320	£470	£3,500	£612	£650	£959,048

purchase price. If VAT is not chargeable, the sum can be deducted from the purchase price but not the auctioneer's and solicitor's fees. Table 8.6 gives details of the vendor's net proceeds for properties selling from £350 up to £1,000,000.

AUCTION CHECKLIST:
For the vendor

If you are thinking about bringing your property to auction, the following checklist will help you tackle it step by step.

1 Is your property right for offering by auction? ☐

2 Choose your auction house carefully after some research. ☐

3 Note your chosen auctioneer's terms carefully. ☐

4 Check on the amount of fees and when they are due. ☐

5 Check on the nature of the agency. ☐

6 Look through the terms and any supporting literature in great detail. ☐

7 Make sure the terms and the nature of the agency are in writing. ☐

8 Instruct your solicitor fully and early. ☐

9 Liaise thoroughly with the auctioneer and your solicitor to ensure the details in the catalogue are correct and not misleading. ☐

10 Agree the guideline figures with the auctioneer. ☐

11 Discuss the revision of those guidelines as marketing proceeds. ☐

12 Check the details of your property are correct after you have been provided with a copy of the printed catalogue. ☐

13 Be sure you have disclosed any personal interest under the Estate Agents Act. ☐

14 Discuss the wisdom or otherwise of accepting any pre-auction offers if any have been received by your auctioneer. ☐

15 If you accept a pre-auction offer make sure your solicitor and the purchaser move to a quick exchange of contracts. ☐

16 Fix the reserve at least three or four days before the sale. Do not leave it until the last minute. ☐

17 If you attend the sale do not bid yourself unless you have made a special arrangement with the auctioneer. ☐

18 Listen to the bidding carefully and watch the audience to assess the amount of interest in your lot. ☐

19 If you are sure the lot has sold, go out and celebrate but remember approximately one in every hundred lots do not proceed to completion, even when the gavel has fallen in the auction room. ☐

20 If your lot has not sold, remember the auctioneer will usually have authority to sell it at your reserve price thereafter. Review this instruction if you feel it is not appropriate. ☐

21 Liaise with your auctioneer in the period after the auction to consider changing your reserve and to help him in post-auction negotiations. ☐

22 In normal circumstances, expect your solicitor to complete the sale and for you to receive your money in approximately 28 days. ☐

9 'We bought at auction' — what buyers have to say

By now, you will be well-equipped to face your first auction. But how have others fared with the auction process? To give you a flavour of what it is like, the following people's experiences illustrate what they thought and felt about buying a property at auction.

1. Caroline Titley bought two semi-detached Victorian houses for her business

Caroline Titley runs her own business in Ashton-under Lyme. She needed a property for her business and decided it would be more advantageous to buy than to rent, as it was cheaper.

'I found the property from an estate agent, not the auctioneer. It is a Victorian property comprising two semi-detached houses and is around 150 years old. We bought the whole property and inhabit one half for our business and have a tenant in the other half. This was the first property that my partner and I had bought at auction and we made the bids ourselves. We had been to an auction before, so we were familiar with the process.

It was originally offered for sale in one auction but failed to receive a single bid and was withdrawn. The agent said the owner was seeking an asking price of £85,000 and that it was going to auction again in three weeks' time. We thought we might get it cheaper at auction rather than negotiating the sale there and then.

At the second auction, I asked how much the reserve price was and was given a guideline figure of £70,000 to £75,000. We thought that given the lack of interest in the property at the first auction, if we bid up to the guideline then no one would bid any higher. The bidding process went smoothly. I wasn't too apprehensive about it and I had my business partner with me although he did not want to do the actual bidding when it came to it. It started at £70,000. I was so surprised when someone bid against me. It was all over in a matter of minutes, but I was equally surprised that just before the property reached £85,000 the other bidder dropped out.

'We didn't go over what we could afford'

In the end, we got it for the price we were prepared to pay and we didn't go over what we could afford. I was really pleased that we had acquired the property and I would certainly purchase commercial property at auction again and recommend others to use an auction to do the same.'

2. Don Lee paid 33% less buying his house at auction

Don Lee lives in Manchester and has bought two residential houses at separate auctions.

'I was living in Manchester and noticed there was a number of run-down properties in the inner city part of Manchester. They had been built as private houses in 1982/3 and there had been problems with them simply because the people who had bought them could not pay their mortgage. They were quickly vandalised and went down in value like the rest of the property market.

I noticed that the auctioneers had managed to get hold of a few of these properties and they were going for about £14,000 which was pretty good even then. I waited for the best of the houses to come along which was an end one overlooking a public space with a pleasant view. I went to auction a couple of times before to get the feel for it and to see what the prices were like. I thought just before Christmas would be a good time to buy because people haven't got a lot of spare money and have other things on their mind and as it turns out I was proved right.

'Closing Order' –

Where the local authority feels that a property is unsuitable for occupation, they issue a 'Closing Order' which prevents the property being used. It is often possible to agree a schedule of repairs with the local authority, upon completion of which they will allow the property to be used for occupation once more.

'Planning Brief' –

Certain planning authorities for particular sites or areas often prepare a 'brief' for that area indicating the type and nature of development which they will be inclined to permit.

LONDON

STRETTONS of E1 at New Connaught Rms, WC2, Apr 19

E1 — 18 Pevensey Hse, Ben Johnson Rd. S/C mais, 4 rms. L, P	**30,000**
50 Cephas Ave. End terr hse, 6 rms. Closing order. F, P	**53,000**
37 New Rd. Terr w/shop bdg. 2 floors. Let £2,068 pa. 2 floors, 388 & 410 sq ft with P. F	**55,000**
E3 — 104 Fairfoot Rd. Bdg plot. PP 2 flats. F, P	**15,000**
111 Grove Rd. Terr hse, 5 rms. F, P	**54,000**
13 Grafton Hse, Wellington Way. 2nd floor, S/C flat, 3 rms. L, P	**17,500**
E5 — 5/7 Chatsworth Rd. 2 adj shops. RUP 2 S/C flats, 4 & 5 rms. Let £3,120 PAX. Closing Order. F	**40,000**
4 Cricketfield Rd. S/C flat, 2 rms. L, P	**25,500**
19 Elderfield Rd. End terr hse, 9 rms. PP flat, mais, 2 garages. Closing order. F, P	**43,000**
30 Glenarm Rd. 2nd floor, S/C studio flat. L, P	**15,500**
103 Mount Pleasant Lane. S/C flat, 3 rms. L, P	**23,000**
E6 — 132 Charlemont Rd. RUP S/C flat, 2 rms. L, P	**20,500**
58 Dickens Rd. End terr hse, 3 bed. F, P	**35,000**
130 Masterman Rd. Terr hse, 2 bed. F, P	**36,500**
St Andrews Hall, Roman Rd. Derelict hall, site 0.10 a. Planning brief for 2 hses. F, P	**31,000**
E7 — 165 Capel Rd. Corner bdg, 6 rms, part used as clinic. PP 2 hses & garages on rear land. F, P	**66,500**
7 Neville Rd. End terr bdg as 3 S/C flats. 1 LGR, 1 studio flat & 1 x 3 rms with P. For completion. F	**36,500**
75 Pevensey Rd. Terr hse as 2 flats, 3 rms. F, P	**38,000**
7 Reginald Rd. Corner shop, rear rm. RUP, 3 rms. F, P	**35,000**
21 Shaftesbury Rd. Terr hse, 2 bed. F, P	**35,500**
E8 — 234 Dalston Lane. 4 storey hse, 10 rms, 2 store rms. F, P	**55,000**
376C Kingsland Rd. RUP S/C mais, 3 rms. L, P	**22,000**
113 Shacklewell Lane. Shop, rear rm. S/C mais, 3 rms. P	**28,500**
E10 — 287 High Rd. Shop, rear rm, basement, mais, 4 rms, garage. F, P	**60,000**
E12 — 32 Salisbury Rd. Terr hse, 3 bed. F, P	**36,500**
E13 — 198 Balaam St. S/C flat, 3 rms. L, P	**18,000**
163 Grange Rd. Terr hse, 6 rms. F, P	**34,500**
50 London Rd. S/C flat, 2 rms. L, P	**14,000**
31 Maud Rd. Terr hse as S/C flat, 3 rms & S/C mais, 3 rms. F, P	**41,000**
Tabernacle Ave. Site 0.16 a. Planning brief for development. F, P	**16,000**
E14 — 46 Chapel House St. Terr hse, 3 bed. F, P	**60,000**

Illustration 8. Estates Gazette auction results

122

'I was surprised they did not go for more'

There was a certain tension at the auction. However, the property failed to reach its reserve and was withdrawn at auction. I negotiated a price of £12,000 for it after the auction and it only needed another £1,000 to put it into liveable condition. I was surprised they did not go for more.

The auction itself was run very well. I had been before so I knew they were good and entertaining (it's the best bit of free entertainment in Manchester). I did all the legal side myself and the conveyancing.

'I paid 33% less'

The main advantage to me of buying at auction has got to be the price. Compared with the prices going through high street estate agents I paid 33% less. That is perhaps a bit more than usual – I think 25% is a bit nearer the mark. However, I realised I was buying a vandalised property and knew what I was getting. I didn't buy a pig in a poke – you can do that – there is always that risk.

I bought another house recently and was surprised when it was knocked down to me for £24,000 as I was expecting to pay up to £25,000. I did think at one stage that I might not get the property although I was prepared to bid £1000 more than I paid for it. For this second house, similar properties are costing almost twice as much. I was surprised it went for what it did do. I was well pleased with it.

'I would definitely buy another property at auction'

I would definitely buy another property at auction and have no hesitation recommending others to buy at auction provided they understand the risks and have no worries. You must ask why the property is going for sale at auction and what (if anything) is wrong with it and satisfy yourselves that you are not buying a pig in a poke. You have got to be prepared to do your own research. For example, I had to check that I was not buying a property over a coal mine. I knew the reason for the sale – that the property was foreclosed and put up for auction by a building society.'

3. Michael Kirby is a chartered surveyor who buys commercial property for clients

'The latest property I bought was a Railtrack goods yard which I was buying on behalf of tenants as an investment property. It was let to them on short leases. The property is used for open storage of coal, pallets, and cars.

I have bought one or two properties before, on behalf of clients and I made all the bidding myself.

We did try to bid for the property beforehand. This was unsuccessful and it was suggested that we go to the auction where the price we got it for was slightly above what we originally bid beforehand. If you bid beforehand, you can open up a situation and show your hand so you must be careful.

I didn't start the bidding. There were one or two other bidders lower down. I let them have their say and then came in at the end. We bid twice and the second time it stopped, my bid being the highest bid. I thought the auctioneer might withdraw it because it was only slightly higher than we had bid before the auction. I thought it probably hadn't reached the reserve. But then the gavel came down and I knew it was ours.

From a purchaser's point of view, I would have said you were going to get quite a good deal at auction, particularly in this climate. It all depends on the day because you never know who else is going to bid. In our case we didn't think there would be anyone else interested, but there was. We assume that we bought it at the reserve.

'I always try to do a deal beforehand'

I always try to do a deal beforehand because you never know what opposition you are going to come up against at auction. But you should never show your hand in case it does go to auction. The vendor is generally only going to accept a higher price before the auction.

For a house or a plot of land that is good you can be outbid if people get carried away. The professional who is buying property will not get

LOT 150
21 Marsala Road, Lewisham, London SE13
BY ORDER OF MORTGAGEES IN POSSESSION

A Freehold Mid Terrace House

TENURE
Freehold

LOCATION
The property is located on the east side of Marsala Road close to its junction with Ellerdale Street. The local amenities and shopping facilities of Lewisham are within reach. Communications exist via Ladywell British Rail Station, the A20 and the A2 to Central London and the M2 motorway.

DESCRIPTION
The property comprises a mid terrace house arranged over ground and first floors with gardens to both the front and rear.

ACCOMMODATION

Ground Floor	First Floor
Two Reception Rooms	Three Bedrooms
Kitchen/Breakfast Room	Bathroom with WC
Separate WC	

A south London family residence for under £50,000? This could have been yours for £46,000.

carried away but the average punter can tend to get carried away quite easily.

You can sometimes get a better deal at auction especially from lots that get withdrawn. Once you have reached your highest price you hope that the property hasn't reached the vendor's reserve and you can do a deal afterwards. You can get quite good deals that way.

Years ago it wasn't the done thing to buy property at auction but now it is more the norm especially on repossessions and investments. It's a quick way to buy a property. It gets the deal done.'

4. Michael Roe has bought two houses successfully at auction

'It is usually cheaper to buy property at auction'

'I bought a two-up, two-down terrace. I saw the property originally from the auctioneer's catalogue and went to view it from that. I have bought three properties at auction and so I was fairly familiar with the procedures. The great advantage to me is that it is usually cheaper to buy property at auction.

I have bought properties that are in some state of disrepair. They always wanted modernising and bringing up to date. In deciding what price to bid I tend to take an overall view. I check local sale prices and work out how much it will cost me to bring it up to date. I am usually prepared to pay so much at auction and if it goes for that price, I will buy it.

You always feel a little apprehensive before you go in. You go in with nothing and come home with something else. It was a fair investment, but it wasn't a big enough sum to worry me very much. The ones I've gone for I've got. I didn't feel I was going to lose the property during the auction.

With the latest one, I waited until the other bids had been made and then came in at the end. I only made one bid, and that was the last bid that succeeded. I was pleased to get it.

Buying at auction is very straightforward. If I could see houses that were being sold at comparable prices in comparable areas I would buy privately. But buying at auction is a way of ensuring I don't have to pay more than I need to pay. You want to make sure you acquire your property at a bargain level and auctions are the way.'

Appendices

AGREEMENT
(Incorporating the Standard Conditions of Sale (Third Edition))

Agreement date	: 29th September 2000
Seller	: James Middleton, 4 Howarth Street, Clacton
Buyer	: John Crow 8 Barking Way Cambridge
Property (freehold/leasehold)	: 76 Oldview Winterleigh Devon
Root of title/Title Number	: 638291
Incumbrances on the Property	: None
Title Guarantee (full/limited)	: Full
Completion date	: 29th October 2000
Contract rate	: 4% over Barclays Base Rate
Purchase price	: £16,000
Deposit	: £1,600
Amount payable for chattels	: Nil
Balance	: £14,400

The Seller will sell and the Buyer will buy the Property for the Purchase price.
The Agreement continues on the back page.

WARNING	Signed
This is a formal document, designed to create legal rights and legal obligations. Take advice before using it.	Seller/Buyer

Appendix 1. Agreement (Incorporating the Standard Conditions of Sales (Third Edition))

STANDARD CONDITIONS OF SALE (THIRD EDITION)

(NATIONAL CONDITIONS OF SALE 23rd EDITION, LAW SOCIETY'S CONDITIONS OF SALE 1995)

1. GENERAL

1.1 Definitions

1.1.1 In these conditions:
- (a) "accrued interest" means:
  - (i) if money has been placed on deposit or in a building society share account, the interest actually earned
  - (ii) otherwise, the interest which might reasonably have been earned by depositing the money at interest on seven days' notice of withdrawal with a clearing bank
  less, in either case, any proper charges for handling the money
- (b) "agreement" means the contractual document which incorporates these conditions, with or without amendment
- (c) "banker's draft" means a draft drawn by and on a clearing bank
- (d) "clearing bank" means a bank which is a member of CHAPS Limited
- (e) "completion date", unless defined in the agreement, has the meaning given in condition 6.1.1
- (f) "contract" means the bargain between the seller and the buyer of which these conditions, with or without amendment, form part
- (g) "contract rate", unless defined in the agreement, is the Law Society's interest rate from time to time in force
- (h) "lease" includes sub-lease, tenancy and agreement for a lease or sub-lease
- (i) "notice to complete" means a notice requiring completion of the contract in accordance with condition 6
- (j) "public requirement" means any notice, order or proposal given or made (whether before or after the date of the contract) by a body acting on statutory authority
- (k) "requisition" includes objection
- (l) "solicitor" includes barrister, duly certificated notary public, recognised licensed conveyancer and recognised body under sections 9 or 32 of the Administration of Justice Act 1985.
- (m) "transfer" includes conveyance and assignment
- (n) "working day" means any day from Monday to Friday (inclusive) which is not Christmas Day, Good Friday or a statutory Bank Holiday.

1.1.2 When used in these conditions the terms "absolute title" and "office copies" have the special meanings given to them by the Land Registration Act 1925.

1.2 Joint parties

If there is more than one seller or more than one buyer, the obligations which they undertake can be enforced against them all jointly or against each individually.

1.3 Notices and documents

1.3.1 A notice required or authorised by the contract must be in writing.

1.3.2 Giving a notice or delivering a document to a party's solicitor has the same effect as giving or delivering it to that party.

1.3.3 Transmission by fax is a valid means of giving a notice or delivering a document where delivery of the original document is not essential.

1.3.4 Subject to conditions 1.3.5 to 1.3.7, a notice is given and a document delivered when it is received.

1.3.5 If a notice or document is received after 4.00pm on a working day, or on a day which is not a working day, it is to be treated as having been received on the next working day.

1.3.6 Unless the actual time of receipt is proved, a notice or document sent by the following means is to be treated as having been received before 4.00pm on the day shown below:
- (a) by first-class post: two working days after posting
- (b) by second-class post: three working days after posting
- (c) through a document exchange: on the first working day after the day on which it would normally be available for collection by the addressee.

1.3.7 Where a notice or document is sent through a document exchange, then for the purposes of condition 1.3.6 the actual time of receipt is:
- (a) the time when the addressee collects it from the document exchange or, if earlier
- (b) 8.00am on the first working day on which it is available for collection at that time.

1.4 VAT

1.4.1 An obligation to pay money includes an obligation to pay any value added tax chargeable in respect of that payment.

1.4.2 All sums made payable by the contract are exclusive of value added tax.

2. FORMATION

2.1 Date

2.1.1 If the parties intend to make a contract by exchanging duplicate copies by post or through a document exchange, the contract is made when the last copy is posted or deposited at the document exchange.

2.1.2 If the parties' solicitors agree to treat exchange as taking place before duplicate copies are actually exchanged, the contract is made as so agreed.

2.2 Deposit

2.2.1 The buyer is to pay or send a deposit of 10 per cent of the purchase price no later than the date of the contract. Except on a sale by auction, payment is to be made by banker's draft or by a cheque drawn on a solicitors' clearing bank account.

2.2.2 If before completion date the seller agrees to buy another property in England and Wales for his residence, he may use all or any part of the deposit as a deposit in that transaction to be held on terms to the same effect as this condition and condition 2.2.3.

2.2.3 Any deposit or part of a deposit not being used in accordance with condition 2.2.2 is to be held by the seller's solicitor as stakeholder on terms that on completion it is paid to the seller with accrued interest.

2.2.4 If a cheque tendered in payment of all or part of the deposit is dishonoured when first presented, the seller may, within seven working days of being notified that the cheque has been dishonoured, give notice to the buyer that the contract is discharged by the buyer's breach.

2.3 Auctions

2.3.1 On a sale by auction the following conditions apply to the property and, if it is sold in lots, to each lot.

2.3.2 The sale is subject to a reserve price.

2.3.3 The seller, or a person on his behalf, may bid up to the reserve price.

2.3.4 The auctioneer may refuse any bid.

2.3.5 If there is a dispute about a bid, the auctioneer may resolve the dispute or restart the auction at the last undisputed bid.

3. MATTERS AFFECTING THE PROPERTY

3.1 Freedom from incumbrances

3.1.1 The seller is selling the property free from incumbrances, other than those mentioned in condition 3.1.2.

3.1.2 The incumbrances subject to which the property is sold are:
- (a) those mentioned in the agreement
- (b) those discoverable by inspection of the property before the contract
- (c) those the seller does not and could not know about
- (d) entries made before the date of the contract in any public register except those maintained by HM Land Registry or its Land Charges Department or by Companies House
- (e) public requirements.

3.1.3 After the contract is made, the seller is to give the buyer written details without delay of any new public requirement and of anything in writing which he learns about concerning any incumbrances subject to which the property is sold.

3.1.4 The buyer is to bear the cost of complying with any outstanding public requirement and is to indemnify the seller against any liability resulting from a public requirement.

3.2 Physical state

3.2.1 The buyer accepts the property in the physical state it is in at the date of the contract unless the seller is building or converting it.

3.2.2 A leasehold property is sold subject to any subsisting breach of a condition or tenant's obligation relating to the physical state of the property which renders the lease liable to forfeiture.

3.2.3 A sub-lease is granted subject to any subsisting breach of a condition or tenant's obligation relating to the physical state of the property which renders the seller's own lease liable to forfeiture.

3.3 Leases affecting the property

3.3.1 The following provisions apply if the agreement states that any part of the property is sold subject to a lease.

3.3.2
- (a) The seller having provided the buyer with full details of each lease or copies of the documents embodying the lease terms, the buyer is treated as entering into the contract knowing and fully accepting those terms
- (b) The seller is to inform the buyer without delay if the lease ends or if the seller learns of any application by the tenant in connection with the lease; the seller is then to act as the buyer reasonably directs, and the buyer is to indemnify him against all consequent loss and expense
- (c) The seller is not to agree to any proposal to change the lease terms without the consent of the buyer and is to inform the buyer without delay of any change which may be proposed or agreed
- (d) The buyer is to indemnify the seller against all claims arising from the lease after actual completion; this includes claims which are unenforceable against a buyer for want of registration
- (e) The seller takes no responsibility for what rent is lawfully recoverable, nor for whether or how any legislation affects the lease
- (f) If the let land is not wholly within the property, the seller may apportion the rent.

3.4 Retained land

3.4.1 The following provisions apply where after the transfer the seller will be retaining land near the property.

3.4.2 The buyer will have no right of light or air over the retained land, but otherwise the seller and the buyer will each have the rights over the land of the other which they would have had if they were two separate buyers to whom the seller had made simultaneous transfers of the property and the retained land.

3.4.3 Either party may require that the transfer contain appropriate express terms.

4. TITLE AND TRANSFER

4.1 Timetable

4.1.1 The following are the steps for deducing and investigating the title to the property to be taken within the following time limits:

Step	Time Limit
1. The seller is to send the buyer evidence of title in accordance with condition 4.2	Immediately after making the contract
2. The buyer may raise written requisitions	Six working days after either the date of the contract or the date of delivery of the seller's evidence of title on which the requisitions are raised whichever is the later
3. The seller is to reply in writing to any requisitions raised	Four working days after receiving the requisitions
4. The buyer may make written observations on the seller's replies	Three working days after receiving the replies

The time limit on the buyer's right to raise requisitions applies even where the seller supplies incomplete evidence of his title, but the buyer may, within six working days from delivery of any further evidence, raise further requisitions resulting from that evidence. On the expiry of the relevant time limit the buyer loses his right to raise requisitions or make observations.

4.1.2 The parties are to take the following steps to prepare and agree the transfer of the property within the following time limits:

Step	Time Limit
A. The buyer is to send the seller a draft transfer	At least twelve working days before completion date
B. The seller is to approve or revise that draft and either return it or retain it for use as the actual transfer	Four working days after delivery of the draft transfer
C. If the draft is returned the buyer is to send an engrossment to the seller	At least five working days before completion date

4.1.3 Periods of time under conditions 4.1.1 and 4.1.2 may run concurrently.

4.1.4 If the period between the date of the contract and completion date is less than 15 working days, the time limits in conditions 4.1.1 and 4.1.2 are to be reduced by the same proportion as that period bears to the period of 15 working days. Fractions of a working day are to be rounded down except that the time limit to perform any step is not to be less than one working day.

4.2 Proof of title

4.2.1 The evidence of registered title is office copies of the items required to be furnished by section 110(1) of the Land Registration Act 1925 and the copies, abstracts and evidence referred to in section 110(2).

4.2.2 The evidence of unregistered title is an abstract of the title, or an epitome of title with photocopies of the relevant documents.

4.2.3 Where the title to the property is unregistered, the seller is to produce to the buyer (without cost to the buyer):
- (a) the original of every relevant document, or
- (b) an abstract, epitome or copy with an original marking by a solicitor of examination either against the original or against an examined abstract or against an examined copy.

4.3 Defining the property

4.3.1 The seller need not:
- (a) prove the exact boundaries of the property
- (b) prove who owns fences, ditches, hedges or walls
- (c) separately identify parts of the property with different titles
further than he may be able to do from information in his possession.

4.3.2 The buyer may, if it is reasonable, require the seller to make or obtain, pay for and hand over a statutory declaration about facts relevant to the matters mentioned in condition 4.3.1. The form of the declaration is to be agreed by the buyer, who must not unreasonably withhold his agreement.

4.4 Rents and rentcharges

The fact that a rent or rentcharge, whether payable or receivable by the owner of the property, has been or will on completion be, informally apportioned is not to be regarded as a defect in title.

4.5 Transfer

4.5.1 The buyer does not prejudice his right to raise requisitions, or to require replies to any raised, by taking any steps in relation to the preparation or agreement of the transfer.

4.5.2 If the agreement makes no provision as to title guarantee, then subject to condition 4.5.3 the seller is to transfer the property with full title guarantee.

4.5.3 The transfer is to have effect as if the disposition is expressly made subject to all matters to which the property is sold subject under the terms of the contract.

4.5.4 If after completion the seller will remain bound by any obligation affecting the property, but the law does not imply any covenant by the buyer to indemnify the seller against liability for future breaches of it:
(a) the buyer is to covenant in the transfer to indemnify the seller against liability for any future breach of the obligation and to perform it from then on, and
(b) if required by the seller, the buyer is to execute and deliver to the seller on completion a duplicate transfer prepared by the buyer.

4.5.5 The seller is to arrange at his expense that, in relation to every document of title which the buyer does not receive on completion, the buyer is to have the benefit of:
(a) a written acknowledgement of his right to its production, and
(b) a written undertaking for its safe custody (except while it is held by a mortgagee or by someone in a fiduciary capacity).

5. PENDING COMPLETION

5.1 Responsibility for property

5.1.1 The seller will transfer the property in the same physical state as it was at the date of the contract (except for fair wear and tear), which means that the seller retains the risk until completion.

5.1.2 If at any time before completion the physical state of the property makes it unusable for its purpose at the date of the contract:
(a) the buyer may rescind the contract
(b) the seller may rescind the contract where the property has become unusable for that purpose as a result of damage against which the seller could not reasonably have insured, or which it is not legally possible for the seller to make good.

5.1.3 The seller is under no obligation to the buyer to insure the property.

5.1.4 Section 47 of the Law of Property Act 1925 does not apply.

5.2 Occupation by buyer

5.2.1 If the buyer is not already lawfully in the property, and the seller agrees to let him into occupation, the buyer occupies on the following terms.

5.2.2 The buyer is a licensee and not a tenant. The terms of the licence are that the buyer:
(a) cannot transfer it
(b) may permit members of his household to occupy the property
(c) is to pay or indemnify the seller against all outgoings and other expenses in respect of the property
(d) is to pay the seller a fee calculated at the contract rate on the purchase price (less any deposit paid) for the period of the licence
(e) is entitled to any rents and profits from any part of the property which he does not occupy
(f) is to keep the property in as good a state of repair as it was in when he went into occupation (except for fair wear and tear) and is not to alter it
(g) is to insure the property in a sum which is not less than the purchase price against all risks in respect of which comparable premises are normally insured
(h) is to quit the property when the licence ends.

5.2.3 On the creation of the buyer's licence, condition 5.1 ceases to apply, which means that the buyer then assumes the risk until completion.

5.2.4 The buyer is not in occupation for the purposes of this condition if he merely exercises rights of access given solely to do work agreed by the seller.

5.2.5 The buyer's licence ends on the earliest of: completion date, rescission of the contract or when five working days' notice given by one party to the other takes effect.

5.2.6 If the buyer is in occupation of the property after his licence has come to an end and the contract is subsequently completed he is to pay the seller compensation for his continued occupation calculated at the same rate as the fee mentioned in condition 5.2.2(d).

5.2.7 The buyer's right to raise requisitions is unaffected.

6. COMPLETION

6.1 Date

6.1.1 Completion date is twenty working days after the date of the contract but time is not of the essence of the contract unless a notice to complete has been served.

6.1.2 If the money due on completion is received after 2.00pm, completion is to be treated, for the purposes only of conditions 6.3 and 7.3, as taking place on the next working day.

6.1.3 Condition 6.1.2 does not apply where the sale is with vacant possession of the property or any part and the seller has not vacated the property or that part by 2.00pm on the date of actual completion.

6.2 Place

Completion is to take place in England and Wales, either at the seller's solicitor's office or at some other place which the seller reasonably specifies.

6.3 Apportionments

6.3.1 Income and outgoings of the property are to be apportioned between the parties so far as the change of ownership on completion will affect entitlement to receive or liability to pay them.

6.3.2 If the whole property is sold with vacant possession or the seller exercises his option in condition 7.3.4, apportionment is to be made with effect from the date of actual completion; otherwise, it is to be made from completion date.

6.3.3 In apportioning any sum, it is to be assumed that the seller owns the property until the end of the day from which apportionment is made and that the sum accrues from day to day at the rate at which it is payable on that day.

6.3.4 For the purpose of apportioning income and outgoings, it is to be assumed that they accrue at an equal daily rate throughout the year.

6.3.5 When a sum to be apportioned is not known or easily ascertainable at completion, a provisional apportionment is to be made according to the best estimate available. As soon as the amount is known, a final apportionment is to be made and notified to the other party. Any resulting balance is to be paid no more than ten working days later, and if not then paid the balance is to bear interest at the contract rate from then until payment.

6.3.6 Compensation payable under condition 5.2.6 is not to be apportioned.

6.4 Amount payable

The amount payable by the buyer on completion is the purchase price (less any deposit already paid to the seller or his agent) adjusted to take account of:
(a) apportionments made under condition 6.3
(b) any compensation to be paid or allowed under condition 7.3.

6.5 Title deeds

6.5.1 The seller is not to retain the documents of title after the buyer has tendered the amount payable under condition 6.4.

6.5.2 Condition 6.5.1 does not apply to any documents of title relating to land being retained by the seller after completion.

6.6 Rent receipts

The buyer is to assume that whoever gave any receipt for a payment of rent or service charge which the seller produces was the person or the agent of the person then entitled to that rent or service charge.

6.7 Means of payment

The buyer is to pay the money due on completion in one or more of the following ways:
(a) legal tender
(b) a banker's draft
(c) a direct credit to a bank account nominated by the seller's solicitor
(d) an unconditional release of a deposit held by a stakeholder.

6.8. Notice to complete

6.8.1 At any time on or after completion date, a party who is ready able and willing to complete may give the other a notice to complete.

6.8.2 A party is ready able and willing:
(a) if he could be, but for the default of the other party, and
(b) in the case of the seller, even though a mortgage remains secured on the property, if the amount to be paid on completion enables the property to be transferred freed of all mortgages (except those to which the sale is expressly subject).

6.8.3 The parties are to complete the contract within ten working days of giving a notice to complete, excluding the day on which the notice is given. For this purpose, time is of the essence of the contract.

6.8.4 On receipt of a notice to complete:
(a) if the buyer paid no deposit, he is forthwith to pay a deposit of 10 per cent
(b) if the buyer paid a deposit of less than 10 per cent, he is forthwith to pay a further deposit equal to the balance of that 10 per cent.

7. REMEDIES

7.1 Errors and omissions

7.1.1 If any plan or statement in the contract, or in the negotiations leading to it, is or was misleading or inaccurate due to an error or omission, the remedies available are as follows.

7.1.2 When there is a material difference between the description or value of the property as represented and as it is, the injured party is entitled to damages.

7.1.3 An error or omission only entitles the injured party to rescind the contract:
(a) where it results from fraud or recklessness, or
(b) where he would be obliged, to his prejudice, to transfer or accept property differing substantially (in quantity, quality or tenure) from what the error or omission had led him to expect.

7.2 Rescission

If either party rescinds the contract:
(a) unless the rescission is a result of the buyer's breach of contract the deposit is to be repaid to the buyer with accrued interest
(b) the buyer is to return any documents he received from the seller and is to cancel any registration of the contract.

7.3 Late completion

7.3.1 If there is default by either or both of the parties in performing their obligations under the contract and completion is delayed, the party whose total period of default is the greater is to pay compensation to the other party.

7.3.2 Compensation is calculated at the contract rate on the purchase price, or (where the buyer is the paying party) the purchase price less any deposit paid, for the period by which the paying party's default exceeds that of the receiving party, or, if shorter, the period between completion date and actual completion.

7.3.3 Any claim for loss resulting from delayed completion is to be reduced by any compensation paid under this contract.

7.3.4 Where the buyer holds the property as tenant of the seller and completion is delayed, the seller may give notice to the buyer, before the date of actual completion, that he intends to take the net income from the property until completion. If he does so, he cannot claim compensation under condition 7.3.1 as well.

7.4 After completion

Completion does not cancel liability to perform any outstanding obligation under this contract.

7.5 Buyer's failure to comply with notice to complete

7.5.1 If the buyer fails to complete in accordance with a notice to complete, the following terms apply.

7.5.2 The seller may rescind the contract, and if he does so:
(a) he may
(i) forfeit and keep any deposit and accrued interest
(ii) resell the property
(iii) claim damages
(b) the buyer is to return any documents he received from the seller and is to cancel any registration of the contract.

7.5.3 The seller retains his other rights and remedies.

7.6 Seller's failure to comply with notice to complete

7.6.1 If the seller fails to complete in accordance with a notice to complete, the following terms apply.

7.6.2 The buyer may rescind the contract, and if he does so:
(a) the deposit is to be repaid to the buyer with accrued interest
(b) the buyer is to return any documents he received from the seller and is, at the seller's expense, to cancel any registration of the contract.

7.6.3 The buyer retains his other rights and remedies.

8. LEASEHOLD PROPERTY

8.1 Existing leases

8.1.1 The following provisions apply to a sale of leasehold land.

8.1.2 The seller having provided the buyer with copies of the documents embodying the lease terms, the buyer is treated as entering into the contract knowing and fully accepting those terms.

8.1.3 The seller is to comply with any lease obligations requiring the tenant to insure the property.

8.2 New leases

8.2.1 The following provisions apply to a grant of a new lease.

8.2.2 The conditions apply so that:
"seller" means the proposed landlord
"buyer" means the proposed tenant
"purchase price" means the premium to be paid on the grant of a lease.

8.2.3 The lease is to be in the form of the draft attached to the agreement.

8.2.4 If the term of the new lease will exceed 21 years, the seller is to deduce a title which will enable the buyer to register the lease at HM Land Registry with an absolute title.

8.2.5 The buyer is not entitled to transfer the benefit of the contract.

8.2.6 The seller is to engross the lease and a counterpart of it and is to send the counterpart to the buyer at least five working days before completion date.

8.2.7 The buyer is to execute the counterpart and deliver it to the seller on completion.

8.3 Landlord's consent

8.3.1 The following provisions apply if a consent to assign or sub-let is required to complete the contract.

8.3.2 (a) The seller is to apply for the consent at his expense, and to use all reasonable efforts to obtain it
(b) The buyer is to provide all information and references reasonably required.

8.3.3 The buyer is not entitled to transfer the benefit of the contract.

8.3.4 Unless he is in breach of his obligation under condition 8.3.2, either party may rescind the contract by notice to the other party if three working days before completion date:
(a) the consent has not been given or
(b) the consent has been given subject to a condition to which the buyer reasonably objects.
In that case, neither party is to be treated as in breach of contract and condition 7.2 applies.

9. CHATTELS

9.1 The following provisions apply to any chattels which are to be sold.

9.2 Whether or not a separate price is to be paid for the chattels, the contract takes effect as a contract for sale of goods.

9.3 Ownership of the chattels passes to the buyer on actual completion.

SPECIAL CONDITIONS

1. (a) **This Agreement incorporates the Standard Conditions of Sale (Third Edition). Where there is a conflict between those Conditions and this Agreement, this Agreement prevails.**

    (b) **Terms used or defined in this Agreement have the same meaning when used in the Conditions.**

2. **The Property is sold subject to the Incumbrances on the Property and the Buyer will raise no requisitions on them.**

3. **Subject to the terms of this Agreement and to the Standard Conditions of Sale, the Seller is to transfer the property with the title guarantee specified on the front page.**

4. **The chattels on the Property and set out on any attached list are included in the sale.**

5. **The Property is sold with vacant possession on completion.**

(or) ~~The Property is sold subject to the following leases or tenancies~~

5.   Condition 2.2.2 and 2.2.3 are deleted. The Deposit is to be held by the Seller's solicitors as Agents for the Seller.

6.   The Seller has no personal knowledge of the property and the Buyer shall not raise any enquiries or requisitions relating thereto.

7.   The provisions of Standard Condition 5.1.2 shall not apply.

Seller's Solicitors   : Jones and Ashwood
Bradford Square
Clacton

Buyer's Solicitors   : Smith and Westby
Blake Crescent
Cambridge

CON. 29 (1994)
To be submitted in duplicate

ENQUIRIES OF LOCAL AUTHORITY (1994 EDITION)

Please type or use BLOCK LETTERS

Search No..
The Replies are given on the attached sheet(s)

Signed ....
                                    Proper Officer

Date...

A.
To

B.
Property

C.
Other roadways, footpaths and footways

D.
A plan in duplicate is attached   YES/NO

Optional Enquiries are to be answered (see Box G)   YES/NO

Additional Enquiries are attached in duplicate on a separate sheet   YES/NO

E.
Fees of £   are enclosed.

Signed :

Date :

Reference :

Tel. No. :

F.
Reply to

A. Enter name and address of District or Borough Council for the area. If the property is near a Local Authority boundary, consider raising certain Enquiries (e.g. road schemes) with the adjoining Council.

B. Enter address and description of the property. A plan in duplicate must be attached if possible and is insisted upon by some Councils. Without a plan, replies may be inaccurate or incomplete. A plan is essential for Optional Enquiries 18, 37 and 38.

C. Enter name and/or location of (and mark on plan, if possible) any other roadways, footpaths and footways (in addition to those entered in Box B) for Enquiry 3 and (if raised) Enquiries 19 and 20.

D. Answer every question. Any additional Enquiries must be attached on a separate sheet in duplicate and an additional fee will be charged for any which the Council is willing to answer.

E. Details of fees can be obtained from the Council or The Law Society.

F. Enter name and address of the person or firm lodging this form.

G. Tick which Optional Enquiries are to be answered.

PLEASE READ THE NOTES ON PAGE 4.

G.

	Optional Enquiries
	17. Road proposals by private bodies
	18. Public paths or byways
	19. Permanent road closure
	20. Traffic schemes
	21. Advertisements
	22. Completion notices
	23. Parks and countryside
	24. Pipelines
	25. Houses in multiple occupation
	26. Noise abatement
	27. Urban development areas
	28. Enterprise zones
	29. Inner urban improvement areas
	30. Simplified planning zones
	31. Land maintenance notices
	32. Mineral consultation areas
	33. Hazardous substance consents
	34. Environmental and pollution notices
	35. Food safety notices
	36. Radon gas precautions
	37. Sewers within the property
	38. Nearby sewers

Appendix 2.   Enquiries of Local Authority (1994 Edition)

PART I—STANDARD ENQUIRIES
(APPLICABLE IN EVERY CASE)

DEVELOPMENT PLANS PROVISIONS

Structure Plan([1])

1.1.1 What structure plan is in force?

1.1.2 Have any proposals been made public for the alteration of the structure plan?

Local Plans([1])([2])

1.2.1 What stage has been reached in the preparation of a local plan?

1.2.2 Have any proposals been made public for the alteration or replacement of a local plan?

Old Style Development Plan

1.3 What old style development plan is in force?

Unitary Development Plan([1])

1.4.1 What stage has been reached in the preparation of a unitary development plan?

1.4.2 Have any proposals been made public for the alteration or replacement of a unitary development plan?

Non-Statutory Plan

1.5.1 Have the Council made public any proposals for the preparation or modification of a non-statutory plan?

1.5.2 If so, what stage has been reached?

Policies or Proposals for the Property

1.6 Do any of the above plans (including any proposed alterations or replacements) indicate:
  (a) a designation of primary use or zoning for the property or the area, or
  (b) a specific proposal which includes the property?

Land required for Public Purposes

1.7 Is the property included in any of the categories of land specified in Schedule 13 paras 5 and 6 of the T&CP Act 1990?

DRAINAGE

Foul Drainage

2.1.1 To the Council's knowledge, does foul drainage from the property drain to a public sewer?([3])([4])

2.1.2 If yes, does the property drain into the public sewer through:
  (a) a private drain alone, or
  (b) a private drain and then a private sewer?([3])([4])([5])

Surface Water Drainage

2.2.1 To the Council's knowledge, does surface water from the property drain to:
  (a) a public sewer, or
  (b) a highway drain?([3])([4])([5])

2.2.2 If the answer to 2.2.1(a) or (b) is yes, does the surface water drain to it through:
  (a) a private drain alone, or
  (b) a private drain and then a private sewer?([3])([4])([5])

Statutory Agreements and Consents

2.3.1 Is there in force an agreement under s.22 of the Building Act 1984 for drainage of any part of the property in combination with another building through a private sewer?

2.3.2 Except as shown in the Official Certificate of Search, is there in force an agreement or consent under s.18 of the Building Act 1984 for the erection of a building or extension of a building over or in the vicinity of a drain, sewer or disposal main?([4])

Adoption Agreement

2.4.1 To the Council's knowledge, is any sewer serving, or which is proposed to serve, the property the subject of an agreement under s.104 of the Water Industry Act 1991 for the sewer to become vested in the sewerage undertaker?([5])([6])

2.4.2 If so, is such an agreement supported by a bond or other financial security?([6])

Sewerage Undertaker

2.5 Please state the name and address of the sewerage undertaker.

MAINTENANCE OF ROADS ETC.

Publicly Maintained

3.1 Are all the roadways, footpaths and footways referred to in Boxes B and C on page 1 maintainable at the public expense within the meaning of the Highways Act 1980?([7])

Resolutions to make up or adopt

3.2 If not, have the Council passed any resolution to:
  (a) make up any of those roadways, footpaths or footways at the cost of the frontagers, or
  (b) adopt any of them without cost to the frontagers?
  If so, please specify?([7]).

Adoption Agreements

3.3.1 Have the Council entered into any subsisting agreement relating to the adoption of any of those roadways, footpaths or footways? If so, please specify?([6])

3.3.2 Is any such agreement supported by a bond or other financial security?([6])

ROAD SCHEMES

Trunk and Special Roads

4.1.1 What orders, draft orders or schemes have been notified to the Council by the appropriate Secretary of State for the construction of a new trunk or special road, the centre line of which is within 200 metres of the property?

4.1.2 What proposals have been notified to the Council by the appropriate Secretary of State for:
  (a) the alteration or improvement of an existing road, involving the construction, whether or not within existing highway limits, of a subway, underpass, flyover, footbridge, elevated road or dual carriageway, the centre line of which is within 200 metres of the property, or
  (b) the construction of a roundabout (other than a mini-roundabout([8])), or the widening of an existing road by the construction of one or more additional traffic lanes, the limits of construction of which are within 200 metres of the property?

Other Roads

4.2 What proposals of their own([9]) have the Council approved for any of the following, the limits of construction of which are within 200 metres of the property:
  (a) the construction of a new road, or
  (b) the alteration or improvement of an existing road, involving the construction, whether or not within existing highway limits, of a subway, underpass, flyover, footbridge, elevated road, dual carriageway, the construction of a roundabout (other than a mini-roundabout([8])), or the widening of an existing road by the construction of one or more additional traffic lanes?

Road Proposals Involving Acquisition

4.3 What proposals have the Council approved, or have been notified to the Council by the appropriate Secretary of State, for highway construction or improvement that involve the acquisition of the property?

Road Proposals at Consultation Stage

4.4 What proposals have either the Secretary of State or the Council published for public consultation relating to:
  (a) the construction of a new road indicating a possible route the centre line of which would be likely to be within 200 metres of the property, or
  (b) the alteration or improvement of an existing road, involving the construction, whether or not within existing highway limits, of a subway, underpass, flyover, footbridge, elevated road, dual carriageway, the construction of a roundabout (other than a mini-roundabout([8])), or the widening of an existing road by the construction of one or more additional traffic lanes, the limits of construction of which would be likely to be within 200 metres of the property?

OUTSTANDING NOTICES

5. What outstanding statutory notices or informal notices have been issued by the Council under the Public Health Acts, Housing Acts, Highways Acts, Building Acts([10]) or Part III of the Environmental Protection Act 1990?
(This enquiry does not cover notices shown in the Official Certificate of Search or notices relating to matters covered by Enquiries 13 or, if raised, 31, 34 or 35.)

BUILDING REGULATIONS

6. What proceedings have the Council authorised in respect of an infringement of the Building Regulations?

---

(1) The present development plan system requires structure plans by the County Council in the non-metropolitan areas, as well as local plans by District Councils. County Councils also deal with minerals and waste plans. In Greater London and the metropolitan areas, Unitary Development Plans are prepared by the relevant London Borough or metropolitan district council.

(2) Local plan includes action area plan.

(3) Any reply will be based on the statutory sewer map provided to the Council by the sewerage undertaker and any other records which the Council may hold.

(4) If the reply is "Not Known", the enquiry should be raised directly with the sewerage undertaker.

(5) The sewerage undertaker is not responsible for the maintenance of private drains or private sewers connecting a property to the public sewer.

(6) An adoption or vesting agreement requires adoption or vesting to take place only when the developer complies with his obligations under that agreement and the enquirer should make separate enquiries as to such compliance and should satisfy himself as to the adequacy of any bond or other financial security for such compliance.

(7) An affirmative answer does not imply that the public highway directly abuts the boundary of the property.

(8) A mini-roundabout is a roundabout having a one-way circulatory carriageway around a flush or slightly raised circular marking less than 4 metres in diameter and with or without flared approaches.

(9) This enquiry refers to the Council's (including where appropriate the County Council's) own proposals but not those of other bodies or companies; the latter are covered by Enquiry 17 in Part II.

(10) For property in Greater London, this includes the London Building Acts.

PLANNING APPLICATIONS AND PERMISSIONS
Applications and Decisions
7.1 Please list:
  (a) any entries in the Register of planning applications and permissions,
  (b) any applications and decisions in respect of listed building consent, and
  (c) any applications and decisions in respect of conservation area consent.

Inspection and Copies
7.2 If there are any entries:
  (a) how can copies of the decisions be obtained?
  (b) where can the Register be inspected?

NOTICES UNDER PLANNING ACTS
Enforcement and Stop Notices
8.1.1 Please list any entries in the Register of enforcement notices and stop notices.
8.1.2 If there are any entries:
  (a) how can copies of the notices be obtained?
  (b) where can that Register be inspected?

Proposed Enforcement or Stop Notice
8.2 Except as shown in the Official Certificate of Search, or in reply to Enquiry 8.1.1., has any enforcement notice, listed building enforcement notice, or stop notice been authorised by the Council for issue or service (other than notices which have been withdrawn or quashed)?

Compliance with Enforcement Notices
8.3 If an enforcement notice or listed building enforcement notice has been served or issued, has it been complied with to the satisfaction of the Council?

Other Planning Notices
8.4 Have the Council served, or resolved to serve, any breach of condition or planning contravention notice or any other notice or proceedings relating to a breach of planning control?

Listed Building Repairs Notices, etc.
8.5.1 To the knowledge of the Council, has the service of a repairs notice been authorised?
8.5.2 If the Council have authorised the making of an order for the compulsory acquisition of a listed building, is a "minimum compensation" provision included, or to be included, in the order?
8.5.3 Have the Council authorised the service of a building preservation notice?[11]

DIRECTIONS RESTRICTING PERMITTED DEVELOPMENT
9. Except as shown in the Official Certificate of Search, have the Council resolved to make a direction to restrict permitted development?

ORDERS UNDER PLANNING ACTS
Revocation Orders etc.
10.1 Except as shown in the Official Certificate of Search, have the Council resolved to make any Orders revoking or modifying any planning permission or discontinuing an existing planning use?

Tree Preservation Order
10.2 Except as shown in the Official Certificate of Search, have the Council resolved to make any Tree Preservation Orders?

COMPENSATION FOR PLANNING DECISIONS
11. What compensation has been paid by the Council under s.114 of the T&CP Act 1990 for planning decisions restricting development other than new development?

CONSERVATION AREA
12. Except as shown in the Official Certificate of Search, is the area a conservation area?

COMPULSORY PURCHASE
13. Except as shown in the Official Certificate of Search, have the Council made any order (whether or not confirmed by the appropriate Secretary of State) or passed any resolution for compulsory acquisition which is still capable of being implemented?[12]

AREAS DESIGNATED UNDER HOUSING ACTS ETC.
Clearance
14.1 Has any programme of clearance for the area been:
  (a) submitted to the Department of the Environment, or
  (b) resolved to be submitted, or
  (c) otherwise adopted by resolution of the Council?
Housing
14.2 Except as shown in the Official Certificate of Search, have the Council resolved to define the area as designated for a purpose under the Housing Acts? If so, please specify the purpose.

SMOKE CONTROL ORDER
15. Except as shown in the Official Certificate of Search, have the Council made a smoke control order or resolved to make or vary a smoke control order for the area?

RAILWAYS
16. What proposals have been notified to the Council, and what proposals of their own have the Council approved, for the construction of a railway (including light railway or monorail) the centre line of which is within 200 metres of the property?

PART II—OPTIONAL ENQUIRIES
(APPLICABLE ONLY AS INDICATED ON PAGE ONE)
ROAD PROPOSALS BY PRIVATE BODIES
17. What proposals by others[13] have the Council approved for any of the following, the limits of construction of which are within 200 metres of the property:
  (a) the construction of a new road, or
  (b) the alteration or improvement of an existing road, involving the construction, whether or not within existing highway limits, of a subway, underpass, flyover, footbridge, elevated road, dual carriageway, the construction of a roundabout (other than a mini-roundabout[8]), or the widening of an existing road by the construction of one or more additional traffic lanes?

PUBLIC PATHS OR BYWAYS
18. Is any public path, bridleway or road used as a public path or byway which abuts on[7] or crosses the property shown in a definitive map or revised definitive map prepared under Part IV of the National Parks and Access to the Countryside Act 1949 or Part III of the Wildlife and Countryside Act 1981? If so, please mark its approximate route on the attached plan[14].

PERMANENT ROAD CLOSURE
19. What proposals have the Council approved for permanently stopping up or diverting any of the roads or footpaths referred to in Boxes B and C on page 1?

TRAFFIC SCHEMES
20. In respect of any of the roads referred to in Boxes B and C on page 1, what proposals have the Council approved, but have not yet put into operation, for:
  (a) waiting or loading restrictions,
  (b) one-way streets,
  (c) prohibition of driving,
  (d) pedestrianisation, or
  (e) vehicle width or weight restrictions?

ADVERTISEMENTS
Entries in Register
21.1.1 Please list any entries in the Register of applications, directions and decisions relating to consent for the display of advertisements.
21.1.2 If there are any entries, where can that Register be inspected?

Notices, Proceedings and Orders
21.2 Except as shown in the Official Certificate of Search:
  (a) has any notice been given by the Secretary of State or served in respect of a direction or proposed direction restricting deemed consent for any class of advertisement?
  (b) have the Council resolved to serve a notice requiring the display of any advertisement to be discontinued?
  (c) if a discontinuance notice has been served, has it been complied with to the satisfaction of the Council?
  (d) have the Council resolved to serve any other notice or proceedings relating to a contravention of the control of advertisements?
  (e) have the Council resolved to make an order for the special control of advertisements for the area?

COMPLETION NOTICES
22. Which of the planning permissions in force have the Council resolved to terminate by means of a completion notice under s.94 of the T&CP Act 1990?

---

(11) The Historic Buildings and Monuments Commission also have power to issue this type of notice for buildings in London Boroughs, and separate enquiry should be made of them if appropriate.
(12) This enquiry refers to the Council's own compulsory purchase powers and not those of other bodies.
(13) This enquiry refers to proposals by bodies or companies (such as private developers) other than the Council (and where appropriate the County Council) or the Secretary of State.
(14) A plan of the property must be supplied by the enquirer if this enquiry is to be answered.

PARKS AND COUNTRYSIDE

Areas of Outstanding Natural Beauty

23.1 Has any order under s.87 of the National Parks and Access to the Countryside Act 1949 been made?

National Parks

23.2 Is the property within a National Park designated under s.7 of the National Parks and Access to the Countryside Act 1949?

PIPELINES

24. Has a map been deposited under s.35 of the Pipelines Act 1962, or Schedule 7 of the Gas Act 1986, showing a pipeline laid through, or within 100 feet (30.48 metres) of, the property?

HOUSES IN MULTIPLE OCCUPATION

25. Is the property included in a registration of houses scheme (houses in multiple occupation) under s.346 of the Housing Act 1985, containing control provisions as authorised by s.347 of that Act?

NOISE ABATEMENT

Noise Abatement Zone

26.1 Have the Council made, or resolved to make, any noise abatement zone order under s.63 of the Control of Pollution Act 1974 for the area?

Entries in Register

26.2.1 Has any entry been recorded in the Noise Level Register kept pursuant to s.64 of the Control of Pollution Act 1974?

26.2.2 If there is an entry, how can copies be obtained and where can that Register be inspected?

URBAN DEVELOPMENT AREAS

27.1 Is the area an urban development area designated under Part XVI of the Local Government Planning and Land Act 1980?

27.2 If so, please state the name of the urban development corporation and the address of its principal office.

ENTERPRISE ZONES

28. Is the area an enterprise zone designated under Part XVIII of the Local Government Planning and Land Act 1980?

INNER URBAN IMPROVEMENT AREAS

29. Have the Council resolved to define the area as an improvement area under s.4 of the Inner Urban Areas Act 1978?

SIMPLIFIED PLANNING ZONES

30.1 Is the area a simplified planning zone adopted or approved pursuant to s.83 of the T&CP Act 1990?

30.2 Have the Council approved any proposal for designating the area as a simplified planning zone?

LAND MAINTENANCE NOTICES

31. Have the Council authorised the service of a maintenance notice under s.215 of the T&CP Act 1990?

MINERAL CONSULTATION AREAS

32. Is the area a mineral consultation area notified by the county planning authority under Schedule 1 para 7 of the T&CP Act 1990?

HAZARDOUS SUBSTANCE CONSENTS

33.1 Please list any entries in the Register kept pursuant to s.28 of the Planning (Hazardous Substances) Act 1990.

33.2 If there are any entries:
(a) how can copies of the entries be obtained?
(b) where can the Register be inspected?

ENVIRONMENTAL AND POLLUTION NOTICES

34. What outstanding notices or informal notices have been issued by the Council under the Environmental Protection Act or the Control of Pollution Act?
(This enquiry does not cover notices under Part III of the EPA, to which Enquiry 5 applies).

FOOD SAFETY NOTICES

35. What outstanding statutory notices or informal notices have been issued by the Council under the Food Safety Act?

RADON GAS PRECAUTIONS

36.1 Is the property in an area where radon precautions are required for new dwellings?

36.2 If so, are full or secondary precautions required?

SEWERS WITHIN THE PROPERTY [3][14]

37. Does the statutory sewer map show, within the boundaries of the property as depicted on the attached plan, a public sewer or disposal main, a sewer in respect of which a vesting declaration has been made but which has not yet come into force, or a drain or sewer which is the subject of an agreement under s.104 of the Water Industry Act 1991?

NEARBY SEWERS [3][14]

38. Please either:
(a) state whether the statutory sewer map shows public foul and surface water sewers within 100 feet (30.48 metres) of the property [15], or
(b) supply a copy extract from the statutory sewer map showing any public sewers in the vicinity of the property[16].

---

[15] The sewer map does not show the relative levels of the sewers and the property.
[16] If the Council supplies an extract from the sewer map, the notation should be carefully checked and any queries should be clarified with the Council or the sewerage undertaker.

GENERAL NOTES

(A) Unless otherwise indicated, all these enquiries relate to the property as described in Box B on page 1, and any part of that property, and ''the area'' means any area in which the property is located.

(B) References to ''the Council'' include references to a predecessor Council and to a Committee or Sub-Committee of the Council acting under delegated powers, and to any other body or person taking action under powers delegated by the Council or a predecessor Council. The replies given to certain enquiries addressed to District Councils cover knowledge and actions of both the District Council and the County Council.

(C) References to an Act, Regulation or Order include reference to (i) any statutory provision which it replaces and (ii) any amendment or re-enactment of it.

(D) References to any Town and Country Planning Act, Order or Regulation are abbreviated, eg ''T&CP Act 1990''.

(E) The replies will be given after the appropriate enquiries and in the belief that they are in accordance with the information at present available to the officers of the replying Council(s), but on the distinct understanding that none of the Councils, nor any Council officer, is legally responsible for them, except for negligence. Any liability for negligence shall extend for the benefit of not only the person by or for whom these Enquiries are made but also a person (being a purchaser for the purposes of s.10(3) of the Local Land Charges Act 1975) who or whose agent had knowledge, before the relevant time (as defined in that section), of the replies to these Enquiries.

(F) This form of Enquiries is approved by The Law Society, the Association of County Councils, the Association of District Councils and the Association of Metropolitan Authorities and is published by their authority.

GENERAL TERMS AND CONDITIONS CONCERNING
DOMESTIC NON-STRUCTURAL SURVEY

Our basis of valuation is the open market value for existing use defined below. It is based on the Royal institution of Chartered Surveyors guidance notes on the Valuation of Assets (3rd edition).

Our instructions do not extend to the carrying out of any form of structural survey of the building and our inspection was intended to be for valuation purposes only.

Open market value means the best price at which an interest in property might reasonably be expected to have been sold and completed unconditionally for cash consideration on the date of valuation assuming:

a   a willing seller;

b   that prior to the date of valuation there had been a reasonable period (having regard to the nature of the property and the state of the market) for the proper marketing of the interest for the agreement of price and terms and for the completion of the sale;

e   that the state of the market, level of values and other circumstances were, on any earlier assumed date of exchange of contracts, the same as the date of the valuation and:

d   that no account will be taken of any additional bid by a purchaser with a special Interest.

Full Investigation of title, tenure, covenants, rights of way etc., normally involving the services of a solicitor have **NOT** been earned out.

We strongly recommend that your solicitors be shown a copy of this report and if any of our observations or conclusions conflict with their report on Title then we should be informed as there may be a possibility that our valuation will require amendment.

We have relied upon the information supplied to us by yourselves or your advisers as detailed in the section of the Report and Valuation concerning tenure and we have no knowledge (express or implied) of any restrictive, adverse or other covenants, wayleaves, rights of way or of light or of support, emergency escape routes, access and facilities for repairs, maintenance and replacement or other easements, options, conditions (positive or negative), third party rights or any prescriptive rights enjoyed by the owner or occupier of the property or over the property for the benefit of other property or of any unusual or onerous rights, restrictions or outgoings which may in any way affect the value of the property. We do not accept responsibility for any inaccuracies mis-statements or fact or omissions in information provided to us.

Where a plan is attached we have shown what visually appear to be the boundaries of the property but we have no knowledge (express or implied) of the responsibilities for fencing and legal advice should be sought upon that aspect, if required. We have therefore assumed that such boundaries show the true extent of the property. We know of no potential or existing boundary or other disputes or claims. Any site, floor, yard or similar areas should be considered approximate.

Where possible we make oral enquiries of the relevant Local Authority. Where the Local Authority refuses to assist us we will inform you and we will review our valuation when a solicitor provides us with a copy of the Local Authority Search.

Information provided in relation to Town & County Planning or highway matters is the result of these informal enquiries made of the offices of the Local Authority which we have assumed are correct. We have had to assume that the property was constructed with the appropriate planning and any other consents necessary and in accordance with appropriate building regulations and that it is being used for a purpose or purposes compatible with its permitted planning use, ie its apparent current use. We confirm however that the property is prima facie suitable for the purposes for which we have been informed that planning permission is held.

We have assumed that the property and its value is unaffected by any additional matters which would be revealed by a full written Local Search reply and replies to the usual enquiries: or by any outstanding requirement of insurance companies. We assume that the property and its value are not affected by any statutory notice and that the property nor any construction thereon or its or their condition nor its use or intended use is not or will not be unlawful or in breach of any covenant or be an actionable wrong claimed by any person.

The Environmental Protection Act 1990 requires local authorities to establish Contaminated Land Registers. We have not investigated whether the site is, or has been, in the past contaminated or whether it is on such a register, and your legal advisers should investigate whether the subject property is on the register before you enter into any legal commitment to purchase. Our valuation is on the assumption that the land is not contaminated and is not on the register.

We have not inspected the woodwork or other parts of the structure which are covered, unexposed or inaccessible and we are therefore unable to report that any such part of the properly is free from defect, the examination and testing of the electrical, gas, oil or other fuel or energy supplies and installations to include all wiring, cables, pipe and conduit, switches, plugs, fuses and tap and water and drainage systems and plumbing, heating and ventilating installations are outside our instructions and consequently no opinion nor any assurance or guarantee whatsoever to their existence condition or suitability is made or given.

We recommend that any Guarantees which have been given for any of the services should be checked for validity and effectiveness.

We can give no opinion or warranty nor any assurance or guarantee whatsoever that any part of any construction on the property does not have in any form whatsoever any rot, disease, beetle or other attack or metal corrosion or fatigue or any other defects. We have not reported minor or trivial repairs required. We have not inspected any roof or floor voids or spaces or wall cavities and wall-ties.

In properties of all ages where metal or wire wall ties are incorporated in cavity walls, recent research has shown that these may be in poor condition. It is beyond the scope of our survey to inspect such wall ties as such an inspection requires specialist equipment. Failure of the wall ties is generally not detectable without special inspection unless it has resulted in bulging or cracking of the walls. We therefore accept no liability for wall tie failure which is not externally apparent. If required, we can supply the names of specialist firms who have fibre optic inspection equipment capable of carrying out internal inspections of any wall cavities.

Since it would require major excavation, we have not carried out any examination of the foundations to the property and have not judged the quality of the support provided. No examination or test has been carried out on any of the buildings to check if any high alumina cement, calcium chloride additive, blue asbestos, sea dredged aggregates, wood-wool slabs as permanent shutterings. calcium silicate bricks or crocodilite or any other deleterious or other materials which is generally accepted as not being good and sound and for the purpose has been used. We have assumed for the purposes of our Report and Valuation that any such investigation will not disclose the presence of any such materials. We cannot therefore report that the property is free from risk from these problems.

We have not carried out nor commissioned a site investigation or geographical or geophysical survey and therefore can give no opinion or warranty or assurance or guarantee whatsoever that the ground has sufficient load bearing strength to support the existing constructions or any other construction that may be erected upon it in the future. We also cannot give any opinion or warranty or assurance or guarantee that there are no underground mineral or other workings beneath the site or in its vicinity or that there is any fault or disability underground which could or might affect the existing property or any future or current construction thereon, or pollute the local environment.

We are not aware of the content of any environmental audit or other environmental investigation or soil survey which may have been carried out on the property and which may draw attention to any contamination or the possibility of any such contamination, In undertaking our work, we have assumed that no contaminative or potentially contaminative uses have ever been carried out on the property. We have not carried out any investigations into past or present uses or either the property or of any neighbouring land to establish whether there is any potential for contamination from these uses or sites to the subject property and have therefore assumed that none exists, nor have we had regard to the contents of any Register of Land which may be subject to contamination.

Should it however be established subsequently that contamination exists at the property or on any neighbouring land or that the premises have been or are being put to a contaminative use, or that the property is on the Register, this might reduce the values no reported.

In arriving at our opinion as to the value we have not take into account any item in the nature of tenant's fixtures and fittings, plant equipment, goodwill, vehicles and machinery, materials, work in progress or stock in trade upon the property at the time of our inspection.

Our valuation does not take into account any matters concerning the consideration of or the incidence of taxation whether in the nature of stamp duty, capital gains tax, income tax, value added tax, corporation tax, development land tax, or any other tax or levy (whether national or local) that may arise or be taken into account on any transaction. Nor does the valuation have regard to any incidental costs of sale that might arise on a disposal.

No allowance has been made to reflect any liability to taxation that may arise on disposal nor for any costs associated with disposal. No allowance has been made to reflect any liability to repay any grants or taxation allowances that may arise on disposal.

Within the constraints of the various clauses above we have brought all defects or problems known to us arising under these clauses to your attention.

We are willing to supply but without any responsibility whatsoever, the names and addresses of specialists known to us for you to instruct independently and/or to arrange surveyors and reports on any matter upon which we are unable to report under any paragraph hereof.

This report shall be for private and confidential use of the clients for whom the report is undertaken and should not be reproduced in whole or in part or relied upon by third parties for any use without the express written authority of the Surveyors.

We confirm that at the date hereof we have brought to your attention all the facts which have been disclosed to us or which we might reasonably be expected to know and which may reduce the amount of our valuation or the prompt realisability of the property over the next twelve months including inter alia the reduced period remaining in a lease and/or the effect of Landlord and Tenant legislation.

If we have quoted a forced sale value we have assumed that the property is fully marketed and thereafter auctioned at a public auction within three to four months of the commencement of the marketing exercise.

Our surveyor will be pleased to discuss any points mentioned in this report.

THIS LEASE made the   day of   2000
<u>BETWEEN</u>

1. <u>BLOWERS PROPERTY COMPANY LIMITED</u> whose registered office is at 8 Market Street Hardwick Cheshire (hereinafter called "the Landlord" which expression where the context so admits includes the estate owner or estate owners for the time being of the reversion of the premises hereby demised expectant on the terms hereby granted)

2. ROBERT COLE of 17 Collins Close Takley M49 7ZY (hereinafter called "the Tenant" which expression where the context so admits includes his successors in title)

<u>NOW THIS DEED WITNESSETH</u> as follows:-

1. <u>IN</u> consideration of the rents and covenants and conditions hereby reserved and contained and on the part of the Tenant to be paid performed and observed the Landlord hereby demises unto the Tenant <u>ALL THAT</u> the premises more particularly described in the First Schedule hereto <u>TOGETHER WITH</u> the rights set forth in the said First Schedule <u>EXCEPT AND RESERVED</u> as is more particularly mentioned in the said First Schedule (hereinafter called "the premises") <u>TO HOLD</u> except and reserved as aforesaid unto the Tenant from the 1st day of September 199 for a term of <u>THREE YEARS YIELDING AND PAYING</u> therefore yearly and so in proportion for any time less than a year without any deduction whether demanded or not the yearly rent of <u>THREE THOUSAND FIVE HUNDRED POUNDS</u> per annum exclusive of Value Added Tax such yearly rent to be paid by equal quarterly payments in advance on the usual quarter days in every year the first payment in respect of the period from the   day of   Two thousand to the quarter day next following the date hereof to be made on the execution hereof

2. <u>THE TENANT</u> for himself and his assigns and to the intent that the obligations shall continue throughout the term hereby granted <u>HEREBY COVENANTS</u> with the Landlord as follows that is to say:-

(a) To pay the reserved yearly rent at the times and in the manner aforesaid without deduction or abatement whatsoever

(b) To pay and discharge all rates taxes duties charges assessments impositions and outgoings whether parliamentary parochial local or of any other description which are now or may at any time hereafter be taxed charged or imposed under or payable in respect of the premises or on the owner or occupier in respect thereof and a due proportion to be determined by the Landlord of all such rates taxes duties charges impositions assessments and outgoings which may be payable in respect of the premises together with other premises or may be payable by the Landlord in respect of the premises or other premises

(c) To pay for all gas electricity and water consumed on the premises and to observe and perform at the Tenant's expense all present and future regulations and requirements of the gas electricity and water supply boards and to keep the Landlord indemnified against non-payment breach non-observance or non-performance thereof

(d) To pay to the Landlord interest on all sums (including rent) payable by the tenant under the provisions hereof at the rate of 4% above the base rate of Barclays Bank Plc for the time being in force after as well as before any judgment from the due date (or if no date is specified in this Deed) from the date of demand until payment and in the case of reviewed rent from the date upon which such review fell due

(e) As to the inside and as to the outside during the third year and at the expiration or sooner determination of the said term (but not twice in any period of twelve consecutive months) to paint colour grain paper varnish wash and otherwise treat all the inside and outside parts of the premises and all additions thereto and will also carry out all such work in a proper and workmanlike manner with materials of good quality and do all painting with two coats of good quality paint of a colour to be approved by the Landlord

(f)   To repair and throughout the term to keep in good and substantial repair (including decorative condition) the exterior and interior of the premises and all additions thereto and all (if any) ways roads yards toilets passages stairs pavements paths forecourts car parks sewers drains pipes watercourses cables wires and conduits fences party walls party structures party fences walls easements quasi-easements or other appurtenances or conveniences which belong to or are used for or by or for the benefit of the premises in common with other premises near or adjoining thereto

(g)   At the expiration or sooner determination of the said term peaceably and quietly to yield up unto the Landlord the premises in such a state of repair and condition as accords with the due performance by the Tenant of his covenants and obligations herein

(h)   In the event of any of the drains sewers or watercourses in the premises being damaged or becoming choked or stopped-up owing to careless use by the Tenant or its employees or licensees the Tenant will pay the cost incurred by the Landlord in repairing the said drains sewers or watercourses or cleansing and clearing them from obstruction

(i)   At all times during the said term to observe and comply in all respects with the provisions and requirements of any and every enactment (which expression in these covenants includes as well any and every Act of Parliament already or hereafter to be passed as any and every ordinary regulation and bye-law already or hereafter to be made under or in pursuance of any such Act) so far as they relate to or affect the premises or any additions or improvements thereto or the user thereof for the purpose of any manufacture process trade or business or the employment or residence therein of any person or persons or any fixtures machinery plant or chattels for the time being affixed thereto or being thereupon or used for the purposes thereof and to execute all works and provide and maintain all arrangements which by or under any enactment or by any government department local authority or other public authority or duly authorised officer or Court of competent jurisdiction acting under or in pursuance of any enactment are or may be directed or required to be executed provided and maintained at any time during the said term upon or in respect of the premises or any additions or improvements thereto or in respect of any such user thereof or employment or residence therein of any person or persons or fixtures machinery plant or chattels as aforesaid whether by the Landlord or Tenant thereof and to indemnify the Landlord at all times against all costs charges and expenses of or incidental to the execution of any works or the provision or maintenance of any arrangements or directions as required as aforesaid and not at any time during the said term to do or omit or suffer to be done or omitted on or about the premises any act or thing by reason of which the Landlord may under any enactment incur or have imposed upon them or become liable to pay any penalty damages compensation costs charges or expenses

(j)   To pay and satisfy any charge that may hereafter be imposed under the Planning Acts in respect of the carrying out or maintenance by the Tenant of any such operations or the institution or continuance by the Tenant of any such use as aforesaid

(k)   At all times hereafter to indemnify and keep indemnified the Landlord against all actions proceedings costs expenses claims and demands in respect of any act matter or thing contravening the provisions of the Planning Acts or any of them as aforesaid

(l)   To permit the Landlord at any time within six calendar months next before the expiration or sooner determination of the said term to enter upon the premises and to fix and retain without interference upon any suitable part or parts thereof a notice board for reletting the same or at any time during the term in the case of a notice board for the selling of the Landlord's reversion and that the Tenant will not remove or obscure the same and to permit all persons by order in writing of the Landlord to view the premises at all convenient hours in the daytime without interruption

(m) The Tenant will not use the premises or any part thereof nor permit the same to be used otherwise than for general industrial and commercial purposes or for such other use as the Landlord may from time to time approve in writing such approval not to be unreasonably withheld in the case of proposed use that does not conflict with the principles of good estate management

(n) Not to do or permit to be done on the premises or any part thereof anything which shall or may be or become or cause an annoyance nuisance damage inconvenience disturbance injury or danger to the Landlord or the owners lessees or occupiers of any premises in the neighbourhood and will not permit or suffer (i) any sale by auction to be held upon the premises (ii) anyone to sleep therein And to keep the Landlord fully and effectually indemnified against all actions proceedings damages costs expenses claims and demands whatsoever arising out of or in consequence of any breach or non-observance of this covenant

(o) Not to grant any easement right or privilege in respect of the premises or any part thereof to any adjoining owner or occupier and not to share any of the same with any such person or persons

(p) (i) The Tenant will not assign transfer charge underlet or part with the possession of part only of the premises in contradistinction from the whole thereof

(ii) The Tenant will not assign transfer charge underlet or part with the possession of the whole of the premises without the previous consent of the Landlord but such consent shall not be unreasonably withheld to an assignment or underletting of the whole of the premises to a respectable and responsible person or persons or limited company at the annual prevailing market rent thereof at the time being (without taking a fine or premium) and in any event being not less than the rent hereby reserved and not less than the due proportion thereof which rents will on request be notified to the Landlord from time to time PROVIDED THAT:

(a) any assignee or underlessee shall enter into a formal written licence with the Landlord at the cost of the Tenant prior to such assignment or underlease taking place which licence shall contain a covenant by the assignee or underlessee with the Landlord to observe and perform the terms of this Lease as if they had been a party hereto (save for the payment or the rent hereby reserved in the case of an underletting)

(b) in the event of an assignment or underletting of the whole to a limited company the Landlord shall be entitled to insist upon a responsible guarantor becoming liable under the terms of this Lease and/or the Underlease as the case may be the form of such guarantee to be prescribed by the Landlord

(c) any permitted Underlease shall contain an absolute prohibition against further underletting charging or parting with possession and shall contain a covenant on the part of such underlessee not to assign or mortgage such underlease without the consent of the Landlord and shall be in a form approved by the Landlord such consent and approval not to be unreasonably withheld

(d) any permitted Underlease shall exclude the security of tenure provisions of the Landlord and Tenant Act 1954 such exclusion to be supported by the usual Court Order and a copy thereof supplied to the Landlord

(q) To give to the Landlord or its solicitors notice in writing of every assignment assent transfer underlease mortgage or charge (within one calendar month of the same) relating to the premises and to pay their registration fee being not less than £25 plus Value Added Tax at the appropriate rate

(r) Not to deposit or permit to be deposited any rubbish waste or refuse except in proper recepticles to be kept on the premises nor to form any refuse dump or rubbish or scrap heap on the premises (or in any yard passageway road pavement staircase or balcony adjacent thereto) but to remove not less frequently than once a » nth all refuse rubbish and scrap which may have accumulated on the premises and all used cans tins boxes and other containers and generally keep the premises free from noxious weeds deposits of materials or refuse and not to bring or keep or suffer to be brought or kept upon the premises anything which is or may become in the reasonable opinion of the Landlord untidy unclean unsightly or in any way detrimental to the amenity of the neighbourhood and within two weeks to comply with the requirements of any written notice or restore any amenity injured as aforesaid and in the event of the Tenant failing to comply with such notice the Landlord shall be entitled to enter upon the premises and carry out any works necessary to comply with such notice and to recover the cost thereof from the Tenant as a liquidated debt PROVIDED THAT this sub-clause shall not apply to scrap metal stored or placed on the premises in connection with the Tenant's business carried on there

(s) That nothing of a dangerous or explosive nature (oil being deemed to come within this description) shall be placed or kept or suffered to be placed or kept upon the premises or any part thereof PROVIDED THAT this sub-clause shall not apply to any such substances which are kept on the premises in connection with the normal running of the Tenant's business

(t) (i) To repay to the Landlord on demand all costs charges and expenses which may be incurred or sustained by the Landlord by reason or in consequence of any damage done to any part of the premises attributable to any act neglect or default of the Tenant its employees or agents

(ii) To indemnify and keep indemnified the Landlord from all liability in respect of any injury to or the death of any person damage to any property moveable or immoveable arising directly or indirectly out of the repair state of repair and condition or any alteration to or to the user hereinbefore permitted of the premises and from all proceedings costs claims and demands of whatsoever nature in respect of any such liability or alleged liability of the Landlord

(u) To keep the premises and all additions thereto insured at all times throughout the tenancy in the joint names of the Landlord and the Tenant from loss or damage by fire flood storm tempest riot civil commotion and other risks and special perils normally insured under a comprehensive policy on property of the same nature as the premises in some insurance office or with underwriters to be approved by the Landlord in a sum equal to the full reinstatement value thereof from time to time throughout the said term together with architects and surveyors professional fees and two years loss of rent and to make all payments necessary for the above purposes within seven days after the same shall respectively become due and to produce to the Landlord or its agents on demand the policy or policies of such insurance and the receipts for each such payment and to cause all monies received by virtue of any insurance (other than monies received in respect of loss of rent) to be forthwith laid out in rebuilding and reinstating the premises or any part thereof in respect of which such monies shall have become payable or have been received to the satisfaction in all respects of the surveyor for the time being of the Landlord and to make up any deficiency out of its own monies PROVIDED ALWAYS

(i)   that if the rebuilding or reinstatement of the buildings or any part thereof shall be frustrated all such insurance monies (other than aforesaid) relating to the building or part in respect of which the frustration occurs shall belong to the Landlord and

(ii)   that if the Tenant shall at any time fail to keep the premises insured as aforesaid the Landlord may do all things necessary to effect and maintain such insurance and any monies expended by it for that purpose shall be repayable by the Tenant on demand and be recoverable forthwith by action

(v)   To permit the Landlord and its surveyors or agents with or without workmen and others at any reasonable time upon giving five days previous notice (except in emergency) to enter upon the premises and every part thereof to view the state and condition of the same and of all defects decays and wants of reparation there found and for which the Tenant shall be liable under the covenants herein contained to give to the Tenant notice in writing requiring it to make good the same

(w)   Within two months next after every such notice as aforesaid (or immediately in case of emergency) to repair well and substantially and make good all defects decays and wants of reparation of the premises at the Tenants own cost absolutely PROVIDED ALWAYS that if the Tenant shall fail to comply with the requirements of any such notice as aforesaid or be in default for over two months in the performance of any of the covenants hereinbefore contained or relating to the maintenance and repair of the premises it shall be lawful for the Landlord (but without prejudice to the right of re-entry hereinafter contained) or its respective contractors agents or workmen to enter upon the premises at any time after the expiration of such two months or immediately in case of emergency and to execute such repairs and work and the costs thereof (including any charges and professional fees incurred in connection therewith and any value added tax thereon) shall be repaid by the Tenant on demand as rent in arrear and in default shall be forthwith recoverable by action and the Landlord shall have liberty to enter upon the premises at any time to execute repairs to any adjoining premises

(x)   The Tenant will pay all costs charges and expenses (including solicitors costs and surveyors fees) incurred by the Landlord of or incidental to the preparation and service of and the compliance by the Tenant with any notice given under section 146 of the Law of Property Act 1925 or the provisions of this Lease requiring the Tenant to comply with or remedy a breach of any of the covenants herein contained notwithstanding that forfeiture when claimed for any breach of covenant may be avoided otherwise than by relief granted by the Court

(y)   The Tenant will not at any time during the said term without first obtaining the written licence of the Landlord make any alteration or addition whatsoever either externally or internally in or to the premises and will pay to the Landlord the amount of any solicitors architects and surveyors fees incurred by the Landlord in connection with the application for and grant of such licence PROVIDED ALWAYS that the Tenant shall if so required by the Landlord at the expiration or sooner determination of the said term reinstate the premises to the condition thereof prior to the making of such permitted alteration or addition

(z)   That in addition to the rent fees and other payments of whatsoever nature which are or shall be reserved or which are or may become payable pursuant to the provisions of this Lease (hereinafter in this clause called "the Payments") by or on behalf of the Tenant to the Landlord or any person acting on its behalf the Tenant shall pay any Value Added Tax which is or may at any time hereafter become payable in respect of the Payments and such Value Added Tax shall be recoverable by distress in the same way as rent in arrear

(aa) To pay the Landlord~s solicitors costs and disbursements including any Value Added Tax thereon of and incidental to (a) the preparation and completion of this Lease and the Counterpart thereof including the stamp duty on the said Counterpart (b) any applications for consent required by the terms of this Lease made by the Tenant whether or not such consent is given

(bb) Not to permit any oil to escape from the premises onto the land of any adjoining owner or occupier and to indemnify and keep indemnified the Landlord from all liability in respect of such escape as aforesaid

3. THE LANDLORD HEREBY COVENANTS WITH THE TENANT that the Tenant paying the said yearly rent hereby reserved and observing and performing the covenants conditions and agreements hereinbefore contained on the part of the Tenant to be observed and performed shall and may quietly enjoy the premises during the said term without any interruption by the Landlord or persons lawfully claiming under the Landlord

4. The drainage system used or intended to be used by any adjoining or neighbouring plots or properties in common with the premises shall at all times be maintained and kept in repair at the joint expense of the Tenant and the owners or occupiers of the said adjoining or neighbouring plots or properties the Tenant paying a fair proportion of such expense such proportion to be determined conclusively by the Landlord and (subject to the operation of any other provisions contained herein) all gutters downspouts rights of way passage water drainage support air and light and other easements or quasi-easements and other commodities and things which may be used jointly by the said adjoining plots or properties with the premises or any buildings thereon shall continue to be used and enjoyed by the Tenant and owners or occupiers of such adjoining plots or properties and the liability expense and reservations for the use and enjoyment thereof shall be deemed to have been hereby granted and reserved and the owners of the dominant tenement shall henceforth pay a fair proportion of the cost of keeping in repair the things and commodities on the servient tenement of which the owner or occupier for the time being of the dominant tenement enjoys the use

5. PROVIDED ALWAYS AND IT IS HEREBY AGREED AND DECLARED as follows:-

(a) It shall be lawful for the Landlord at any time during the said term to develop alter or rebuild any adjoining or neighbouring property in any manner whatsoever notwithstanding that the same may obstruct or interfere with the access of light or air to the premises or any part thereof or to any building for the time being thereon

(b) If and whenever the said yearly rent hereinbefore reserved (which includes any additional rent under Clause 1 hereof) or any part of such rent shall be in arrear for twenty-one days after the same shall become payable (whether any legal demand therefor shall have been made or not) or if and whenever the Tenant shall at any time fail or neglect to perform or observe any of the covenants conditions or agreements herein contained and on the part of the Tenant to be performed and observed or if while the premises or any part thereof shall remain vested in the Tenant the Tenant (or any assign of the Tenant being an individual) shall become bankrupt or shall compound or make any arrangement with his or their creditors or shall suffer any of their effects to be taken in execution or if the Tenant or any assign of the Tenant being a limited company shall enter into liquidation whether compulsory or voluntary (except for the purpose of reconstruction or amalgamation~ then and in any such case it shall be lawful for the Landlord or any person or persons duly authorised by the Landlord in that behalf into or upon the premises or any part thereof in the name of the whole to re-enter and the premises peaceably to hold and enjoy thenceforth as if these presents had not been made without prejudice to any right of action or remedy of the Landlord in respect of any antecedent breach of any of the covenants by the Tenant hereinbefore contained

(c) The Landlord shall not be responsible to the Tenant for the acts neglects or defaults or misfeasances of any servant or employee of the Landlord nor for any accidental damage which may at any time during the said term be done to the premises or to any of the goods or property of the Tenant thereon or suffered by the Tenant or its servants occupants or visitors to the said premises by reason of any act neglect or default of any other tenant in the Landlord's adjoining or neighbouring premises or of any such servant or employee as aforesaid in breach neglect or non-fulfilment of his duty or arising by the reason of the defective working accidental stoppage or breakdown of any pipes appliances apparatus lifts or other machinery in or connected with or used for the purpose of such adjoining or neighbouring premises or any part thereof

(d) It shall be lawful for the Landlord at any time or times hereafter to use or permit to be used any other building or buildings belonging to the Landlord for business purposes or such other purposes and generally in such manner as the Landlord may think fit and to make or cause or permit to be made any alterations therein or additions thereto for the purpose of any such user as aforesaid or for any other purpose And that the Landlord shall not be or become under any liability to the Tenant nor shall the Tenant make any objection claim or complaint in respect of ny noise disturbance or other nuisance that may be occasioned by the making of any alterations or additions to or the execution of any work executed by or with the sanction of the Landlord in any part or parts of any such building or buildings as aforesaid or by the carrying on of any business whatsoever thereon or therein .

6.   IT IS HEREBY AGREED that except where the context forbids (a) the expression "the Landlord" hereinbefore contained shall be deemed to include the party hereto of the first part and the successors and assigns of the Landlord or other the person or persons for the time being entitled to the reversion of the premises expectant on the determination of the term hereby granted (b) the expression "the Tenant" hereinbefore contained shall be deemed to include the party hereto of the second part and the successors and assigns of the Tenant or of any other the person or persons in whom the said term of years shall for the time being be vested (c) words importing the singular shall include the plural and vice versa and (d) where there are two or more persons included in the expression "the Tenant" covenants expressed to be made by the Tenant shall be deemed to be made by such persons jointly and severally

7.   THIS LEASE shall incorporate the regulations as to notices contained in section 196 of the Law of Property Act 1925 provided that any notice will be deemed to have been properly served on the Tenant if left at the premises in an envelope addressed to the Tenant

IN WITNESS of which this Deed was executed and is delivered on and takes effect from the day and year first before written

THE FIRST SCHEDULE
("the premises")

ALL THAT piece or parcel of land situate at 8 Black Street Leadenham Manchester as the same is shown for the purposes of

identification only edged red on the attached plan <u>EXCEPTING</u> <u>AND</u>
<u>RESERVING</u> in favour of the Landlord:

(i)   the right of passage and running of water soil gas and
electricity as heretofore used and enjoyed from any other
building and land of the Landlord and by other Tenants through
the sewers drains cables channels pipes and conduits on in or
under the premises

(ii)   the right to lay construct use and maintain gas water steam and
other pipes drains sewers electric telegraph telephone and other
wires and cables and appliances (with necessary inspection
chambers) through under or upon the premises or any part thereof
and the right for the Landlords and their surveyors agents and
workmen from time to time and at all reasonable times with
materials and tools to enter upon the premises to carry out the
works aforesaid and also for the purposes of having access to
valves cleaning repairing replacing and renewing the said pipes
drains wires cables and appliances and also for the purposes of
executing repairs or alterations to the adjacent or neighbouring
lands and buildings of the Landlords making good to the
reasonable satisfaction of the Tenant all damage done to the
premises by reason of the carrying out of any such works

(iii) full right and liberty at any time hereafter as need or occasion
shall arise to execute any works or erections or carry out any
repairs or to alter or rebuild any adjacent or neighbouring lands
and buildings of the Landlord and to use the adjacent or
neighbouring lands and buildings in any manner and for the
purposes as the Landlords may think fit notwithstanding that the
access of light and air to the premises may thereby suffer
interference

<u>THE</u> <u>COMMON</u> <u>SEAL</u> of BLOWERS   )
PROPERTY COMPANY LIMITED was   )
affixed in the presence of:-   )

Director's Name ....
                                                              Director's Signature

Director's Name ....
                                                              Director's Signature

Signed by the Tenant

Robert Cole ....

In the presence of

Witness (signature) ....

Name (capitals) ....

Occupation ....

Address ....

....

....

....

'Under the Hammer' Property Records

established 1905

"Under the Hammer" is a publication consisting of fortnightly reports of forthcoming auctions and also the results of residential, commercial & industrial, agricultural, development property and investment property auctions.

"Under the Hammer" covers 5 major areas:

Area 1
West Midlands, South Staffordshire, Warwickshire, Oxfordshire, Shropshire and Hereford & Worcester, Northamptonshire and Cambridgeshire:

Area 2
Derbyshire, North Staffordshire, Nottinghamshire, Leicestershire, Northamptonshire and Cambridgeshire:

Area 3
Greater Manchester, Lancashire, Cumbria, Merseyside, Cheshire and Clwyd:

Area 4
Northumberland, Tyne & Wear, Durham, Cleveland; North, South and West Yorkshire; Humberside, and North Derbyshire:

Area 5
Gloucestershire, Avon, Somerset, Wiltshire, Gwent and Glamorgan.

Subscription rates: £45.00 half yearly per area or £95.00 half yearly all areas.
For full details of our services, including our "Annual Property Values" Digest available separately for each area please apply to:

Under the Hammer (Property Records) Ltd.
70 Rowheath Road
Kings Norton
Birmingham B30 2EX   Tel: 0121 680 6832   Fax: 0121 680 6888

Appendix 5. Details of Under the Hammer

The relevant Statutory Instrument 1991 No 859 (Provision of Information) Regulations enacted under the Estate Agents Act 1979 reads:

Additional information as to services

2- (1) The following additional information is hereby prescribed and shall be given by an estate agent to his client, that is to say as to the services -

   (a) which the estate agent is himself offering, or intends to offer, to any prospective purchaser of an interest in the land; or

   (b) which he knows a connected person or (in a case where he or a connected person would derive a financial benefit from the provision of the service) another person is offering, or intends to offer, to any prospective purchaser of an interest in the land.

   (2) The additional information referred to in paragraph (1) above shall be given at the time and in the manner specified in Regulations 3 and 4 below.

Time of giving information

3- (1) The time when an estate agent shall give the information specified in section 18(2) of the Act, as well as the additional information prescribed in Regulation 2 above, is the time when communication commences between the estate agent and the client or as soon as is reasonably practicable thereafter provided it is a time before the client is committed to any liability towards the estate agent.

   (2) The time when an estate agent shall give the details of any changes to the terms of the contract between himself and his client as are mentioned in section 18(3) of the Act, is the time when, or as soon as is reasonably practicable after, those changes are agreed.

Manner of giving information

4   The additional information prescribed in Regulation 2 above and the information required to be given under section 18(2) and (3) of the Act shall be given by the estate agent in writing.

Explanation of terms concerning client's liability to pay remuneration to an estate agent

5 (1) If any of the terms 'sole selling rights', 'sole agency, and 'ready willing and able purchaser' are used by an estate agent in the course of carrying out estate agency work, he shall explain the intention and effect of those terms to his client in the manner described respectively below, that is to say –

   (a) 'sole selling rights', by means of a written explanation having the form and content of the statement set out in paragraph (a) of the Schedule to these Regulations;

   (b) 'sole agency', by means of a written explanation having the form and content of the statement set out in paragraph (b) of the Schedule to these Regulations; and

   (c) 'ready willing and able purchaser', by means of a written explanation having the form and content of the statement set out in paragraph (c) of the Schedule to these Regulations:

   Provided that if, by reason of the provision of the contract in which those terms appear, the respective explanations are in any way misleading, the content of the explanation shall be altered so as accurately to describe the liability of the client to pay remuneration in accordance with those provisions.

   (2) Any other terms which, though differing from those referred to in paragraph (1) above, have a similar purport or effect shall be explained by the estate agent to his client by reference to whichever of paragraphs (a), (b) or (c) of the Schedule to these Regulations is appropriate, subject also to the proviso to paragraph (1) above.

   (3) The explanation of the terms mentioned in paragraphs (1) and (2) above shall be given by the estate agent to his client in a document setting out the terms of the contract between them (whether that document be a written or printed agreement, a letter, terms or engagement or a form, and whether or not such document is signed by any of the parties), and shall be given at the time specified in Regulation 3(1) and (2) above.

Prominence etc. of explanation

6 (1) Subject to the proviso to Regulation 5(1) and (2) above, the explanations set out in the Schedule to these Regulations shall be reproduced in the documents embodying them in the same form as they appear in that Schedule and without any material alterations or additions to the text, and shall be shown prominently, clearly and legibly.

   (2) The wording of such explanations shall be given no less prominence than that given to any other information in the document setting out the terms of the contract (as more particularly described in Regulation 5 (3) above) between the estate agent and his client apart from the heading thereto, trade names, names of the parties and numbers or letting subsequently inserted therein in handwriting or in type.

THE SCHEDULE

Explanation of certain terms (a)

(a) Sole selling rights

SOLE SELLING RIGHTS

You will be liable to pay remuneration to us, in addition to any other costs or charges agreed, in each of the following circumstances -

if (unconditional contracts for the sale of the property are exchanged) (b) in the period during which we have sole selling rights, even if the purchaser was not found by us but by another agent or by any other person, including yourself;

if (unconditional contracts for the sale of the property are exchanged) (b) after the expiry of the period during which we have sole selling rights but to a purchaser who was introduced to you during that period or with whom we had negotiations about the property during that period.

(b) Sole agency

SOLE AGENCY

You will be liable to pay remuneration to us, in addition to any other costs or charges agreed, if at any time (unconditional contracts for the sale of the property are exchanged) (b)-

with a purchaser introduced by us during the period of our sole agency or with whom we had negotiations about the property during that period; or

with a purchaser introduced by another agent during that period.

(c) Ready, willing and able purchaser

READY, WILLING AND ABLE PURCHASER

A purchaser is a 'ready, willing and able' purchaser if he is prepared and is able to (exchange unconditional contracts for the purchase of your property). (c)

You will be liable to pay remuneration to us, in addition to any other costs or charges agreed, if such a purchaser is introduced by us in accordance with your instructions and this must be paid even if you subsequently withdraw and (unconditional contracts for sale are not exchanged), irrespective of your reasons.

Appendix 6   Terms of the Estate Agents Act 1979 governing provision of information and explanation of terms

Allen & Harris
Auction Administration Centre for Wales
7a Heol-y-Deri, Rhiwbina, Cardiff CF4 6HA
Tel: 029 2062 5626 Fax: 029 2062 5632
Catalogue request line: 09069 118846
Results fax line (touchtone): 0991 118819
Results fax line (non-touchtone): 0660 222223
Website: www.rsaproperty.co.uk/auctions

Allen & Harris
Newfield House, Vicarage Lane
Blackpool, Lancashire FY4 4EW
Tel: 01253 607634 Fax: 01253 607777
Website: www.rsaproperty.co.uk/auctions

Allsop & Co (Residential Department)
100 Knightsbridge, London SW1X 7LB
Tel: 020 7494 3686 Fax: 020 7581 3058
E-mail: post@allsop.co.uk
Website: www.allsop.co.uk
Catalogue request line: 0906 5151510
Auction live link: 09003 411262
Audio guide price line: 09067 110450
Audio results line: 09067 110451
Results fax line: 09067 110200
Buyers fax guide on: 09067 110201
Legal documents line: 020 7494 3686
Audio results: refer catalogue

Allsop & Co (Commercial Department)
27 Soho Square, London W1V 6AX
Tel: 020 7437 6977 Fax: 020 7437 8984
E-mail: post@allsop.co.uk
Website: www.allsop.co.uk
Catalogue request line: 0115 972 6222
Auction live link: 09003 411262
Guide prices & results fax line: 09067 110202
London & SE regional fax list: 09067 110203
SW, E & W Mids, E Anglia fax list: 09067 110204
Yorks, Humbs, NW,Wales, N, Scot fax list: 09067 110205
High yield prop fax line: 09067 110206

Andrews & Robertson
27 Camberwell Green, London SE5 7AN
Tel: 020 7703 2662 Fax: 020 7708 2453
Individual results phone line: 09067 110455
Auction results fax line: 09067 110235

Astley Samuel Leeder
49 Mansel Street, Swansea SA1 5TB
Tel: 01792 655891 Fax: 01792 476926

Athawes Son & Co
203 High Street, Acton, London W3
Tel: 020 8992 0056/0122 Fax: 020 8993 0511
Guide price & results fax line: 09067 110209

Bacons
71/73 St Peter's Avenue
Cleethorpes DN35 8HF
Tel: 01472 691905 Fax: 01472 691267
Website: www.bacons.co.uk
Also two offices in Grimsby
(Tel: 01472 351126/351127)

Barnard Marcus
Auction Office, Commercial House
64/66 Glenthorne Road
London W6 0LR
Tel: 020 8741 9990/9001
Fax: 020 8741 2188/2168
Audio guide prices: 09067 110460
Audio results: 09067 110461
Fax guide prices: 09067 110210
Fax results: 09067 110461
Catalogue hotline: 0906 5226631 (£1.50/min!)
Auction live link: 0900 3411262
E-mail: auctions.bm@rsaproperty.co.uk
Website:
www.rsaproperty.co.uk/auctions/barnardmarcus

Bigwood
43a Calthorpe Road, Edgbaston
Birmingham B15 1TS
Tel: 0121 456 2200 Fax: 0121 456 4008
Auction Line: 0121 625 0489
Website: www.bigwoodassociates.uk.com

Bond Wolfe
Victoria House, 290-292 High Street
West Bromwich
West Midlands B70 8EN
Tel: 0121 525 0600 Fax: 0121 525 8660
Results faxline: 09067 110075

Boultons Harrisons
54 John William Street
Huddersfield HD1 1ER
Tel: 01484 515029 Fax: 01484 450025

Butters
49/53 Trinity Street
Hanley, Stoke-on-Trent ST1 5LX
Tel: 01782 261511 Fax: 01782 202159
Results faxline: 09067 110252
Website: www.charlesbutters.co.uk

Caxtons
5 Clarendon Place
King Street, Maidstone
Kent ME14 1BQ
Tel: 01622 609050
Auction results fax line: 09067 110 299

Clarke Hillyer
163/165 Hoe Street
Walthamstow, London E17 3AL
Tel: 020 8521 6121 Fax: 020 8521 0382

Colliers Conrad Ritblat Erdman
Milner House
14 Manchester Square
London W1A 1BA
Tel: 020 7935 4499 Fax: 020 7487 1810
London results fax line: 09067 110213
Manchester results fax line: 09067 110254

Cottons
361 Hagley Road, Edgbaston
Birmingham B17 8DL
Tel: 0121 247 2233 Fax: 0121 247 1233
E-mail: auctions@cottons.co.uk

Countrywide Property Auctions
144 New London Road
Chelmsford, Essex CM2 0AW
Tel: 01245 344133 Fax: 01245 358985
Catalogue request line (Local rate):
0870 240 1140
London results fax line: 09067 110214
Leeds results fax line: 09067 110215
Manchester results fax line: 09067 110216
Durham results fax line: 09067 110249
Birmingham results fax line: 09067 110250
Plymouth results fax line: 09067 110251

Darlows
Auction Department, 5 North Street
Newport NP20 1JZ
Tel: 01633 250485 Fax: 01633 220909
Website: www.darlows.co.uk
Auction results fax line: 0991 118804

Dedman Property Services
'Hillsboro', 377 Southchurch Road
Southend-on-Sea, Essex SS1 2PQ
Tel: 01702 467000 Fax: 01702 460929
Auction enquiry line: 01702 311010
E-mail: auctions@dedman.net
Website: www.auctioninfo.co.uk
Results fax line: 09067 110238

Drewery & Wheeldon
Rebrook House, 124 Trinity Street
Gainsborough, Lincolnshire DN21 1JD
Tel: 01427 616118 Fax: 01427 811070

Drivers & Norris
407-409 Holloway Road
London N7 6HP
Tel: 020 7607 5001 Fax: 020 7609 5031
Guides & results fax line: 09067 110217
E-mail: auction@drivers.co.uk
Website: www.drivers.co.uk

Eddisons
Pennine House, Russell Street
Leeds LS1 5RN
Tel: 0113 243 0101 Fax: 0113 242 1364
Results faxback line: 09067 110222
E-mail: property@eddcom.co.uk
Website: www.eddcom.co.uk
Offices in Bradford and Huddersfield

Edwin Evans
253 Lavender Hill
Battersea, London SW11 1JW
Tel: 020 7228 5864 Fax: 020 7223 7637
Guide price fax line: 09067 110218
Guide price audio line: 09067 110458
Results fax line: 09067 110219
Results audio line: 09067 110459
Catalogue request line: 09067 110590

Clive Emson
8 Cavendish Way, Bearstead
Maidstone, Kent ME15 8XY
Tel: 01622 630033 Fax: 01622 630036
Results fax line: 09067 110237
Results audio line: 09067 110454
Results by post: 09068 517744
E-mail: clive@emson.demon.co.uk
Website: www.auctioninfo.co.uk

Fox & Sons
HQ & Brighton Auction Centre
117/118 Western Road, Brighton BN1 2AE
Tel: 01273 321300 Fax: 01273 204756
Covering East Sussex, West Sussex and
bordering areas of Surrey and Kent.

Southampton Auction Centre
32-34 London Road
Southampton SO15 2TB
Tel: 023 80338066 Fax: 023 80225479
Covering Hampshire, Dorset, Wiltshire, the Isle of
Wight and south-west Surrey.

Catalogue request line 09067 110582
Guide prices and entries
fax line: 09067 110246
Recent results (last two sales)
fax line: 09067 110247

Austin Gray
123-125 & 135-137 Dyke Road
Hove, East Sussex BN3 1TJ
Tel: 01273 232232 Fax: 01273 232233
Results faxline: 09067 110236
E-mail: property@austingray.co.uk

Chris Guttridge
20 High Street, Wath Upon Dearne
Rotherham, South Yorkshire S63 7QG
Tel: 01709 872247 Fax: 01709 877397

Hamilton Osborne King
32 Molesworth Street, Dublin 2
Tel: 00 353 1 618 1300 Fax: 00 353 1 676 7066
E-mail: info@hok.ie
Website: www.hok.ie

Frederick G Hair & Son
200 London Road, Southend on Sea SS1 1PJ
Tel: 01702 432255 Fax: 01702 337846
Guides/Results fax line: 09067 110253
E-mail: hairandson@iclweb.com
Website:
www.propertylive.co.uk/hairandson
Website: www.auctioninfo.co.uk
Offices also in Westcliff-on-Sea, Leigh-on-Sea
and Thorpe Bay.

Halifax National Property Auctions
National Auction Division, Halifax House
28 High Street, Kegworth
Derby DE74 2DA
Tel: 01509 680701 Fax: 01509 670888
Website: www.halifax.co.uk
Birmingham results fax line: 0906 5867173
Bolton results fax line: 0906 5867174
Bristol results fax line: 0906 5867175
Cardiff results fax line: 0906 5867176
Leeds results fax line: 0906 5867178
Catalogue request line: 09067 530166

Handleys
10 Blenheim Walk, Leeds LS2 9AQ
Tel: 0113 246 9090 Fax: 0113 246 9100
E-mail: auctions@handleys.com
Website: www.handleys-leeds.com

Harman Healy
340 Grays Inn Road
London WC1X 8BJ
Tel: 020 7833 5885 Fax: 020 7833 5995
Results fax line: 09067 110224
Auction Live Link: 09003 426507

Healey & Baker
29 St George Street
Hanover Square, London W1A 3BG
Tel: 020 7629 9292 Fax: 020 7514 2360
E-mail: jcornwell@healey-baker.com
Website: www.healey-baker.com
Guide prices faxline: 09067 110285
Results fax line: 09067 110221
Audio guide price lines: 020 7514 0745 to 0751

Mark Jenkinson & Son
8 Norfolk Row, Sheffield S1 2PA
Tel: 0114 276 0151 Fax: 0114 275 6370
Website: www.markjenkinson.co.uk

Jones Lang LaSalle
22 Hanover Square, London W1A 2BN
Tel: 020 7493 6040 Fax: 020 7399 5637
Guide price fax line: 020 7399 5399
Results fax line: 020 7399 5399
Catalogue request line: 020 7399 5399
E-mail: uk.auctions@joneslanglasalle.com
Website:http://reach.joneslanglasalle.com

Lambert & Foster
77 Commercial Road, Paddock Wood
Tonbridge, Kent TN12 6DR
Tel: 01892 832325 Fax: 01892 834700
Website: www.lambertandfoster.co.uk

Larards
33 Lowgate, Hull HU1 1PB
Tel: 01482 223311
Fax: 01482 618131

**Longden & Cook Commercial and Edward
Mellor**
182 London Road
Hazel Grove
Stockport
Cheshire SK7 4DQ
Tel: 0161 230 1740
Fax: 0161 419 9933
E-mail: auction@auctioneers-lcc.co.uk
Website: www.auctioneers-lcc.co.uk

D.J. Manning
Carriden, Bo'ness, West Lothian EH51 9SF
Tel: 01506 827693
Fax: 01506 826495

Miller Metcalfe
56 Bradshawgate, Bolton BL1 1DW
Tel: 01204 535 353 Fax: 01204 362 945
Catalogue request line: 01204 525 150
Website: www.millermetcalfe.co.uk

Morgan Beddoe
147 Whiteladies Road, Clifton, Bristol BS8 2QT
Tel: 0117 946 7100
Fax: 0117 946 7111
Website: www.morgan-beddoe.co.uk

Morgan Evans & Co
Head Office, 28-30 Church Street
Llangefni, Anglesey LL77 7DU
Tel: 01248 723303 Fax: 01248 750146
Property Office: 01248 716816
Website: www.property-wales.uk/morganevans

Morton & Flanagan Ltd
Main Street, Words, Dublin
Tel: 00 353 1 840 4011 Fax: 00 353 1 840 4459

Nelson Bakewell
25 Sackville Street, London W1X 2HQ
Tel: 020 7544 2000 Fax: 020 7544 2222
Auction line: 020 7544 2244
Results fax line: 09067 110229
Catalogue request line: 0115 946 5715
E-mail: auction@nelson-bakewell.com
Website: www.nelson-bakewell.com

Keith Pattinson
(Auction Office) 210 High Street
Newcastle upon Tyne NE3 1HN
Tel: 0191 213 0550 Fax: 0191 222 0314
Website: www.pattinson.co.uk

Royal & SunAlliance
Newfield House, Vicarage Lane
Blackpool, FY4 4EW
Tel: 01253 607600 Fax: 01253 607777
Website: www.rsaproperty.co.uk/auctions

FPD Savills
139 Sloane Street, London SW1X 9AY
Tel: 020 7824 9091 Fax: 020 7824 9062
Results fax line: 09067 110220
Catalogue hotline: 0906 538 3458 (60p/min)
E-mail: ccolemansmith@fpdsavills.co.uk
Website: www.fpdsavills.co.uk

FPD Savills
4 St Peter's Gate,
Nottingham NG1 2JG
Tel: 0115 934 8000 Fax: 0115 934 8001/2
Guide price & results fax line: 09067 110223
Catalogue hotline: 0906 863 3458 (60p/min)
E-mail: ccolemansmith@fpdsavills.co.uk
Website: www.fpdsavills.co.uk

Seel & Co
The Crown House, Wyndham Crescent
Canton, Cardiff CF11 9UH
Tel: 029 2034 2721 Fax: 029 2023 7544
Catalogue request line: 029 2034 2721
E-mail: property@seel-and-co.demon.co.uk

Sherry FitzGerald
13 Merrion Row, Dublin 2
Tel: 00 353 1 661 6198 Fax: 00 353 1 661 3755
Website: www.sherryfitz.ie

Shonki Brothers
55 London Road, Leicester LE2 OPE
Tel: 0116 254 3373 Fax: 0116 258 4491

Strettons (incorporating Stickley & Kent)
Auction Office, Central House
189-203 Hoe Street, Walthamstow
London E17 3AP
Tel: 020 8520 8383 Fax: 020 8520 7306
E-mail:auctions@strettons.co.uk
Website: www.strettons.co.uk
Results fax line: 09067 110230
Audio database: 09067 110453
Auction live link: 09003 411262
Recorded lot results: refer catalogue
Catalogue request line: 09003 424806

Sullivan Mitchell
36 St Thomas Street,
Lymington SO41 9NE
Tel: 01590 677555 Fax: 01590 677333
404–406 Garratt Lane, London SW18 4HP
Tel: 020 8944 8899 Fax: 020 8944 8886
Auction results: 09067 110 231

SVA Property Auctions
3a St Vincent Street, Edinburgh EH3 6SW
Tel: 0131 624 6640 Fax: 0131 624 6630
E-mail: sva.auctions@cableinet.co.uk
Website: www.sva-auctions.co.uk

K. Stuart Swash
2 Waterloo Road, Wolverhampton WV1 4BL
Tel: 01902 710626 Fax: 01902 428017

TOPS Property Services Ltd
15-17 Princes Street, Norwich NR3 1AF
Tel: 01603 767050 Fax: 01603 767567
Website: www.ITLhomesearch.com

Venmore Thomas & Jones
44 Stanley Street, Liverpool L1 6AL
Tel: 0151 236 6746 Fax: 0151 255 0403
Auction results fax line: 09067 110243
E-mail: liverpool@vtj.co.uk
Website: www.vtj.co.uk

Ward & Partners
136 Ashford Road, Bearstead
Maidstone, Kent ME14 4NH
Tel: 01622 736736 Fax: 01622 738738
Catalogue hotline: 0906 8020113 (60p/min)
Results faxline: 09067 110245
E-mail: auction.dept@wardandpartners.co.uk
Website: www.arunestates.co.uk/auctions

Weaving & Partners
20 Water Street, Liverpool L2 8TL
Tel: 0151 236 9090 Fax: 0151 236 1144
Results fax line: 09067 110244
E-mail: jmw@weaving.co.uk
Website: www.weaving.co.uk

Willmotts
Willmott House, 12 Blacks Road
Hammersmith, London W6 9EU
Tel: 020 8748 6644 Fax: 020 8748 9300
Results audio line: 09067 110452
Results fax line: 09067 110232

Wilsons Auctions
22 Mallusk Road, Newtownabbey
Belfast BT36 8PP
Tel: 028 9034 2626 Fax: 028 9034 2528
E-mail: auctions@wilsons.attmail.com
Website: www.wilsons-auctions.com

Winkworth Auctions
23 Brighton Road, South Croydon
Surrey CR2 6EA
Tel: 020 8649 7255 Fax: 020 8666 0559
Website: www.winkworth.co.uk
North of England office: 01253 796260
Auction results fax line: 09067 110233
Addendum update line: 09067 110234
Auction live link: 09003 411292

Index

The index covers the main text, but not preliminary pages or appendices. Headings categorise the purchase and sale of property at auction, the principal subjects of the book. **Bold** type within a sequence of page numbers indicates a more significant section; an 'f' after a page number indicates a figure (or figure and text); an 'i' indicates an illustration (or illustration and text); a 't' indicates a table (or table and text).

Visit the Law Pack website...

www.lawpack.co.uk

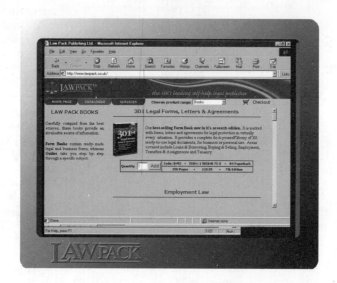

for full information on Law Pack's extensive range of innovative, self-help legal and business publications...

✔ books

✔ kits

✔ forms

✔ software